# THE MACHIAVELLIAN LEGACY

*Also by Joseph V. Femia*

GRAMSCI'S POLITICAL THOUGHT

MARXISM AND DEMOCRACY

# The Machiavellian Legacy

## Essays in Italian Political Thought

Joseph V. Femia
*Reader in Political Theory*
*University of Liverpool*

First published in Great Britain 1998 by
**MACMILLAN PRESS LTD**
Houndmills, Basingstoke, Hampshire RG21 6XS and London
Companies and representatives throughout the world

A catalogue record for this book is available from the British Library.

ISBN 0–333–68937–2

 First published in the United States of America 1998 by
**ST. MARTIN'S PRESS, INC.,**
Scholarly and Reference Division,
175 Fifth Avenue, New York, N.Y. 10010

ISBN 0–312–21511–8

Library of Congress Cataloging-in-Publication Data
Femia, Joseph V.
The Machiavellian legacy : essays in Italian political thought /
Joseph V. Femia.
p. cm.
Includes bibliographical references (p.    ) and index.
ISBN 0–312–21511–8 (cloth)
1. Political science—Italy—History.   2. Machiavelli, Niccolò,
1469–1527—Influence.   I. Title.
JA84.I8F38   1998
320'.092'245—dc21                                                98–20171
                                                                          CIP

This book is printed on paper suitable for recycling and made from fully managed and
sustained forest sources.

10   9   8   7   6   5   4   3   2   1
07   06   05   04   03   02   01   00   99   98

Printed and bound in Great Britain by
Antony Rowe Ltd, Chippenham, Wiltshire

# Contents

# Preface and Acknowledgements

This collection brings together four of my previously published papers and a long introductory essay written especially for the volume. The reprinted pieces are all similar in form and style: each sets out and critically examines the main ideas of a modern Italian political thinker. The introductory chapter deals with Machiavelli in a like manner, but its primary purpose is to consider his impact on the four thinkers discussed in subsequent chapters: Labriola, Gramsci, Mosca and Pareto. My central thesis is that modern Italian thought, whether Marxist or conservative, has been crucially influenced by Machiavelli's hostility to abstract universals and predilection for empirical analysis. A semester as Visiting Fellow in the Department of History at Princeton University allowed me to develop my thoughts on Machiavelli. My thanks are also due to the British Academy for a generous research grant, and to Liverpool University, for giving me the necessary sabbatical leave.

Were I to rewrite the reprinted papers today, some of the conclusions drawn would be slightly modified and the issues covered might differ somewhat. But for the most part I have changed my mind on only a few minor points. Rather than attempting to alter what I have already written, I have used the introductory essay to pinpoint unifying themes and new ideas. I hope that the reprinted papers will be of use to readers who have not seen them in their original form, as well as providing a convenient collection for those who already know them. They first appeared in the following publications:

'Antonio Labriola: a Forgotten Marxist Thinker', in *History of Political Thought*, Vol. 2 (1981), pp. 557–72. Copyright ©, Imprint Academic, Exeter, U.K.

'Gramsci's Patrimony', in *British Journal of Political Science* (July 1983), pp. 327–64 (reprinted with kind permission of Cambridge University Press).

'Mosca Revisited', in *European Journal of Political Research*, vol. 23 (1993), pp. 145–61 (reprinted with kind permission of Kluwer Academic Publishers).

'Pareto's Concept of Demagogic Plutocracy', in *Government and Opposition*, vol. 30, no. 3 (Summer 1995), pp. 370–92.

Acknowledgement is gratefully made to these journals and publishing companies.

Last but not least, I wish to thank my wife, Heather, for her unfailing support and advice.

Joseph V. Femia
Liverpool

# 1 The Machiavellian Legacy

Whatever its other virtues and achievements, Italian political thought has contributed little, if anything, to the formation of liberal democratic theory. Discourse on the abuse of power, on human rights, on the purposes of popular participation – all this is, as Norberto Bobbio once complained, 'alien' to the political culture of his native land.[1] Where are Italy's equivalents of Locke? of Tocqueville? of Madison? of J.S. Mill? When Italian thinkers have reflected in a systematic way on the principles or arrangements of liberal democracy, their aim has usually been denunciation rather than constructive engagement. Italian political philosophy, Bobbio notes, has been dominated, ever since the Renaissance, by the Machiavellian theme of *ragion di stato*, which assumes an eternal conflict between the demands of political life and those of individual conscience. In jurisprudence, the prevalent doctrine remains not the Anglo-Saxon one of natural law, regarding the state as an association founded on a contract of mutual assistance, but the German one of *Rechtsstaat*, whose point of departure is the Hegelian refutation of contractual assumptions. Within this doctrine there is no room for abstract freedoms or explicit limits on political intervention, since the state is deemed to have an irreducibly 'ethical' component, giving it priority over the individual. Italian political *science*, Bobbio continues, has been no friendlier to the values of liberal democracy. In thrall to the idea of inevitable elite rule (also Machiavellian in provenance), its most distinctive 'discovery' is that democracy is more myth than reality.

Bobbio points out that of the three traditional theories of the state – (1) the state as force, (2) the state as a focus of collective and inherited morality, and (3) the state as guarantor of universal rights – Italian thought has favoured the first and second, and consistently denigrated the third. Underlying this set of preferences is an aversion to the abstract individual of liberal political philosophy, the decontextualized possessor of 'natural rights' and transcendent ethical truths. For Bobbio, this disrespect for Enlightenment ideals sometimes takes (unintentionally) comical form, as when Gentile, the chief proponent of 'actual idealism',[2] assured potential rebels that law is by definition just, and therefore no law can be unjust. With this display of circular reasoning, his 'absolute spiritualism was transformed into absolute positivism'.[3]

1

Bobbio's observations are correct as far as they go, but his preoccupation with liberal individualism prevents him, I think, from penetrating to the heart of the matter. The distinguishing characteristic of modern Italian political thought is not, in my opinion, its worship of the state, but its dismissal of transcendence. This trait is discernible in all four thinkers covered in the following chapters. On the one hand, we have Mosca and Pareto, progenitors of elite theory and (to their critics) fascism's assault on parliamentary democracy. On the other hand, we have Gramsci and Labriola, theoreticians of neo-Hegelian Marxism and (to their critics) communist totalitarianism. What I intend to demonstrate in this opening chapter is that these four thinkers, despite their evident differences, worked from an identical Machiavellian premise, one that accounted for some remarkable similarities in their respective approaches to political life. What united them, at bottom, was their hostility to 'essentialism', to the positing of *a priori* goals, imposed on men by God or nature, and revealed to us by holy scripture or abstract reason. For the theorists in question, as for Machiavelli before them, there were no unconditional values or norms, no universally valid modes of conduct, no supra-historical 'essences', distinct from the observable attributes of human beings. This immanentism, or worldly humanism, had two major implications, one methodological and the other substantive. First, it encouraged attachment to an empirical method of analysis. Our four thinkers all refused to reach conclusions by deduction from first principles. In their view, factual reality was the basis for all knowledge. Accordingly, they rejected the unproven (and unprovable) belief – quite self-evident to Christian, Hegelian and orthodox Marxist 'theologians' – that the world formed a rational structure. The second implication of their worldly humanism was political realism. Each theorist endeavoured to dispel illusions about politics, to unmask the myths of *both* reactionaries *and* utopian visionaries. It was their common conviction that man was an inveterate spinner of fancies and delusive images, concealing the true nature of events. *Au fond*, politics was a clash of particular interests and particular 'utilities', a struggle for brute advantage, hidden by veils of euphemism. As Marxists, Gramsci and Labriola obviously *hoped* for a brighter future of collective harmony, but they could not entirely free themselves from the legacy of Machiavellian pessimism. They explicitly attacked Marxist utopianism, in a manner reminiscent of Bernstein and other critics of Marxist teleology.

It will not be my argument, in what follows, that the four thinkers were *directly* influenced by Machiavelli. They all read him, of course, and – with the exception of Labriola – commented on his ideas at some length. Their comments were generally favourable (though not uncritical), and one can assume that his writings helped to inspire theirs. But my case will not depend on evidence, whether circumstantial or explicit, of conscious borrowing. Instead, I shall attempt to show that the *deep conceptual structure* of their thought is reflective of Machiavelli's concerns and ideas – in particular, his determination to study man as he is revealed in the historical record rather than man as revealed in the visions of theology and speculative philosophy. It is also my intention to explain why Machiavelli's rejection of abstract universals amounted to a revolutionary change in political thought, making the great Florentine a pivotal figure in the advance of modernity.

My thesis is not entirely original. Edmund Jacobitti, in his study of Italian historicism, has already argued that 'concrete humanism', or 'hostility to abstract Enlightenment natural laws as well as to the transcendent Christian religion, marks the uniqueness and prescience of modern Italian thought'.[4] He reminds us that, for Italian idealist philosophers, the Hegelian *Weltgeist* appeared to embody a superhuman transcendence that belied Hegel's pretensions to concreteness. An immanent and worldly historicism could not prescribe a foreordained course for the historical process. Hegel's 'philosophy of history' represented a poorly disguised return to rationalism and religion, to *filosofia teologizzante* – the type of philosophy that views man from the perspective of the ideal rather than the real. Jacobitti also claims that it was Machiavelli who paved the way for modern humanism by reversing the Christian concepts of 'sin' and 'virtue'. The medieval era had as its theological basis the notion that sin lay in attaching oneself to this life, whereas virtue lay in the negation of the worldly life. Reality, for the Christian, is not 'what is' but 'what ought to be', and therefore its true content is the afterlife the world that conforms to truth and justice. Machiavelli, in contrast, eulogized the man of action, creating and appropriating his own world here on earth.[5]

Although he is primarily interested in Italian idealist philosophers (Croce, the Spaventa brothers, De Sanctis), Jacobitti recognizes that the so-called Hegelian Marxists such as Gramsci and Labriola were also worldly humanists in the Machiavellian tradition. My purpose here is to develop this insight and extend Jacobitti's thesis to the 'classical elitists', whose 'Machiavellianism' is rather more obvious, though insufficiently explored.

Nevertheless, to say that Machiavelli discarded essentialism and teleology is itself controversial, as we shall see. Indeed, to prove that Machiavelli influenced anyone in any way, we must first establish the precise nature of his legacy. This is no mean feat. The original Machiavelli is buried under a vast pile of exposition and argument, containing a bewildering variety of often contradictory interpretations. Was he a cold empirical scientist, the 'Galileo of politics',[6] or a fierce patriot dominated by dreams and emotions?[7] Was he 'chiefly responsible for the spirit of modernity',[8] or a slavish imitator of antiquity, who – in his obsession with classical authors – derived useless maxims from dogmatic axioms,[9] and – according to one interpretation – adhered to a pre-modern cosmology of spirits, prodigies and portents?[10] Was he the anti-Christ,[11] 'a teacher of evil',[12] a malevolent counsellor of tyrants, or a sincere Catholic, the possessor of 'a most resolute and lofty Christian conscience'?[13] Should we describe him as an anguished moralist, who reluctantly divorced the harsh world of politics from the ideal world of ethics,[14] or as an optimistic republican humanist, anxious to spread the spontaneous harmony of a 'citizen democracy'?[15]

Machiavelli himself must shoulder some of the responsibility for this violent disparity of judgements. As a high-ranking diplomat who spent 15 years in the service of the Florentine republic, he lacked the temperament for abstract speculation and did not write with the express purpose of setting out an organic system of political philosophy. Nowhere did he define his terms and basic principles with anything resembling academic rigour. This helps to explain the complexity of Machiavelli's thought, its ambiguity and occasional inconsistency, caused by the intermingling of elements old and new. This complexity, in turn, largely accounts for the exegetical divergences, as innumerable commentators search for some simple formula to impose order on a fundamentally disordered body of work. This, however, is just one type of 'reductionism' in the scholarly literature. Potentially more damaging (to my thesis at least) is what Cassirer calls 'the historian's fallacy',[16] the attempt to dissolve Machiavelli's writings into their historical context. To quote Sir Richard Lodge, 'Machiavelli was writing not only about his own time but for his own time and for no other.'[17] From this viewpoint, to compare his ideas to those of a twentieth-century thinker such as Gramsci is to be guilty of the worst kind of anachronism. Machiavelli neither produced nor intended to produce general maxims that were valid for all times in all places.

But is this actually so? When dealing with an author from the distant past, there is always the danger of translating his meaning into our own categories. Still, as Cassirer argues, no Renaissance philosopher or scientist or artist ever viewed himself in historical perspective. Wholly innocent of the modern tendency to judge everything in terms of its surroundings, the thinkers (and doers) of that era still believed in universal truths.[18] In the case of Machiavelli, there was a special reason why he would not see his own thought as belonging only to Renaissance Italy. To him, all men and all ages were essentially the same – the implication being that history always repeats itself. Even his contemporaries thought his desire to discover recurrent features, at the expense of particular circumstances, a bit excessive. While Machiavelli may have mistaken the significance of his own achievement, the historical record hardly confirms this. To the contrary, instead of disappearing into the grey mists which swallow up the dead things of the past, Machiavelli's works have, as everyone knows, attracted the attention of posterity, provoking almost uninterrupted controversy ever since his death. Bitter hatred and extravagant blame, on the one hand, have been met by unrestrained enthusiasm and lyrical praise, on the other. Surely this suggests the existence of something static in the human condition, something that enables certain historical products to transcend their historical context. At any rate, Machiavelli's legion of admirers and detractors must have felt that the continuity of human experience rendered his ideas relevant to their own time and place.

It is therefore odd that Machiavelli's writings excited little reaction during his lifetime. This is probably because *The Prince*, the work responsible for making his name synonymous with unscrupulousness in politics, was not published until after his death in 1527, though it did circulate widely in manuscript form. Soon after publication, in 1532, the notorious little book became the subject of fierce political invective and moral reprobation. In a climate of growing religious fervour, it was called the Devil's catechism or the Ten Commandments reversed. One of the early denunciations came from the pen of Cardinal Reginald Pole, who, in his *Apologia ad Carolum v. Caesarem*, assailed *The Prince* as a diabolical handbook for sinners. In 1559 *all* of Machiavelli's works were condemned by the Roman Church and placed on the Index. But Catholics held no monopoly on the condemnation of Machiavelli. Protestant theologians, notably the French Huguenot Innocent Gentillet, were also shocked by his political cynicism and attacked him in print. The Machiavelli 'legend of hatred'[19] was most developed in Elizabethan England, where the supposedly demonic character of his thought provided much fodder for poets and playwrights, who perhaps did more than politicians and theologians to propagate the Machiavelli myth. References to the 'murderous Machiavel' were numerous in Elizabethan literature, and everywhere – most graphically in the plays of Shakespeare, Jonson and Marlowe – Machiavellianism meant the incarnation of cunning, hypocrisy, cruelty and gangsterism.[20] By the end of the eighteenth century, however, this judgement was turned upside down. As the modern spirit of nationalism dawned, severe condemnation gave way to awe and veneration. The satanic villain was transmuted into a righteous hero. It was Herder, the German romantic philosopher, who first declared that *The Prince* was not an iniquitous guide for political criminals but an objective study of sixteenth-century Italian politics offered by a patriot as a service to his beleaguered country. If Machiavelli recommended bad behaviour, it was all in a good cause – that of freeing Italy from the foreign invaders. True, some of his counsels were shocking, but only strong medicine would suffice in the context. Machiavelli gradually became a hero, and then a saint, of the Italian *Risorgimento* – an idealistic spokesman for the freedom of his country and the champion of all political virtues.

These incompatible images of Machiavelli correspond to the apparently contrasting messages of his two major works. In *The Prince*, he was prepared to advise both good and bad rulers in a 'value-free' way. If cruelty or treachery was necessary to preserve their power, he did not scruple to recommend it. As for the 'people', they were depicted as an amorphous, anonymous rabble, a collection of isolated *subjects* (as distinct from citizens), who figured negatively: if you dishonoured them, or violated their property or their customs, they might turn against you. In the *Discourses on Livy*, however, Machiavelli makes his republican sentiments plain, calling for the widespread dissemination of civic virtue and specifying mechanisms for the preservation of freedom and the rule of law. One distinguished commentator even refers to the 'political idealism'[21] of the *Discourses*, a description supported by passages such as the one where Machiavelli likens 'the voice of a people' to 'that of God'.[22] The relationship between these two seemingly antithetical books has long been regarded as perhaps the most vexing problem in Machiavelli studies. Matters are not helped by the fact that the books were written at more or less the same time. Exhaustive (and exhausting) scholarship has established that the first part of the *Discourses* was composed in 1513. Machiavelli then interrupted the work after the eighteenth chapter (the chapters are very brief and plentiful) to write *The Prince*, between July and December 1513. In 1515 he returned to the *Discourses*, finishing it in 1517.[23] So how could the faithful servant of the Florentine republic, the author of the *Discourses*, also be the author of a handbook for despots? One solution, first canvassed by Florentines who knew Machiavelli, is that he was a lover of liberty who nevertheless chose to abase himself before the city-state's new Medici masters in the (vain) hope of securing a post in the regime that overthrew the republic.[24] After all, *The Prince* was formally dedicated to Lorenzo 'The Magnificent'. A more charitable interpretation is that Machiavelli, outraged by the foreign occupiers who threatened Florence and humiliated the whole of central and northern Italy, was willing to support *any* government that might preserve Florentine independence, expel the 'barbarians' and take the first steps towards unifying the peninsula. The prospects for a republican revival were, he realized, nil in the existing circumstances; it was therefore necessary to make the best of a bad situation. Moreover, Machiavelli held fast to a cyclical theory of history, according to which a principate was a recurrent and indispensable phase in the life of states.[25] All republics, he tells us in the *Discourses*, are founded by a *single* law-giver,[26] and all republics eventually degenerate. When they do, only tyrannical means can restore them to past glories.[27] Republics may be desirable, but they are not always possible. It is also true that Machiavelli's model for an ideal republic was ancient Rome, an expansionist and predatory state. Indeed, Herbert Butterfield argues that Machiavelli 'did not admire ancient Rome because the Romans had a republic; he admired republican government because it was the form under which ancient Rome had achieved unexampled greatness and power'.[28] According to what is now the received, though not unanimous, opinion, *The Prince* and the *Discourses* 'were in fact interdependent aspects of an organically unified outlook'.[29] The mood and focus vary between one work and another, but both show equally the basic values for which Machiavelli is famous (or infamous), such as indifference to the use of conventionally immoral means for political purposes and the belief that government depends largely on force and guile.

Having dealt with preliminary issues, we are now in a position to consider the central propositions stated or implied in Machiavelli's writings, and to establish parallels between these propositions and modern Italian political thought.

## THE REVOLT AGAINST METAPHYSICS

As a thinker and historical figure, Machiavelli is closely associated with the Renaissance, which is usually reckoned to begin during the mid-1300s (with the poems of Petrarch) and to end some time after the death of Raphael (1520) and before that of Tintoretto (1594). It was, according to Jacob Burckhardt's influential analysis, a distinctive period in human history, with sharp traits that constituted its particular Hegelian *Geist*.[30] The features singled out by Burckhardt and his many acolytes included rationalism, individualism and a keen appreciation of man's this-worldly capacities. Whereas the Middle Ages became a byword for barbarism and suffocating religiosity, the Renaissance was portrayed as a sudden and brilliant flowering of all kinds of spiritual activity. The traditional picture of the Middle Ages and the Renaissance was therefore one of antithesis between darkness and light. Deepening knowledge of medieval life eventually challenged the conventional stereotypes. For example, historians discovered that the imitation of ancient models, supposedly the cause of cultural rebirth in the fourteenth and fifteenth centuries, was already a familiar theme in twelfth-century France, where the Chartres School promoted a revival of 'Latinity'. Some scholars went so far as to claim that *all* Renaissance insights were prefigured in late medieval thought. The subtleties and details of this academic debate need not detain us.[31] Suffice it to acknowledge that history is indeed a continuous process; to divide it into distinctive phases is to impose artificial categories on an inherently shapeless flux of events and ideas. It would be absurd to seek for a point at which the medieval era 'ends' and the Renaissance 'begins'. And yet we must, for the sake of giving coherence to our thoughts, still look for an *intellectual* line of demarcation between the two periods. Talking about the 'Renaissance' is not to foist an arbitrary scheme upon historical reality – one founded on *a priori* reasoning. All that is meant is that in the interpretation of history, the infinitude of isolated facts must be arranged in some coherent pattern and so made accessible to historical analysis. 'Renaissance' and 'Middle Ages' are simply 'ideal-types' in the Weberian sense. Like all ideal-types, they are not faithful reflections of factual reality, but they do, through a process of abstraction, capture something 'essential' about that reality. While there was no sudden intellectual upheaval, mid-fourteenth century Italy did witness the emergence of a form of thought, known as 'humanism', that represented 'a fundamental change in man's outlook on life and the world'.[32] A brief exploration of this new paradigm, if you like, should help us to assess and appreciate Machiavelli's originality.

What were the humanists rebelling against? What was the medieval vision of the world? For a start, it was teleological. In order to understand a thing, we must – said the scholastic philosophers – go back to its first principle and show in what way it has evolved from this principle. The very first principle, the cause and origin of all things, is God, the 'unmoved mover' of the universe. He is the ultimate source of motion, being at rest himself. He transmits his force first to the things that are next to him, to the highest celestial entities. From here the force descends, by degrees, to our own world, the earth. But here we no longer find the same perfection. The higher world, the world of the celestial bodies, is made of an imperishable and incorruptible substance – the ether – and the movements of these bodies are eternal. In our own world, everything is liable to decay or deterioration. There is, it seems, a sharp discontinuity between the lower and higher worlds; they do not consist of the same substance and do not follow the same laws of motion. But the multiplicity of things is held together by a golden chain. All things whatsoever, whether spiritual or material, the choirs upon choirs of angels, man, organic nature, matter – all of them are bound in this golden chain about the feet of God. The essential unity of his creation, however, presupposes a strict hierarchy. The more remote a thing is from the prime mover, from the source of all being, so much the less is its grade of perfection or ethical value. The same principle was assumed to hold for the structures of political and social life. In the religious sphere, we find the ecclesiastical hierarchy that reaches from the Pope, at the summit, to the cardinals, the archbishops, bishops, down to the lower echelons of the clergy. In the state, the highest power, derived from God, is concentrated in the Emperor, who delegates this power to his inferiors, the princes, the dukes, and all the other vassals. The feudal system is an exact image and counterpart of the general hierarchical system: it is an expression and a symbol of the universal cosmic order established by divide wisdom. One must therefore obey one's earthly rulers, though allegiance to God is primary; earthly life is nothing more than a preparation for entering the kingdom of heaven.

The universe was seen as a great allegory, an elaborate system of correspondences, where the different parts were related to one another not so much causally as symbolically. The prevailing worldview was, in sum, teleological (all creation is governed by divine purposes), holistic (everything is organically linked with everything else), hierarchical (both the cosmic and social orders are graded according to degrees of purity or proximity to God), static (God's plan, like God himself, is eternal and unchanging) and other-worldly (man's spirit is nourished by the inner life whose centre lies outside the earthly city and carnal humanity). How and why did this vision of reality change in the period of 'rebirth'?

At the risk of alienating scholars imbued with the traditions of Hegelian or Thomist idealism, we must accept that cultural trans-formations are bound up with attendant, if not antecedent, changes in economic and political institutions. To understand the gradual de-parture from medieval ways of thinking, it is therefore necessary to examine the dynamic forces that were dissolving the medieval social structure, particularly in Italy, the cradle of the Renaissance.

Medieval culture was predominantly feudal and ecclesiastical – the product of a society founded upon an agrarian, land-holding economy. By the beginning of the fourteenth century, that society had already been replaced in Italy by an urban society constructed upon an econ-omic foundation of large-scale commerce and industry, and with rapidly developing capitalist institutions. The growth of capitalism elsewhere in Europe encouraged a parallel development on the polit-ical level, as the medieval conception of the Holy Roman Empire became increasingly obsolete. Beyond the ever-narrowing bounds of the Empire, states were beginning to form, impelled by national senti-ments as well as the need to protect and regulate expanding markets. By Machiavelli's time of writing, national unity was associated with the overthrow of aristocratic privilege and independence and the enhanced authority of monarchies. In Italy, however, national unification did not seem to be an option, despite the early decline of feudalism and a plethora of *condottieri* anxious to enforce their will on the Italian people. During the Renaissance, Italy experienced a col-lapse of traditional authority that was more complete than anywhere else, but no new aggregative force arose from the wreckage. The Empire had ceased to have any real hold on Italian loyalties after the time of Dante (1265–1321). The dominant ideological battle of the Middle Ages between Papacy (supported by the Guelphs) and Empire (supported by the Ghibellines) had drawn to a close in the early four-teenth century. The Great Schism (1375–1415) had brought the Pope and the ecclesiastical hierarchy into discredit. In the resulting vacuum, no single dynasty emerged to embark on a process of Italian unification. Partly because of geography, partly because of the still for-midable *temporal* power of the Church, and partly because of the obstinate traditions of municipal republicanism that took root in the early days of Italian capitalism, centrifugal forces prevailed, especially in the northern and central parts of the peninsula, leading to a number of independent mini-states with apparently incompatible interests. Renaissance Italy became a playground for petty tyrants and oligarchs, rulers with questionable titles to legitimacy. In many cases, individuals with no dynastic claims were the driving force behind revolutions or *coups*, as the absence of an overarching order allowed particularism to flourish. Political success depended on the exercise of superior shrewdness and ruthlessness, since power often had no foun dation in tradition or customary obligation. The political constraints imposed by Christianity, predicated on the assumption that rulers must bow to a higher authority, more or less disappeared in Renaissance Italy, though they were already becoming irrelevant in the late Middle Ages, when the actions of great rulers like the Emperor Frederick II and Philip IV of France offered examples of thoroughly unscrupulous power politics. Even the Church itself, by its inner transformations, by the progressive permeation of the Papacy with worldly political interests, and by the rational perfecting of Papal finances, paved the way for a new secular politics. Whatever the reason, the universal ideas of the medieval *corpus christianum* progressively gave way to a new centre of will concentrated in the state. Certainly, the medieval conception of a universal, organically articulated political order was no longer congruent with Italian circumstances. New forces, entirely unknown to the feudal system, had to be accounted for.

This scene formed the general backdrop of Renaissance art and thought, whose brilliance was epitomized by Machiavelli. Yet his bold ideas were anticipated, in many respects, by the humanists who preceded him. Because humanism was founded on a feeling of profound devotion to classical antiquity, it is commonly assumed that the movement was anti-Christian or neo-pagan. This is a fallacy, much encouraged by the modern misuse of the word 'humanism' to mean 'non-divine', a sort of substitute religion in which 'Man' is the measure of all things. But Renaissance humanism was almost entirely Christian in its roots, and its proponents were overtly or implicitly committed to the teachings of Christ, if not to every dogma of the Catholic Church. In fact, humanism in the Renaissance was *humanitas*, meaning those studies which are 'humane' – worthy of the dignity of man. These were, mainly, grammar, rhetoric, poetry, history and philosophy. Humanism was a cultural and literary movement whose interests were definitely distinct from those of theological studies, but distinction need not imply opposition. However, while it was by no means heretical or impious, humanism contained in its 'programme' some general ideas that threatened prevailing values. One of them was hostility to grand intellectual systems which seek to organize and delimit every possibility within the pattern of a pre-established order. Implicitly challenging established religious cosmology, humanists preferred the conception of an open world, discontinuous and full of contradictions, infinitely various and immune to any kind of systematization. In place of a static world-view, they urged us to recognize 'the plastic mobility of all Being'.[33] Their rejection of a static reality, as presupposed by Scholastic and Aristotelian logic, gave them an empirical bent, which led them to criticize the medieval custom of treating texts as 'oracles from which one had to wrest the secret meaning'.[34] Texts, not factual reality, had become the object of knowledge, and empirical research, any attempt to place texts in *context*, was dismissed by hidebound cultural guardians as impertinence, or worse. Even more subversive was the humanist emphasis on man as the moulder and maker of himself and his world.[35] For example, adjectives such as 'divine' and 'heroic' were increasingly used to describe painters, princes and other mere mortals.[36] There developed a new sense of the human being as agent – as someone responsible for his actions, as the fundamental building block of human society. The stress on human agency was especially visible in humanist historical writings. Whereas medieval historians typically interpreted events in moral and providential terms, regarding success and failure as divine rewards for virtue or divine punishments for sin, humanist historians secularized the interpretation of history, viewing earthly affairs as the outcome of *human* aims, skills and resources.[37]

Moreover, in contrast to the medieval view of man as essentially and exclusively a 'soul', Renaissance writers and artists celebrated the beauty of the human body and produced idealized depictions of it. This renewed respect for human physicality went hand in hand with a refusal to accept monastic isolation and the contemplative life as the highest Christian ideals. Man's vocation lies on this earth, serving one's *patria* and one's friends. For humanists such as Coluccio Salutati and Leonardo Bruni, man reaches his highest perfection through civic activity. The classical insistence on civic virtue and communal well-being was thus completely in harmony with Christian morality. Man shines in his daily construction of the earthly city, in the serious dedication to public life.[38]

What the humanists provided was an unmistakable, if generally implied, critique of the cultural and social values of medieval Christendom, based on their reverence for classical antiquity. In their view, the failings of modern Christian life could mostly be traced to the loss of the classical heritage: the practical wisdom and military power of ancient Italy. As one commentator remarks, 'to celebrate the past was inevitably to criticize the present.'[39] The condemnation of pride and vainglory, for example, had been central to Christian teaching since its beginnings, but humanists saw that reviving ancient traditions of public virtue would be impossible if princes and citizens were not encouraged to attain fame and adulation. The idea of *libido dominandi* (lust for power) was prevalent in Italian Renaissance thinking, as was praise for heroic actions.[40] Indeed, self-assertion words abound in the literature of the period – *gloria, onore, valore, concorrenza* (competition).[41] Although the humanists posed no direct threat to the ecclesiastical polity of the Church, they articulated a new, lay view of Christian society, which fused established Christian values with ancient pagan ones. To a large extent, they were making a virtue of necessity. Renaissance princes were already behaving as if the medieval subordination of political to religious ends was a hopeless anachronism. The *libido dominandi* was an omnipresent reality, while the orthodox Christian injunction to avoid the temptations of wealth and glory became little more than a fig-leaf for society's 'losers'. Given the fluctuating distribution of power between (and within) city-states, people became acutely aware that the political system was not a gift from God but a human artefact. The belief that force was the real key to understanding politics gained currency among the Florentine ruling elite; and, by the time Machiavelli put pen to paper, it was almost universally accepted.[42] One of his diplomatic colleagues, Francesco Guicciardini, formulated the point in his inimitably succinct way: 'State authority is nothing but violence over subjects.'[43] By the end of the fifteenth century, the idea of an immovable, God-given order had been overcome by a more dynamic vision of a world in evolution, in flux, where God (and the Devil) no longer pulled the strings.

It is clear that Machiavelli did not single-handedly destroy the political claims of the late medieval Church. Life itself had already undermined the old assumptions. But more to the point, the theoretical ground for his innovations was prepared by his humanist forerunners. They, not he, invented the contrast between a weak, corrupt and divided contemporary world, and a powerful, united Golden Age of antiquity. The danger of contextual analysis, however, is that a thinker's originality could somehow get lost in the relentless hunt for precursors. Ideas are not like footballs, which are passed from one person to another without being changed in the process. This apparent truism seems to have eluded Allan Gilbert, who decided – after minute historical study – that Machiavelli's *Prince* was a rather commonplace thing, fairly representative, in both thought and style, of treatises written in the familiar genre of advice-books for monarchs, a literary form stretching back to medieval times and quite popular during the Renaissance.[44] Untenable though this argument may be, it does provide a starting point for assessing the precise ways in which Machiavelli's ideas departed from the traditional 'mirror of princes' literature. Another Gilbert, Felix, undertook this task in a renowned article published a year after his namesake's contribution.[45]

The medieval approach to the genre, he maintains, was typified by Egidio Colonna, one of the most influential Aristotelians of the late thirteenth century, who argued purely deductively from general propositions and assumptions regarding the nature of the universe. In his way of thinking, the whole of man's earthly existence is coordinated with the life beyond. From this premise, he deduces the prince's place in the world. The prince is the intermediary between God and man, and the attributes of rulership must flow from this proposition. Princes, for instance, should not aim to acquire honour, power or wealth; instead, they should set an example to their subjects by following the principles of natural justice.[46] At first glance, says Gilbert, the humanists seem to have nothing in common with Colonna. While for Egidio the good ruler's reward was a sublime position in the next world, for the humanists his reward was fame. Furthermore, the humanists introduced a new methodology. They based their arguments on historical examples rather than abstract theoretical speculation. The examples, needless to say, were taken exclusively from antiquity, particularly ancient Rome. Yet, Gilbert continues, careful study of humanist writings on the prince 'will reveal a number of traits which they have in common with the medieval conception'. Like the medieval authors, the humanists attempted to describe the *ideal* prince. In both cases, the qualities of this model sovereign were determined by unrealistic political assumptions. The tasks of the *quattrocento* prince were confined, like those of his medieval counterpart, to the administration of innate justice and the maintenance of peace. Consequently, the just and humane king or prince remained the ideal.[47] But, as suggested above, in the humanist catalogue of princely attributes, purely worldly ones, such as *magnificentia* and *majestas*, took their place beside the religious ones. The former type, moreover, were considered from the point of view of their empirical effects, their advantages and disadvantages being weighed. *Liberalitas*, say, was regarded not so much as a good-in-itself but as a means of consolidating the power of the ruler. Patrizi (1412–94) and Pontano (1426–1503) even began to raise the question whether princely virtues might be in some respects different from those of private citizens, but they did not take it seriously enough to supply a systematic answer or to work out a consistent doctrine of political necessity. Although they had glimpses of a unique political morality, Machiavelli's humanist predecessors 'invariably started by accepting the traditional identity between the ideal prince and the ideal human being'. There is no real appreciation of the power struggles and egoistic purposes which dominate political life. The *quattrocento* princeship literature remained enclosed within the Christian framework, where man's ultimate purpose is to attain a state of grace, and where the rational course of action is always the moral one, dictated by natural law.[48]

Machiavelli did indeed adapt the logical structure of *The Prince* to the conventional literary form of the advice-book genre, but – as we shall see clearly – he removed all traces of the idealized human personality from his portrait of the prince. Conventional Christian concerns yielded to reasons of state. Machiavelli's deviance is nicely illustrated by his redefinition of the pivotal concept of *virtù*. For the humanists, *virtù* was essentially equivalent to 'virtue' as we understand it – a moral good, indicating a humane, prudent, wise form of behaviour. For Machiavelli, *virtù* was more like a force of nature, including in its meaning such things as 'ambition', 'drive', 'courage', 'energy', 'will-power' and 'shrewdness'. While he agreed with the humanists that the prince must personify *virtù*, he did not see *virtù* and lack of scruple as in any way contradictory. He removed the word's Christian associations.[49] In fact, the Latin cognate, *virtus* (with its connotations of patriotism, manliness and courage), resembles *virtù* in the special Machiavellian sense. Machiavelli's subversion is also evident in his use of the historical method. Like the humanists, his aim was to apply classical wisdom to the problems of his own time. It was an axiom of Renaissance thinking that the study of classical antiquity held lessons for the modern world, and that ancient Rome had a unique exemplary status. But humanists were certain that Roman texts, in particular, embodied prudential *and* ethical principles of eternal value. The idea was to extract exempla of good and evil, effective and ineffective conduct. Machiavelli, on the other hand, wanted to draw only pragmatic, not distinctively moral, lessons from the ancient past. It does not necessarily follow, however, that he harboured a burning hostility to Christian ethics. Of all the interpretations of Machiavelli, the most influential remains the one first advanced by Croce, who argued that the Florentine's essential contribution to the history of human thought was his clear separation of politics from morality, his recognition that the former had an existence and logic independent of other spheres of life, and that this 'autonomy' was vital to the proper functioning of the state. Politics is therefore 'beyond good and bad morals'; it is *a*moral, since it engenders its own laws against which it is 'futile to rebel', laws 'which cannot be banished from the world with holy water'.[50] Machiavelli thereby rejected the medieval concept of 'unity' and became – in the words of Federico Chabod – 'one of the pioneers of the modern spirit'.[51]

Of course, the traditional paradigm of 'oneness' had already been breached by Renaissance artists, who saw their task as imitating nature in itself, and not inasmuch as it mirrors the power of God. Long before Machiavelli created the hero of politics, the Renaissance had acclaimed the hero of art, a person dominated by artistic, as distinct from religious, imagination. In a similar if more brutal manner, Machiavelli sought to circumscribe the controlling Christian *Weltanschauung* by rival claims and values which were grounded in experience. If he was willing to countenance cruelty, fraud, and deceit, it was because he saw politics as a form of activity unconditioned by any assumptions or aims of a Christian character. This did indeed represent a decisive break with tradition. Time and again, medieval philosophers had quoted the sayings of St Paul that all power derives from God. Humanist thinkers before Machiavelli at least paid lip-service to the divine origin of the state, but he disdained to make even that concession. What Copernicus, his contemporary, achieved in the realm of cosmology, Machiavelli achieved in the sphere of politics. The Polish astronomer replaced the Aristotelian cosmological system – the conventional orthodoxy – with a new system where we no longer find a division between the 'higher' and 'lower' worlds. All movements whatever, the movements of the earth and those of celestial bodies, obey the same universal rules. For Machiavelli, too, there are no privileged points in the universe, no 'above' and 'below'. The same principles and natural laws hold in the physical and political orders alike. It is often remarked that he employs phrases and analogies of a positively naturalistic or medical character. References to 'natural necessity' and 'the nature of things' occur frequently in his analyses of political forces.[52] In order to describe the state, he is forever racking his brains for expressions that compare it to a plant, roots and all,[53] and for similes in which its development is likened to the development of a human body – so much so that he came to adopt a naturalistic view of the state itself, attributing to it the qualities of a natural phenomenon: birth, growth, decline and death.[54] There may be a contradiction between this deterministic naturalism and Machiavelli's insistence that a *virtuoso* politician can decisively shape events. But perhaps not, since Machiavelli sees the politician as a sort of doctor, who uses his skill to expel bad 'humours' from the body politic and restore it to health, though it is still destined – like the human body – to decay and perish.[55]

For Machiavelli, the universe is not governed by Reason or Mind; the structure of reality is basically a system of physical motions. To all appearances, this world-view might seem to align Machiavelli with the Marxist materialists excoriated by Gramsci and Labriola. Plekhanov and Bukharin also presumed that human events were governed by the very laws that determined external nature. But, in positing communism as the inevitable goal of history, they implicitly embraced Hegelian teleology and thus betrayed the logic of their naturalistic premises. What makes Machiavelli so remarkable, as Berlin has pointed out, is that he rejects teleology altogether. The only natural laws he mentions are laws of physical necessity. He makes no reference to any ideal order, to any doctrine of man's place in the great chain of being, to any far-off event towards which creation moves. He has no notion of human development or progress in pursuit of ends ordained by God or by nature. Even his theory of cyclical recurrences and repetitions in history, Berlin notes, 'is not metaphysically guaranteed'.[56] Rather, such *corsi* and *ricorsi* occur 'by chance'. Although cyclical changes are necessary and follow an unalterable sequence (they are not random), they have not been planned by any being, nor do they serve any fixed design. In using the word 'chance', Machiavelli wants to say that these cycles take place because of the natural inclinations of men in groups and not because of any 'essence', or 'final cause', governing human society or human individuals.[57] According to Berlin, the originality of Machiavelli's viewpoint can hardly be exaggerated. For one of the deepest assumptions of Western political thought, scarcely questioned before Machiavelli, is the doctrine 'that there exists some single principle which not only regulates the course of the sun and the stars, but prescribes their proper behaviour to all animate creatures'. Central to this doctrine 'is the vision of an impersonal Nature or Reason or cosmic purpose, or of a divine Creator whose power has endowed all things and creatures each with a specific function; these functions are elements in a single harmonious whole, and are intelligible in terms of it alone'. The tendency to fit all existence into a 'unifying monistic pattern' survived Machiavelli's attack and came to underpin the various forms of rationalism, 'religious and atheistic, metaphysical and scientific, transcendental and naturalistic', that have dominated Western – but not Italian – thought since Machiavelli's death.[58]

The idea that abstract speculation or divine revelation could give us access to the secrets of the universe was anathema to Machiavelli. He did not seek 'the meaning of flux outside the flux'.[59] Quite the reverse. He was the first prophet of a humanism that allowed man to work out, on his own, apart from religion, natural law, or any extraterrestrial limit whatsoever, the operative principles of the human order. Machiavelli foresaw the lay state, purged of the medieval concentration on eternity, on the salvation of souls, and grounded in practical concerns. Eschewing abstract universals, he exalted man's active and independent spirit, creating and appropriating the external world. Man's behaviour is neither determined nor constrained by transcendent forces or norms. Everything is reducible to human dimensions and passions. Machiavelli offers us history without mysteries, history as a series of physical events. Men unite or become enemies in the same way as some waters join or separate, bodies fall, and so on. In common with nature, human history embodies no meaning, only endlessly repetitive cycles. The hunger for constants, for universal moral truths, originating in God's will or in pure reason, is therefore based on a fatal misconception. There are no standards outside history. What we call absolute values are relics of traditional metaphysics – an invention of man dressed up as an invention of God. Terms like 'justice', 'good', 'bad' are merely conventional and arise from the existential needs of human beings living in communities. 'Good' behaviour is simply behaviour that enjoys approbation because long experience teaches us that its effects are usually beneficial; 'bad' behaviour, conversely, is simply behaviour that invites disapprobation because equally long experience teaches us that its effects are usually harmful. Likewise, 'justice' stems from man's fear of suffering evil at the hands of others; the concept refers to a set of rules and principles that evolve to deal with this concern, and there is no reason why they should not differ, in content if not in form, from one civilization to another.[60] This is why, for Machiavelli, law is an 'external' thing; it is not handed down by God to the mortals made in his immortal image, nor does it derive from moral purposes that are inherent in human nature. Law is nothing but a form of command, rooted in superior force or superior craft.

But, as noted earlier, this 'secular' interpretation of Machiavelli is not universally accepted. There *are* commentators – a small minority, to be sure – who view him as a sincere, if iconoclastic, Catholic, blessed with a profound sense of the eternal and determined to maintain the link between politics and religion. A classic statement of this interpretation was made, some years ago, by Felice Alderisio. What *his* Machiavelli admired about the ancient Romans was not their paganism but their 'fear of divinity', along with their ability to combine piety with martial and civic virtues.[61] Those who deny that Machiavelli possessed a 'resolute and lofty Christian conscience' perpetuate 'a vulgar legend'.[62] True, he wanted to combat the 'deformations' of Catholic dogma, especially its 'fanatical disavowal' of earthly things and its indifference to the common good. Much like later reformers, he urged a 'more vigorous, more ample, more humane, and more elevated interpretation' of Christianity, one that could rescue the Church from its doctrinal distortions, on the one hand, and its secular corruption, on the other. So far from rejecting the primacy of religion, he regarded it as 'the immanent and transcendent end' of the state. Our purpose on earth is to carry out 'the divine plan', and this requires 'active participation' in social life, the accomplishment of mundane tasks assigned by God.[63] If Alderisio is right, Machiavelli would not have felt embarrassed in the company of that other (and somewhat younger) scourge of ecclesiastical misdeeds, Martin Luther.

This 'Christian' interpretation of Machiavelli seemed to become moribund until it was revived in 1989 by Sebastian De Grazia. *The Prince*, he informs us, comprises 'significant metaphysical and theological statements'.[64] As for the *Discourses*, it is 'a fundamental work in the political theory of religion', since it seeks to end the *de facto* duality of Church and state. Machiavelli's apparent criticisms of Christianity are really attacks on dishonest prelates and priests for debasing the founding principles of Christ:

> Niccolò pits the spiritual authority of the founder against the institutional trappings of the Church. Whenever the teachings of the Church deviate from Christ and God's religion, by implication, the papacy is illegitimate and its reputation false; popes, prelates, and clergy have lost their spiritual authority.[65]

Machiavelli's God 'loves men who are just, merciful, and charitable to their neighbours'.[66] He is 'the creator, the master deity, providential, real, universal ... a force transcendent, separate from but operative in the world'.[67] Our daily activities are drenched in celestial design. On

De Grazia's analysis, Machiavelli believes that all religions except Christianity are false; it alone is 'the true faith'.[68]

Alderisio and De Grazia are right to claim that Machiavelli did not wish to separate politics from religion. Indeed, he saw the latter as indispensable to the smooth functioning of the state. Thus he advises princes and republican leaders alike 'to maintain the ceremonies of their religion uncorrupt and hold them always in veneration', for 'one can have no greater indication of the ruin of a province than to see the divine cult disdained'.[69] States are 'secure and happy' only when they are 'rooted in religion'.[70] He even praises Numa Pompilius for *inventing* the ancient Roman religion in order to tame 'a very ferocious people' and to 'reduce it to civil obedience'.[71] But what such remarks express is an *instrumental* approach to religion, indifferent to its truth-value. Most readers do not find a profound sense of the eternal and the transcendent in Machiavelli's work; rather, they are struck by its spiritual emptiness. When pronouncing on the necessity of cruelty and deceit, Machiavelli never exhibits any of the moral doubt or tormenting anxiety that besets a conscience turned in upon itself, and he accordingly ascribes to the various expressions of faith an entirely political significance. While religion may well constitute the foundation of national life, what counts, in his estimation, is not religious sentiment in itself, not its intrinsic value as a palliative for disturbed souls, but its incidental practical value as a check on social corruption and disorderly conduct. Religion is identified with its outward form, as revealed in its ceremonies and institutions; and the moral influence it exerts is, for Machiavelli, that of a coercive force, proceeding from above, subjecting human minds to a firm discipline and assisting in the fulfilment of civic obligations. There is no need for religion to rest on truth, provided that it is socially effective.[72] Religion is thus deprived of its mystical and spiritual content; it is nothing more than a useful fiction, whose worth depends entirely on its capacity to promote solidarity and cohesion.

So his hostility to the Papacy, his desire to see the Church of Rome reformed, was prompted by motives quite different from those that inspired the dissenters and reformers of the time. The Catholic Church, in Machiavelli's opinion, was to be condemned for its *practical* failings, not because it had strayed from the path of true righteousness. First of all, its transparently hypocritical commitment to financial accumulation and territorial aggrandizement had caused Italians to lose 'all devotion and all religion – which brings with it infinite inconveniences and infinite disorders'. Furthermore, the Papacy had kept

Italy divided. For it was too weak to unite the entire peninsula, yet strong enough to prevent others from doing so, 'for fear of losing dominion over its temporal things'.[73] But he was not just opposed to the corrupt antics of the Papacy; he also attacked Christianity as such and contrasted its degenerate values with the noble values enshrined by pagan religion. As if anticipating Nietzsche, he levelled at Christianity the now familiar reproach of having made men humble, unmanly and feeble. Christian dogma held that beatific vision, not worldly success, was the *summum bonum*. But, in a predatory world, what society could flourish or even persist if all its citizens displayed the traditional Christian virtues of humility and passivity? If good men pursue an other-worldly image of human excellence, they will surely fall prey to 'criminal men'. With romantic longing, he gazed towards the strength, grandeur and beauty of life in antiquity, and towards the principles of its *mondana gloria*. Machiavelli promoted the ideal of a 'new man', in whom grandeur of spirit (*grandezza dell'animo*) and strength of body (*fortezza del corpo*) combined to create heroism. Betraying not the slightest sign of reluctance or compunction, the Florentine broke with the spiritualizing ethic of Christianity, which deprecated the natural impulses of the senses. It is true that he regarded this as a 'false' understanding of Christ's message, and that he denounced those who had 'interpreted our religion according to idleness [*ozio*] and not according to virtue [*virtù*]'.[74] The fact remains, however, that Machiavelli valued 'our religion' only in an instrumental sense. His commitment to Christianity was cultural rather than doctrinal or emotional.

The Christian psychology of sin and redemption is nowhere to be found in his two major works. The idea of sin in Machiavelli has nothing in common with the idea of sin as breaking a commandment of God. Instead, 'sins' are political errors, often committed by rulers who try to obey Christian ethics when objective circumstances require mercilessness or deception.[75] Nor do we find the usual Christian imagery of divine and diabolic intervention in earthly affairs. He never invoked a supernatural will to explain the ultimate reason for things. A brief excursion here into Machiavelli's discussion of 'fortune' would help to illustrate this point. The classic expression of the role that fortune had in the medieval system is to be found in a famous passage of Dante's *Inferno*.[76] Men, we learn, are in the habit of speaking of fortune as if she were an irrational and independent being. But such a conception is the result of human blindness. Whatever fortune does, she does not in her own name but in that of a higher power. She is an *ancilla dei*, an agent of divine providence. She may be pitiless and indiscriminate in her bestowal of gifts, but her very indifference to human merit in the disposition of her rewards serves to remind us that the goods of this life are unworthy of our pursuit, that the quest for worldly riches and glory is of no account in the final scheme of things, and that we must therefore free ourselves from such unworthy distractions in order to seek our heavenly home. This Christian element is removed in Machiavelli's description. He revives the pagan conception of an irrational, essentially uncontrollable goddess, who may nevertheless smile on the *vir*, the man of true manliness, the paragon of courage and audacity. Yet, on the other side, Machiavelli introduces a modern element. Fortune, in his writings, is not so much a supernatural figure as a literary device to describe the logic of events, the external constraints on human behaviour, the web of earthly accidents in their inexorable succession. Nevertheless, for rhetorical purposes, he often personifies fortune – in the manner that lingered on through the Middle Ages from ancient times – as a fierce goddess. Like all women, however, she can be 'mastered' through 'boldness'.[77] While the imagery is arresting, its practical meaning is opaque. How can we 'master' an irresistible force? Machiavelli obviously has some difficulty reconciling his predilection for action ('free will must not be denied') with his belief in fortune, which, by definition, lies beyond man's rational control. He resolves the matter (to his own satisfaction at least) by saying 'that even if fortune is the arbiter of half our actions, she still allows us to control the other half' – assuming that we can seduce her with our courage and imagination.[78]

Machiavelli's preference for the classical, as opposed to the Christian, version of fortune highlights an interesting point. While he evinced little of the Christian psyche, he shared with the Middle Ages the conviction that truth had revealed itself at a precise moment in history, which embodied *in nuce* all the possibilities of development open to man. From the Christian perspective, this led to a longing for a return to the primitive Church and for a 'revival' of evangelical poverty and purity. To Machiavelli, the defining moment was ancient Rome, whose political ways, intelligently transplanted, could 'redeem' the den of iniquity that was modern Italy. Machiavelli, one could say, subverted the Christian mentality by mimicking it. But he never risked losing his audience by purging Christian symbols from his language. Those searching for references to 'God' and 'heaven' in his writings will not be disappointed, though he deploys these words in a figurative or declamatory sense, almost as rhetorical weapons.

Moreover, he remained wedded to the appropriate Christian vocabulary of exhortation and disapprobation, using it for his own un-Christian ends. Terms such as 'sin' and 'redemption' were given a secular meaning, but – ever the rhetorician – he knew that the feelings they evoked derived from their Christian origins. Machiavelli brought theology down to earth. Grace became *virtù*, the state took the place of the Church, and patriotic duty was substituted for obedience to God. Salvation was to be sought in this life, not the next. Alderisio and De Grazia seem to mistake surface appearances for underlying reality. Machiavelli was at heart a heathen. Neither his friendliness towards religion nor his occasional resort to Christian terminology makes him a true believer.

Machiavelli, it is fair to conclude, stood at the forefront of the modernist rebellion against medieval ways of thinking. He did not dream of universal monarchies or the eternal hereafter; nor did he concern himself with the salvation of souls or the contemplation of God's handiwork. It is the unprecedented *earthliness* of his thought that provides the crucial link with the twentieth-century theorists discussed in this volume. They all believed, with Machiavelli, that true understanding can come only from an objective assessment of man as he is, not as he ought to be. This focus on the tangible, the concrete, entailed a rejection of abstract universals, of transcendent 'essences' and absolute moral truths, residing in human beings by virtue of some supernatural realm. The moral and religious beliefs that we accept as axiomatic are therefore our own, albeit unconscious, creation.

Machiavelli's desire to reduce the spiritual world to *terra firma* was, of course, one that he shared with Marx. For some unknown reason, the intriguing similarities between these two great thinkers are almost invariably ignored by scholars. Not by Croce, however. He professed himself 'astonished' that no one had ever thought to call Marx the 'Machiavelli of the proletariat'.[79] Marx, in Croce's opinion, embodied 'the best traditions of Italian political science', not just 'the firm assertion of the principle of force, of struggle, of power', but also 'caustic opposition' to 'the so-called ideals of 1789'. Echoing Machiavelli, Marx dismissed moralistic sermons about political rectitude as so much idle chatter. By disputing the gospel of bourgeois liberalism, he tore down the abstract barriers – philosophical and moral – to the proletarian conquest of power.[80] It was this Machiavellian urge to demystify abstractions that especially fascinated Marx's two glittering Italian disciples. Central to historical materialism, on Labriola's interpretation, was the destruction of all speculative faiths and all cosmic beliefs:

The nature of man, his historical making, is a practical process ...
The realistic process leads first from life to thought, not from thought
to life. It leads from work, from the labor of cognition, to understanding as an abstract theory, not from theory to cognition. It leads from
wants ... to the creation of the poetical myth of supernatural forces,
not vice-versa ... Historical materialism, then, or *the philosophy of
practice* ... gives the last blow to all forms of idealism which regard
actually existing things as mere reflexes, reproductions, imitations,
illustrations, results, of so-called *a priori* thought, thought before the
fact. It marks also the end of naturalistic materialism ...[81]

To Labriola (and later, Gramsci), the supernatural was mere poetic
myth. As for the positivist Marxists, who invested matter with covert
spiritual purposes, they were the modern equivalents of older theological thinkers long since overcome by Marx himself. These new 'theologians', peddlers of 'pseudo-scientific metaphysical mumbo-jumbo',
had turned matter into an 'extra-historical truth', 'an abstract universal outside of time and space', a grotesque mirror image of Hegel's
Spirit.[82] If we assume that the philosophical mind is a product of
history, if it is 'a process of creation in perpetuity', in contradistinction
to 'an external entity which does not change', then 'we cannot think
anything except things which we ourselves experience'. *Pace* Marx's
more misguided apostles, it is 'not given to us to know the thing itself,
the inmost nature of things, the final cause and fundamental reason of
phenomena'.[83] The quest for such knowledge is, in Gramsci's ringing
phrase, 'one manifestation of the "search for God"'.[84] Labriola and
Gramsci thus argued for a socialism without metaphysical guarantees
– whether these be found in the Kantian realm of abstract truth or in
the irresistible force of 'History'.[85]

Marxism, so interpreted, is a radical form of anti-essentialism, 'the
absolute secularisation and earthliness of thought',[86] redolent of
Machiavelli's challenge to medieval cosmology. Reason, on this conception, is purely instrumental, the servant of empirical needs. Rather
than inhabiting an autonomous world, where truth or validity is independent of context, reason is bound up with the life activity of the
people. Hence, Gramsci's famously (or infamously) pragmatic conception of 'truth': 'Mass adhesion or non-adhesion to an ideology is the
real critical test of the rationality and historicity of modes of thinking.'[87] To wit, the validity of a social or moral doctrine can be meas-
ured only by its practical success. Does it 'respond to the demands
of a complex, organic period of history'?[88] Does it, in other words,

penetrate popular consciousness through its ability to satisfy existing needs and desires?

Mosca and Pareto were equally dismissive of the notion of a transcendent 'good' and equally concerned to find contextual explanations of moral and political imperatives. Although they are normally considered 'positivists', they had few affinities with the 'religious' sociologies of Spencer and Comte, both of whom assumed that scientific analysis could deliver absolute value judgements. Like their Marxist compatriots, Mosca and Pareto attacked *a priori* reasoning and claimed to move strictly in the field of experience and observation.[89] For the latter thinker, no statement, outside of mathematics and logic, can have definite truth value unless it conforms 'to some experimental reality'. Reason, a purely instrumental faculty, is incapable of discovering some human 'essence' that can tell us how to live.[90] Concepts such as 'justice' and 'goodness' correspond to no cosmic truth about man; they are merely conventional and reflect reasoning 'by accord of sentiments'.[91] Interestingly, Pareto agrees with Gramsci and Labriola that reductive materialism is itself a form of metaphysics, since it elevates matter to the status of an 'absolute'. The proposition that only matter exists issues from 'introspection instead of objective observation'.[92] To combine this proposition with Hegelian teleology, as orthodox Marxists do, 'oversteps the limits of comic absurdity'.[93]

Mosca's anti-metaphysical stance is less explicit though no less central to his thinking. His evolutionary and contextual analysis of moral thinking is reminiscent of Machiavelli's comments on the subject. Neither author attempts to explain morality in terms of divine will or 'right reason'. Morality, to the contrary, develops historically, through a 'long and slow process of elaboration', as people become more civilized and refine their selfish or aggressive impulses to suit the needs of communal life. Also like Machiavelli, Mosca suggests that this morality could differ in substance from one society to another, since ethical norms are expressions of the mass consciousness, which is itself influenced by local customs, traditions and experiences.[94] Similarly, when assessing political and religious doctrines, Mosca does not bother to ask whether they are 'true' in some objective sense; the only relevant question, for him, is whether or not they are successful – and success will depend upon their ability 'to satisfy the needs of the human spirit', which in turn depends upon 'the requirements of time and place'.[95] It follows that Christianity is not necessarily superior to pagan or any other kind of religion. Religious precepts 'emanate from the collective moral sense that is indispensable to all human associations'. Where that sense is weak or undeveloped, or has been allowed to decay through idleness and luxury, the society in question will be barbarous and corrupt, regardless of its formal religious make-up. Conversely, where 'the collective moral sense' is strong, any faith will ensure public order and decency.[96] Machiavelli would have appreciated this relativistic approach to religion.

The Machiavellian idea that the practical success of a moral or social doctrine is the only valid indicator of its 'correctness' is one that unites Labriola and Gramsci, on the one hand, with Mosca and Pareto, on the other. In the struggle for power, the objective 'truth' or 'falsity' of any given normative principle is both irrelevant and impossible to determine (except in the pragmatic sense). There is no divine or otherwise transcendent law, no inescapable human 'essence', that could enable us to decide between different modes of behaviour. Nevertheless, our two schools of thinkers arrived at this conclusion in slightly different ways. The Marxist historicists denied the existence of an independent reality, untouched by human values and categories, against which we could make judgements about 'rightness' or 'wrongness'. What we know about the world will always be filtered through our conceptual framework. Wherever human beings seek knowledge, in other words, they find their own reflection.[97] Mosca and Pareto, as positivists, did postulate an independent world of fact as the ultimate arbiter of our statements about reality. But this factual world can tell us only what *does* happen, not what *ought to* happen. The normative terms of political discourse cannot be validated by scientific analysis; they do not admit of factual proof or disproof.[98]

## THE EMPIRICAL METHOD

Machiavelli's hostility to metaphysics, to *a priori* reasoning, his refusal to appeal to something external to man and history, found expression in his attachment to the empirical method. This, I shall argue, is another component of his legacy to modern Italian thought.

According to a common interpretation of Machiavelli, his principal contribution to intellectual history was to base generalizations on observation of events, not on deduction from first principles. It is said that he was a pioneer of the 'inductive method' – the idea of grounding knowledge on the collection, collation and analysis of what we call facts. This method is contrasted to the medieval practice of seeking explanations by a long process of inference and deduction. Like the ancient Greeks, medieval thinkers were interested in final causes, in what things were for, in purposes. Logic, not controlled observation, was the discipline for resolving theoretical disputes. Machiavelli thus emerges as the first political scientist. For Burnham, no stranger to hyperbole, he shared the methods of Galileo and Darwin and Einstein. His detailed conclusions might sometimes be wrong, but his methods were scientific. Political questions were to be settled by appeal to facts: if these disclose that successful rulers lie frequently and break treaties, then such a generalization takes precedence over an opposite law drawn from some metaphysical dogma which states that all men have an innate love of truth or that truth – in the long run – always triumphs over lies. When the facts decide, it is the principles that must be scrapped. Machiavelli, to Burnham, categorically rejected the type of theory that was simply the elaborate projection of wish fulfilment. Politics, in a manner identical to nature, operates according to fixed laws that impose limits on what we can or cannot achieve.[99]

By the middle of the twentieth century, the elevation of Machiavelli to the same scientific status as Galileo had become a familiar theme among scholars of positivist persuasion. In the opinion of Ernst Cassirer, the supposed prophet of evil 'studied political actions in the same way as a chemist studies chemical reactions ... He never blames or praises political actions; he simply gives a descriptive analysis of them.'[100] Leonardo Olschki supported Cassirer's argument, claiming that Machiavelli, to a far greater extent than any of his contemporaries (including Leonardo da Vinci), possessed a refined scientific instinct. This is because, after the fashion of all great scientists, he started out with an axiomatic assumption that allowed his research findings to fit into a perceptible pattern. Galileo's controlling assumption was that matter is unalterable – eternal and necessary. This axiom has its exact scientific counterpart in Machiavelli's fundamental premise that human nature is always and everywhere the same. If one assumes, as did the cynical Florentine, that all men in all places pursue their own interests in a more or less rational way, then their actions become calculable and predictable. Galileo's concept is no longer accepted in the way he intended, and Machiavelli's view of human nature is obviously open to question. But without these axiomatic propositions, neither man could have formulated his elaborate system of natural or political laws.[101]

Implicit in Olschki's argument is the admission that scientific method cannot rest solely on verifiable observations. The quest for laws or regularities must be guided by suppositions whose truth value is not necessarily validated by experience. To critics of Machiavelli, however, his preconceptions disqualify him from the role of a detached, impartial, scientific observer. While not altogether denying that he has a place in the great transition from teleological abstraction to empirical science, these commentators protest that he tended to wrest conclusions from recalcitrant evidence in a way that was hardly comparable to Galileo's methods of measurement and experimentation. Rather than sifting through the data and allowing generalizations to emerge, 'he is really only making deductions from classical theses concerning human nature or the historical process'.[102] On this interpretation, he looked to history for illustrations of general theorems that were already in his mind, not for data from which to draw such theorems. That Machiavelli 'transformed and stylized facts and events' in order to suit his purposes is now widely accepted.[103] Some unkind observers take an almost malicious pleasure in pointing out his *non-sequiturs* and his selective way with evidence.[104]

Various explanations have been advanced for his alleged failure to discover genuine laws of political behaviour. One focuses on his excessive admiration for Roman values and institutions. He posited a simplistic contrast between ancient virtue and modern corruption, and too easily assumed that pagan modes and attitudes could be resurrected in the bourgeois, Christian Italy that so appalled him. These commitments or prejudices, it is argued, systematically distorted his vision. He was a dreamer, a man of intense passion, emotionally wedded to a revival of ancient glories.[105] This criticism is related to another one: that Machiavelli had a defective sense of historical context, for – contrary to his assumptions – practices and behaviour that are appropriate in situation X are rarely appropriate in situation Y. Machiavelli disputed this because his historical reflections had convinced him that, essentially, human nature was always the same, always defined by the same passions and needs, and therefore likely to produce the same responses and outcomes in a variety of superficially different contexts:

> … whoever wishes to see what has to be considers what has been; for all worldly things in every time have their own counterpart in ancient times. That arises because these are the work of men, who have and always had the same passions, and they must of necessity result in the same effect.[106]

Human psychology acts as a link or common denominator between past and present. Because of its constancy, historical incidents tend to fall into repeating patterns. If we dig deeply enough, supposedly unique situations will reveal themselves as typical occurrences. 'On this view of history,' Butterfield observes, 'change is kaleidoscopic – there is reshuffling and recombination but no transformation of the constituent parts.'[107] The notion that all historical events are interchangeable was initially challenged by Machiavelli's friend, Francesco Guicciardini, a distinguished diplomat and historian in his own right. He did not share Machiavelli's penchant for describing things as 'natural' or 'necessary'; nor did he believe that present reality could be controlled in the light of ancient examples. Although he never questioned Machiavelli's view of the essential fixity of human nature, he nevertheless insisted that conditions and circumstances exhibit differences and exceptions that defeat all attempts to predict the precise consequences of any particular type of political practice or action:

> How wrong it is to cite the Romans at every turn. For any comparison to be valid, it would be necessary to have a city with conditions like theirs, and then to govern it according to their example. In the case of a city with different qualities, the comparison is as much out of order as it would be to expect a jackass to race like a horse.[108]

Where Machiavelli found general principles of absolute clarity, Guicciardini saw infinite complexities that refuted any simple rules.[109] On shifting sands like these, no science of statecraft could take hold.

According to this still influential argument, Machiavelli's scientific ambitions foundered on the diversity and variety of human experience. His quixotic desire to interpret particular events as instances of general causal laws blinded him to the fact that government is not a science but an art – dependent on an imaginative grasp of contextual peculiarities. If his prejudices gained the upper hand, it was because he had set himself an impossible task to begin with. A rather different explanation for his scientific failings, recently developed at length by A.J. Parel, is that his mental outlook fell under the sway of the astrological nonsense that passed for serious thought during the Renaissance.[110] Astrology appeared then both as a 'science' of the stars and as an art of prognosticating their alleged effects on human affairs. Like so many of his contemporaries, Parel's Machiavelli believed that human behaviour was determined by celestial configurations associated with the images of pagan deities – Jupiter, Mercury, Venus, Mars, etc. He accepted the astrological conviction that 'the heavens' are the general cause of all the particular motions – human and natural – occurring in the sublunar world. That is to say, the motions of history as well as of states are subject to the motions of the heavens. Moreover, the celestial intelligences that guide the heavens love to tease or perhaps forewarn men about grave events through revelations, prodigies, and other astral signs. Burnham proclaimed that there 'are no dreams or ghosts in Machiavelli', a thinker who 'lives and writes in the daylight world'.[111] But, in the opinion of Joseph Kraft, 'Machiavelli's daylight world was by no means ghostless'. It was a world of occult forces and interventions, of spirits and portents, far removed from the world of modern science.[112]

To the critics, then, Machiavelli did not take hold of political theory and transport it from speculative realms to a region of empirical observation. Instead, he was a pseudo-scientist who ultimately surrendered to dogma, who could 'see the shape of things only in the mould that his own mind had made for them'.[113] If the critics are right, if he was not a pioneer of the empirical method, if he was not the originator of modern political science, if he was little more than a worshipper of ancient practices and institutions, then my thesis about his enduring influence would have to be modified. But *are* the critics right?

First of all, those who belittle the scientific claims made on his behalf are often guilty of anachronism. In Machiavelli's day, scientific method in our sense – deliberate, systematic, self-conscious – was only in its infancy. Copernicus's great works on astronomy, the turning point for modern science, were not published until after Machiavelli's death. In Machiavelli, as in Leonardo and (indeed) Copernicus, the nature of scientific method is not fully understood; some pre-scientific notions, held over from medieval and ancient metaphysics and theology, are retained. Copernicus himself still thought that the planets must move in circular orbits around the sun because a perfect God would have created none but perfect motion in a circle for the heavenly bodies. Much is made of those few pages where Machiavelli revealed his belief in auguries; yet Johan Kepler, a great astronomer and one of the founders of modern science, a man born *a century after* Machiavelli, was among the best horoscope casters of his time.[114] In any case, Parel exaggerates the significance of Machiavelli's leanings towards astrology. When the matter is explicitly considered in the *Discourses*, our author makes it clear that, for him, the existence of heavenly signs foretelling calamities or other momentous happenings is an *empirical fact* – and one that he professes himself unable to explain.[115] No doubt he confused popular fiction with established fact, but he shared this misapprehension with most of his educated contemporaries. In the same chapter, he mentions the common astrological belief that 'the air is full of intelligences', but pointedly refuses to commit himself to it.[116] Parel also reads too much into Machiavelli's apparent attribution of anthropomorphic qualities to 'the heavens' (*i cieli*). In Italy at the time, it was common to speak of these higher realms as if they had powers and intentions, and it is not clear whether Machiavelli's conformity to conventional speech patterns tells us anything about his cosmological system. Were his words meant to be taken literally? We have already seen how he exhibited the rhetorician's desire to address his audience in their own terms. Perhaps he was simply following a piece of advice he gave to the aspiring prince: be 'a great dissembler', pretend to share the values and prejudices of your subjects even when you do not.[117] So far from being paralysed by superstition, Machiavelli wanted to manipulate it for the purposes of statecraft. Note his praise for Roman military chiefs who cynically interpreted unusual material events as favourable auguries in order to give psychological reassurance to disaffected or hesitant troops.[118] But even if Machiavelli did, to some degree, fall under the spell of astrological speculation, this would not necessarily detract from his scientific reputation. It is perfectly possible for a scientist to adhere to superstitious beliefs, as long as these do not intrude upon his investigation of the physical universe. Newton's theology, for example, included a belief in witchcraft, but there are no pixies in the workings of the 'Newtonian world machine'.[119]

Another observation worth making in defence of Machiavelli is that his methodology was not nearly as unrefined as his critics would have us believe. It is true that his style of argumentation did not lend itself to subtlety. The 'on the one hand this and on the other hand that' approach, so dear to the hearts of academic social scientists, was not in keeping with his personality. He delighted in aphorisms and paradoxes, and was much given to axiomatic pronouncements. Emblematic of the way he thought was his disjunctive prose style, full of either/or formulations. This fondness for strong antitheses had the unfortunate effect of arbitrarily excluding every possibility lying between the poles of the either/or construction. Complex issues are thus reduced to artificial questions. Was virtue or fortune the cause of Rome's greatness? A finely shaded answer is effectively ruled out by the way the question is posed. This disjunctive technique is the appropriate formal expression of a mode of thought which assumes that a *virtuoso* politician will always make prompt and firm decisions, unencumbered by 'ifs', 'ands', and 'buts'. The 'middle way' is to be studiously avoided, irresolution spurned.[120]

Yet such crudity is not the whole story. For Machiavelli often displays a methodological sophistication and a respect for evidence that are curiously overlooked by his critics. One of their complaints, for example, is that he views antiquity as an infallible guide. But he quite explicitly acknowledges that those who laud ancient times frequently suffer from blind spots. Most history, we are reminded, is written by the victors or by those who depend on them, which means that the record of events available to us will, almost without exception, accentuate the positive and gloss over the negative.[121] Expressing self-doubt and self-awareness in equal measure, he writes:

> I do not know thus if I deserve to be numbered among those who deceive themselves; if in these discourses of mine I praise too much the times of the ancient Romans and blame ours.[122]

Although Machiavelli may not have entirely evaded the danger of which he speaks, his affinity for the Roman republic could hardly be described as 'slavish'.[123] In addition, let us not forget that the information available to him about the period was, of necessity, much scantier than our own – a point made in his defence by both Mosca and Pareto. As the latter remarked, 'one cannot blame Machiavelli for accepting the old Roman legends at face value. They were taken as history by everyone in his time.'[124] In assessing the Roman age, we have the accumulated benefits of patient documentary research by a veritable army of historians; he had no such advantage.

It is in any case wrong to assume that he derived his evidence exclusively or even mainly from antiquity. *The Prince* – to take an obviously important example – is full of references to recent history and contemporary politics. One distinguished scholar goes so far as to assert that this work 'reflects Machiavelli's fifteen years' experience in the chancery service', and that the various historical illustrations were strictly for rhetorical effect.[125] Whether or not this assessment is accurate, there is no denying that Machiavelli ordinarily supports his generalizations with examples drawn from several different periods of history. References to Roman and Greek history are often linked with references to Italian and European history comparatively close to his own time. It is reasonable to conclude – in defiance of his critics – that he wanted to guard against mistaking a type of behaviour characteristic of some particular period for a more general historical law. Machiavelli is also careful to point out that diverse conditions often require diverse forms of behaviour. He does not, as some of his critics suggest,[126] put forward infallible maxims of universal applicability, as if contextual factors were of no account. Consider his analysis of 'the difficulties involved in keeping a newly acquired state'. Centralized lands, like the kingdom of Turkey, are difficult to conquer (because the people are united in loyalty and subservience to the ruler), but easy to retain once occupied (because there are no alternative power centres which can provide a focal point for revolt). In contrast, feudal (or quasi-feudal) states, like France, are relatively easy to conquer (since malcontents among the barons can always be found to assist an outside force), but hard to subdue for any length of time (since nobles of ancient lineage, who are loved by their subjects and capable of mounting new insurrections, will remain). Those bent on conquest must bear these subtleties in mind and adjust their behaviour accordingly.[127] Even *within* states, the qualities necessary for successful leadership will vary with circumstances. Machiavelli praises Piero Soderini, leader of the ill-fated Florentine republic that was overthrown in 1512, for his 'humanity and patience', qualities which allowed his fatherland to prosper. But when times changed, and he needed to break with his humble ways, he did not know how to do it, 'so that he together with his fatherland was ruined'.[128]

What is more, when Machiavelli finds that two contrary lines of action have proved successful in analogous circumstances at different periods of the past, he uses this conflicting evidence as a cue for deeper analysis. In the *Discourses*, for example, he shows how Scipio made himself master of all Spain by his 'humanity and mercy', which won him the admiration and friendship of its peoples. Hannibal, on the other hand, produced the same effect in Italy by very different means – 'cruelty, violence, robbery, and every type of faithlessness'. In attempting to explain the discrepancy, Machiavelli concludes that a conquering general has the option of making himself loved or feared. It is immaterial which of these two courses he takes provided he is a man of sufficient abilities to correct whatever inconveniences may arise from the pursuit of either.[129]

Similarly, Machiavelli does not systematically ignore examples that might disprove his *regole generali*; his usual procedure is to explain why they are the exceptions that prove the rule. His reflections on mercenary soldiers nicely illustrate this point. Indulging in typical overstatement, he denounces such troops as 'useless and dangerous', since 'they are disorganized, undisciplined, ambitious, and faithless'. Yet the historical record forces him to concede that 'the Venetians and Florentines did extend their territories in the past through the use of mercenaries'. While his explanations for this anomaly may not have been convincing ('luck' in the case of the Florentines; the modesty of their territorial ambitions in the case of the Venetians), the discussion demonstrates a willingness to confront and deal with contradictory evidence.[130]

None of this is to deny that he was sometimes economical with the truth. But even the most rigorous social scientist will occasionally jump through hoops to reconcile inconvenient data with his theoretical assumptions. Moreover, it is necessary, once again, to look at Machiavelli in context. As an eminent specialist on the Renaissance observes:

> The mental outlook and habits of expression fostered by rhetorical training permeated the culture. Renaissance Italians were not burdened with the cult of sincerity so typical of modern democratic societies; for them, sincerity was a trope like any other. It was more important that speech be appropriate, elegant and effective than that it be strictly true. The rules of decorum in fact called for the *celatio* (concealment) or *suppressio* of the truth, even the *suggestio* of the false, in the appropriate rhetorical situation.[131]

However, while Machiavelli was a product of his culture, he also helped to create something new. For he insisted on contemplating human society and history '*in proprio loco*', independently of metaphysical connections. He never argued about abstract principles. To him, the facts of political life were the only valid political arguments. This is why he could write – when examining the methods used by princes 'to keep their lands secure' – that 'it is impossible to set down definite judgements on all of these measures without considering the particular circumstances of the states where they may be employed'.[132] This statement pretty much epitomizes his empirical *forma mentis*. He categorically rejected the rationalistic procedure – common to this day among political philosophers – of starting from first principles and logically deducing practical propositions from them. Yet this does not mean that he was opposed to abstraction as such. His assertions that all ages are of the same fundamental structure and that all men share an identical nature are empirical inasmuch as they purport to describe an observable reality. But they also involve an element of abstraction from the variety and complications of actual experience. Abstraction in this sense does not destroy Machiavelli's scientific credentials. Analogous methods are followed in all sciences, both physical and social. When Newton introduced the idea of frictionless motion, bodies not acted upon by other forces, he did not imagine that such

things existed exactly as he depicted them. It was a matter of abstract-
ing for the sake of generalizing more adequately.[133] Those who wish to
portray Machiavelli as an *a priori* thinker will have to do more than
simply point out that environment influences human behaviour, or
that historical epochs differ significantly from one another.

But of all the criticisms of Machiavelli, perhaps the silliest is that he
could not have been an objective empirical analyst of human affairs
because of his political passion, his hatred of corruption and his desire
to see the foreign invaders expelled from Italy. Let us concede that
Machiavelli's intention was not merely to *describe* human behaviour or
to expound its enduring patterns or 'laws'. Insofar as he criticizes the
contemporary world without mercy and perpetually tells the states-
men around him how they 'ought' to behave, he does not remain
purely on the level of fact. His works, as everyone knows, abound in
precepts, practical hints, counsels, prescriptions, warnings, and useful
maxims. If he *is* a scientist, he is like a doctor who diagnoses his
patient's illness, then prescribes a remedy based on what has worked
in the past. Indeed, Machiavelli sees the nature of his enterprise in
precisely this way: politics is to be a science, analogous to medicine.[134]
The comparison can be pressed further. Some people make the
unthinking assumption that scientific inquiry cannot be motivated by
practical goals. But this is tantamount to saying that medical
researchers are not scientists. Are those seeking to develop drugs for
AIDS or cancer less than scientific simply because they are driven by
the practical aim of extending human life? Only when the analyst
allows his goals to distort the facts or the correlation between facts
do such value commitments become an impediment to scientific
objectivity.

All things considered, it would not appear excessive to concur with
Baron's judgement that Machiavelli 'laid the groundwork for the
transformation of cosmology'. He represented the transition from a
static/theological to a dynamic/scientific vision of life, where truth is
dependent on the observation of reality and on nothing else.'[135] He
searched not for 'final' causes, emanating from God's design for the
universe, but for 'efficient' causes, grounded in human dispositions
and actions. The question 'why' was replaced by the question 'how'.
This focus on the material world – a corollary of his rejection of teleology – is a striking feature of modern Italian thought.

That Pareto and Mosca saw themselves as social scientists, working
within the anti-metaphysical tradition pioneered by Machiavelli, is
beyond doubt. Rightly or wrongly, both men are associated with the

*fin de siècle* doctrine known as positivism, which, on a minimalist definition, is reducible to two propositions: (1) human behaviour is constrained and determined by inescapable conditions, which can be understood through causal laws; and (2) the way to discover these laws is through the observational techniques used to such good effect in the physical sciences. Machiavelli can be described as an embryonic positivist, inasmuch as he saw his task as one of transforming empirical facts into theoretical precepts. He was not primarily interested in the unique political event, but in laws relating events. Pareto applauded this quest for uniformities in history, noting that 'many maxims of Machiavelli' hold 'as true today as they were in his time'.[136] Those who deny this usually miss the point. While he concerned himself 'with the problem of determining what is going to happen under certain hypothetical circumstances', an eminently scientific mode of discourse, his critics assail him with 'a mass of ethical and sentimental chatter that has no scientific status whatever'.[137] As a self-appointed standard-bearer in the Machiavellian crusade against 'ethical and sentimental chatter', Pareto frequently cites his mentor with approval, complimenting him on his sage observations and scientific methods.[138]

Mosca's attitude to Machiavelli's techniques and findings was less enthusiastic. Unlike his fellow elitist, Mosca was not particularly impressed by *The Prince* – a compendium, as he saw it, of rather dubious generalities. He *was* impressed, however, by the two 'very happy intuitions' that made Machiavelli a great thinker: (1) the idea 'that the explanation of the prosperity and decadence of political organisms is to be sought in the study of events; in other words, in their past history'; and (2) the principle 'that in all peoples who have reached a certain degree of civilization, certain general, constant tendencies are to be found; which means, in other words, that the political nature of man is more or less the same in all times and all places.' Thus, while dismissing many of his forebear's political precepts as of 'little practical value', Mosca nevertheless praised him for his courageous and revolutionary premises.[139] Where the 'Florentine Secretary' fell short was in the excessive burden of expectation he placed upon the historical method. Although he was right to seek 'the great psychological laws that function in all the large human societies', these laws can tell us little about 'the art of attaining power and holding it'. The qualities or circumstances that will lead to success or failure in the political sphere are too multifarious to be covered by general rules – a point that even Machiavelli was forced to concede on occasion.[140]

The well-informed reader may wonder what Mosca and Pareto could possibly have in common with Labriola and Gramsci on the question of science. The two Marxists were both sworn enemies of positivism, which Labriola denounced as an 'epidemic'.[141] Closer inspection, however, indicates that they shared with the classical elitists the Machiavellian predilection for empirical procedures. Needless to say, *all* Marxists are practitioners of the historical method; they go to history to learn the preconditions of insurrection, the mechanics of subversion, and the various permutations of revolutionary strategy. What they cannot do, given the intrinsic environmentalism of their approach, is to endorse Machiavelli's doctrine of a fixed and immutable human nature. Insofar as we can speak of a 'human nature', Gramsci warns, it must be understood as 'the totality of historically determined social relations'.[142] For Gramsci and Labriola, this emphasis on the historical determination of human behaviour meant that Marxism itself must be understood as a form of historicism, inimical to the idea of absolute and eternal laws. Political science must therefore be conceived 'as a developing organism', geared to our evolving needs and assumptions.[143] With this caveat in mind, Gramsci reaches a favourable verdict on Machiavelli's scientific achievement, for it 'represents the philosophy of the time, which tended to the organisation of absolute national monarchies – the political form which permitted and facilitated a further development of the bourgeois productive forces'. It has to be admitted, says Gramsci, that Machiavelli was not a 'pure' scientist, since his scientific efforts were guided by a passionate attachment to specific goals.[144] But Gramsci saw nothing wrong with combining empirical analysis and normative aspirations, as long as the latter originate in real, observable trends and not in the realm of hopes and dreams. He saw himself engaged in just such an enterprise. Because of his stress on human subjectivity, there has been an unfortunate tendency to bracket him with Lukács and other foes of 'bourgeois science'. Nothing could be further from the truth. He explicitly pays homage to 'experimental science', viewing it as a necessary precondition – an ingredient, if you like – of Marxism:

There can be no doubt that the rise of the experimental method separates two historical worlds, two epochs, and initiates the process of dissolution of theology and metaphysics and the process of development of modern thought whose consummation is in the philosophy of praxis.[145]

In attacking positivism, the Marxist historicists intended to discredit a particular approach to social science, not social science itself. They opposed all attempts to construct political or historical theories 'according to criteria built up on the model of natural science', as if one could 'predict' the future of human society in the same way that one predicts the development of the oak tree out of the acorn.[146] Ironically, this manic desire to imitate the physical sciences, initially motivated by a contempt for metaphysical speculation, had resulted in a contempt for empirical evidence, with many Marxists seeing themselves in possession of 'a universal diagram for all things'.[147] What was meant to be a method for illuminating factual reality became an abstract dogma that obscured this reality. But, although one must capture the facts in all their unrepeatable originality, one can still isolate 'certain more general "laws of tendency" corresponding in the political field to the laws of statistics or to the law of large numbers'.[148] It is not, Gramsci assures us, 'a question of "discovering" a metaphysical law of "determinism", or even of establishing a "general" law of causality'. Rather, it is 'a question of bringing out how ... relatively permanent forces ... operate with a certain regularity and automatism'.[149] This ambition to correlate sets of observable facts into generalisations or uniformities places Gramsci and Labriola squarely in the Machiavellian tradition of social scientific analysis.

Indeed, with respect to science, one could plausibly describe the differences between the classical elitists and the Marxist historicists as more rhetorical than real. Both Mosca and Pareto agreed that the 'great complexity' of the phenomena involved in the study of human society makes it difficult to arrive at incontrovertible truths.[150] As Pareto writes, the chief complication for social sciences 'lies in finding ways to unravel tangles of many different uniformities'.[151] Mosca deals with this problem by indicating that we can formulate only tendential regularities, and by suggesting an asymmetry between positive and negative prediction. When examining human society, it is impossible to foresee 'exactly what is going to happen'; we are much better able to predict '*what is never going to happen*'.[152] No more than Gramsci does he believe that the acorn/oak tree model is appropriate for the social sciences. In a similar vein, Pareto admits that social scientific inquiry is 'contingent, relative, yielding results that are just more or less probable'. His assertion that even natural science is 'relative' and 'in part conventional' fits neatly into the Marxist historicist view of the world, which relates the changing paradigms of scientific inquiry to practical needs and relations.[153] Moreover, when Labriola protests against 'scientists whose minds are clouded by mythologies', he is referring primarily to Comte, Pareto's' *bête noire*.[154] Pareto, in like manner, berates the Frenchman (and Spencer) for turning science into a form of religion, complete with absolute value judgements about good and evil.[155] Along these lines, Pareto denigrates the positivist 'theology of Progress' (his words) as a travesty of science, for it implicitly invokes a *telos* rather than an empirical procedure in order to explain social regularities and trends.[156] These remarks on the myth of Progress are reminiscent of the passage where Labriola ridicules those Marxist pseudo-scientists who worship at the feet of '*Madonna Evolution*'.[157]

Finally, it is worth looking at what Pareto has to say about monist views of history. 'Science has no dogmas', he insists, 'and so cannot and must not accept determinism *a priori*.' There may be social situations where, say, economic necessity does seem to be the determining factor, but this can be verified only 'within the limits of the time and space that have been investigated'. Unless we come across a multitude of such situations, we cannot generalize this finding to other social or historical contexts. What the observer will normally discover, in truth, is that 'social facts – that is to say, conditions and effects – are *interdependent*'.[158] Likewise, Labriola declared – and here he speaks for Gramsci as well – that monism, whether of the idealist or materialist variety, represents the triumph of metaphysics over empirical methods.[159] Because it does not accord with the facts of experience, it is, in Mosca's words, 'an article of faith'.[160] Respect for the world of empirical fact and disrespect for those who would turn science into a new metaphysical system, a new faith, served as the connecting link between the Marxist historicists and the classical elitists. And this orientation clearly owes a great deal to their common Machiavellian heritage.

## POLITICAL REALISM

Machiavelli's realism, as much as his commitment to the empirical method, stemmed from his rejection of metaphysics and teleology. If the universe is not governed by Reason or Mind, if the structure of reality is basically a system of physical motion, then effective truth, practical reality, is all there is. There is no natural order of the soul and therefore no natural hierarchy of values. One must take one's bearings by how men live as distinguished from how they ought to live.

With scientific detachment, the objective observer sweeps away the web of illusion men spin round themselves and concentrates on their actual behaviour. What, then, are we talking about when we talk about politics? Man's search for the ideally good society? Not according to Machiavelli, for whom politics was primarily the struggle for power. He was tired of political literature that valued abstract speculation over practical experience – that envisaged perfect princes living in perfect states. Machiavelli expressed this view with memorable bluntness in *The Prince*:

> I depart from the rules set down by others. But since it is my intention to write something of use to those who will understand, I deem it best to stick to the practical truth of things rather than to fancies. Many men have imagined republics and principalities that never really existed at all. Yet the way men live is so far removed from the way they ought to live that anyone who abandons what is for what should be pursues his downfall rather than his preservation; for a man who strives after goodness in all his acts is sure to come to ruin, since there are so many men who are not good.[161]

Unpacking this quotation, we can see that it embodies three distinct propositions, each of which will be discussed in turn: (1) men are not what they seem; despite their professions of good faith, they are generally wicked – at least in their political behaviour; (2) ideal projections, unrelated to practical affairs, are of no use; and (3) survival – the precondition of all other political goods – often requires actions at variance with traditional biblical morality.

**Proposition 1**

Machiavelli's view of human nature was relentlessly pessimistic: 'For this can be said about the generality of men: that they are ungrateful, fickle, dissembling, anxious to flee danger and covetous of gain.'[162] Elsewhere he asserts, succinctly, that 'all men are bad'.[163] Human beings will never be as they are described by those who idealize them. Indeed, Machiavelli's view of human nature was Hobbesian – before Hobbes. Nature, we learn, 'has created men so that they are able to desire everything and are unable to attain everything'. As the desire is always greater than the power of acquiring, 'the result is discontent with what one possesses'. But since all men want more than they have, they are simultaneously frightened that the depredations of others will deprive them of whatever goods they do possess, however meagre or unsatisfying. This explosive combination of insatiable ambition and endemic suspicion is the root cause of political enmities and conflict, within and between states.[164] Political life is normally a battlefield where the strong subdue the weak. Men are reluctant, though, to accept this harsh truth, and try to soften it by constructing beautiful theories that give a veneer of moral justification to our predatory or domineering instincts. While society's rulers may not themselves believe in these doctrines, they would be well-advised to pretend otherwise. For it is a constant Machiavellian theme that a state founded on common values and cultural traditions has a greater chance of survival than one based almost exclusively on naked force.[165] It is rarely sufficient, according to Machiavelli, for political rulers to behave like lions; they must also possess the cunning of a fox, an ability to manipulate the prevailing emotive symbols. Fraud, as well as force, is a necessary component of effective government.[166] Political analysts, however, are obliged to penetrate the fog of pious words and grand principles that enables politicians to befuddle the masses. Following his own advice, Machiavelli took mischievous pride in demystifying the deeds of the ancient Romans, who were, to his mind, great exemplars of dissimulation, the first 'foxes', confounding their external enemies with the most devious diplomacy imaginable.[167] The 'foxes' of antiquity would not have thanked their admirer for this description of their exploits. That deceitfulness could be an aspect of political virtue was simply unthinkable to the Romans. Neither in Virgil's epic poetry nor in Livy's epic history was the dissembler or fraudster allowed to figure other than as a villain. Stoic philosophy, moreover, always sided with the 'good' over the merely useful. Even in their most jingoistic moments, ancient writers were anxious to depict Roman expansion as the divinely ordained extension of law and civilization across the known world. But, for Machiavelli, we will never understand the Romans if we look at them through spectacles coloured by their myths and illusions. Cold-eyed analysis indicates, for example, that 'they made almost all their wars taking the offensive against others and not defending against them'.[168] Where Cicero saw ancient people freely welcoming the Romans because they were the embodiment of justice and fair play, Machiavelli saw the Romans devouring their neighbours through self-conscious power politics. The force and fraud Cicero hated were, in his estimation, the heart and soul of Roman greatness.

While Machiavelli believed that contemporary Italy could be regenerated through a 'rebirth' of the political wisdom and military ethos of ancient Rome, he never advocated a simple imitation of antiquity. His classicism was realistic. He recognized that the Romans themselves were flexible enough to adapt to circumstances and did not permit rigid principles to cramp their style. Nor did he think that ancient Rome offered a perfect model that could endure without change and adaptation. Thus we come to his disdain for utopian ideals.

**Proposition 2**

Central to Machiavelli's realism was the belief that human affairs are never static but in perpetual flux. There is, however, no suggestion of progressive development. The flux is much like the undulating movement of waves – constant motion without a logical end-point. Any idea of a perfect state that could last indefinitely is therefore illusory. The process of change is, as we have seen, repetitive, roughly cyclical. Because human nature alone remains fixed and invariable throughout the centuries, the pattern of social and political change occurs again and again in history, so that by studying the past we learn also about the present and the future. This pattern is familiar to any historian: civilizations arise, prosper, become corrupt and die – unless they can be revived by a wise prince. Machiavelli, exhibiting a precocious form of Hegelian dialectical reasoning, claimed that the very virtues of the good state contain the seeds of its own destruction. For the strong and flourishing state is feared by its neighbours and consequently left in peace. But, alas, 'the cause of the disunion of republics is usually idleness and peace'.[169] Freed from fear and the rigours of war, the populace acquires a taste for luxury and licence. In the absence of external enemies, internal conflicts develop from the most trivial causes and are magnified out of all proportion. Unity and discipline break down; corruption and effeminacy become rife. Decline is inevitable. Usually through conquest, a new, leaner and hungrier state or civilization will eventually replace the degenerate one, only to follow the same road to ruin.[170]

Machiavelli, were he alive, would have agreed with Kant's observation that 'out of the crooked timber of humanity no straight thing was ever made'. Human nature abhors an ideal republic. Indeed, for Machiavelli, no society at all would be possible were it not for the virtuous few whose mental discipline and sense of purpose prevent the rest of us from collapsing into chaos and squalor. Given that most men are weak, stupid and self-obsessed, there will always be those who command and those who serve. The distinction between rulers and ruled is a basic part of political life, and the effective rulers will always be a minority.[171] Machiavelli bore no hostility to popular participation when it was mediated by representatives of superior intellect and courage. Yet he never doubted for a moment 'the uselessness of a multitude without a head'.[172] A people can be 'great' only insofar as they become faithful (if pale) copies of their 'betters'. *Real* power, even in the most democratic of republics, is always in the hands of the few. Machiavelli's imagery effectively conveys his political vision. Throughout his works, the Aristotelian pairing of 'matter' with 'form' incessantly recurs; and wherever the theme is present, the message is the same: that the people, an undifferentiated mass of matter, are nothing without the form stamped upon them by the elite.[173] He underlines the point with images of the builder, the sculptor, and the architect working with their materials.[174]

Although Machiavelli took a dim view of human nature, he was not devoid of political ideals. These, however, were neither wild nor fantastic. He envisaged – to quote Isaiah Berlin – 'men improved but not transfigured, not superhuman'.[175] The purpose of politics is to satisfy people's natural desire for esteem and material gain, not to achieve some transcendent excellence. Statecraft must operate within the limits of human possibilities. A good society is one that enjoys internal peace and security, along with a measure of freedom and prosperity – a society, above all, like the Roman republic.[176] The best state is best because historically tried and proven, not best in an abstract and illusionary sense. If Machiavelli prefers republics over monarchies, this is purely for practical reasons. Republics are, in his opinion, conducive to stability and economic well-being. A good monarch is rare, two good monarchs in succession defy all the odds, but a 'virtuous succession' of able rulers will always exist in a well-ordered republic, since the field of recruitment is wide.[177] Moreover, princes fear men of talent and boldness, and do not, as a rule, offer them preferment. The corrupt and the incompetent thus acquire disproportionate influence, insidiously undermining standards throughout society. In a free city, however, where no single person enjoys absolute authority, men of stature compete openly and on strictly relevant grounds. Through this process of competition, they 'police' one another, thereby preserving the highest standards of probity and efficiency.[178] But, in republics, the public interest is more than an accidental by-product of private transactions; it is an explicit and collective goal, formulated in consultation with the actual 'public'. In monarchical systems, by contrast, the public interest is usually confused with the private interest of the prince.[179]

Whereas the architects of utopianism place man outside history in a social world free of conflicts and tensions so that he can live in perfect concord, Machiavelli accepts the inevitability of man living in time and being subject to its ravages. Continuous strife is an abiding condition of political life. This is a brute fact, but we should welcome it and recognize its creative possibilities. Most intriguing, in this respect, is Machiavelli's discussion of 'the tumults between the nobles and the plebs' in Roman times. With scant regard for conventional wisdom, he identifies the glory of Rome with the perennial conflict between her social classes. People who condemn such discord – all of Machiavelli's contemporaries – 'do not consider that in every republic are two diverse humors, that of the people and that of the great, and that all laws that are made in favour of freedom arise from their disunion'.[180] This is what we would now describe as a classic pluralist argument. Sociologically, the foundation of liberty is a balance of competitive social forces. As human beings are naturally selfish and suspicious, dissension is inevitable. But the continuing clash of opposing groups, if moderated by a common devotion to the *patria*, generates an equally common devotion to liberty. For, where bargaining and compromise are necessary, there develops a climate of tolerance, of give-and-take, of live and let live. Calls for unity are, to Machiavelli, a cover for the suppression of dissent, for the triumph of one social interest, one absolute principle. Roman class divisions, he adds, were also conducive to social *morale* and civic responsibility. Each class gained from the other: the people were elevated to grandeur and heroism when they imitated the nobles, while the nobles, constantly menaced by the people, felt obliged to channel their energies into planning the conquest of other city-states rather than plotting to destroy one another.[181] Machiavelli thinks it self-evident that, if the constitution is so arranged that one or other of these groups is allowed total control, the republic will sink into corruption. If an aristocratic form of government is set up, the rich will rule in their own interests; if there is democracy, the poor will despoil the rich and reduce the polity to penury and licentiousness. The solution, Machiavelli argues, is a mixed constitution, aiming for a balanced equilibrium between opposing social forces.[182]

Reading *The Prince* in isolation might lead one to conclude that Machiavelli preferred absolute monarchy to republican forms of governance. He did not. His conclusion that none but a prince, unfettered by scruple or opposition, could save Italy was dictated by evidence rather than principle. In Machiavelli's view, political choices, like normative theorizing itself, must be grounded in 'the practical truth of things', not in 'fancies'. Although there was nothing utopian about a republic, it was not possible in all circumstances. The unity of theory and practice was Machiavelli's intent. Theory must descend from the ethereal heights of philosophy into the mundane world of affairs. It was this intention that drove him to challenge an assumption fundamental to Western political thought and scarcely questioned by any of his scholastic or humanist predecessors: that political success and the happiness of the people could be guaranteed by the exercise of traditional moral virtues. This brings us to the final proposition.

## Proposition 3

Machiavelli is commonly assumed to be the inventor of *ragion di stato*, but this is not quite true. Political realism was already in the air, as we have seen, and the word 'necessity' dominated the administration and diplomacy of Italian city-states during the fifteenth century. Thinkers and historians, too, apart from Machiavelli, asserted that the only way to learn about politics was through experience. The name Guicciardini springs to mind here – a man who assumed the priority of *ad hoc* solutions over general principles. Even medieval legal theorists and canonists endorsed the idea that 'necessity has no law' to justify the extraordinary acts to which a ruler might resort through force of circumstances. Neither was Machiavelli the first person to discover that immoral behaviour often pays dividends. Chabod makes an interesting distinction between 'virtual' and 'theoretical' Machiavellianism.[183] The former – disregarding moral rules, acting out of expediency, or with a devilish or manipulative cunning – has been practised by monarchs and other rulers from time immemorial. When such behaviour was confined to 'exceptional' circumstances and dedicated to the pursuit of religiously laudable goals, even Thomas Aquinas was willing to condone it as properly Christian. But with Machiavelli, 'virtual' Machiavellianism was transformed into a theoretical precept of universal validity. Actions once deemed exceptional or deviant were now declared commonplace and even admirable. What horrified Machiavelli's readers was not so much his *description* of political life, with its crimes and treacheries, as his apparent determination to teach the *art* of political criminality and treachery, as if the usual moral guidelines had no relevance to politics. He was not talking about the occasional bending of rules, nor about extreme situations requiring extreme measures. Political choice, as Machiavelli presents it, *always* seems to be between evils. Political affairs are perpetually desperate because of the venality and depravity of mankind. Securing a good end – an island of political security in a sea of corruption – will *normally* necessitate violence and betrayal in some shape or form. Political leaders who fight shy of this 'truth' will condemn their citizens or subjects to untold misery.

Machiavelli's many detractors portray him as an advocate of political immorality. A more generous interpretation – the one advanced by Croce – sees him as a defender of political *a*morality. Politics, that is to say, answers to its own logic, follows its own rules and judges actions in accordance with its own standards of success or failure. Croce adds that Machiavelli is torn and tormented by the necessity of doing evil for the sake of good. He did not, on this account, deny the validity of Christian morality, but reluctantly accepted that men with public responsibilities must dirty their hands in a way that could never be justified in the sphere of private relationships.[184]

Croce's thesis became something of a cliché in the secondary literature until the late 1960s, when it was forcefully disputed by Isaiah Berlin. He pointed out that, however troubled Croce may have been by the demonic demands of power, Machiavelli's thought displayed no such anguish. Machiavelli did not have to suspend morality in order to be Machiavelli; he simply had to affirm the tenets of *pagan* morality. Whatever favours the interests of the community is, to a pagan, morally good. Therefore, a pagan statesman can perform Machiavellian deeds with a clear conscience, for he knows morality is on his side. Machiavelli's moral outlook was Greco-Roman, not Christian; public and communal rather than private and individual. He did not emancipate politics from morality so much as introduce 'a differentiation between two incompatible ideals of life, and therefore two moralities'. One values courage, vigour, strength, order and public achievement. The other posits a moral universe where the ideals of charity, mercy, love of God, forgiveness of enemies, contempt for the goods of this world and blessed peace in the hereafter are accorded the highest evaluation. One morality is oriented towards public life and communal happiness; the other towards personal life and salvation in the world to come.[185] Berlin's Machiavelli does not formally condemn Christian morality: the things men call good are indeed good, and words like good, bad, honest, dishonest are used by him as they were in the common speech of his time. He merely says that the unequivocal practice of Christian virtues, especially on the part of rulers, makes it impossible to build a stable, strong and prosperous society. Machiavelli is thus an incipient moral pluralist, forcing us to choose between two sets of ends that are equally 'moral' but mutually exclusive and irreconcilable. 'One can save one's soul, or one can found or maintain or serve a great and glorious state; but not always both at once.'[186]

Other commentators have already noted that Berlin's contrast of two moralities, Christian and pagan, is somewhat simplistic; for there are no ancient moralists, after Socrates, who would condone the kind of behaviour Machiavelli defends in his two famous political treatises.[187] That ancient civilization gave tangible form to his value-preferences is undeniable: heroism and public spirit were glorified, and the other-worldly ideals of Christianity could find little sustenance in pagan religion. Still, no Roman code of morality ever sanctioned cruelty and deceit in the interests of political power. Machiavelli was selective in his paganism, praising its active and aggressive side, while ridiculing those elements that failed to tally with his vision of politics. Self-consciously or not, he wanted to restore pagan values to their pre-philosophical, pre-Platonic meaning. When Plato and Aristotle condemned the Spartan way of life and extolled the *vita contemplativa*, they were quarrelling with the Greek culture they had inherited. Ancient Greece has been dubbed a 'results-culture'.[188] 'Good' intentions were irrelevant, since the only important judgements that could be passed upon a man concerned the way in which he discharged his allotted social function. 'Good' for the Greeks meant 'good at' or 'good for', never good in and of itself. To us, it makes perfect sense to say that a king is 'good but not courageous or clever'. In Homeric times, this assessment would have been dismissed as an unintelligible contradiction. 'Goodness' was, by definition, equivalent to success[189] – an equation that was firmly denied by later pagan philosophers, including Cicero.

If Berlin's thesis falls down because he treats pagan morality as a monolith, Croce's contention that Machiavelli divided politics (the sphere of instrumental values) from morality (the sphere of ultimate values) is equally dubious. It would surely be odd for Machiavelli to accept the universal validity of Christian morality but nevertheless pronounce it inapplicable to such a vast area of human interaction. It makes sense to search for a more natural interpretation of his utterances. A plausible case can be made that, for him, Christian moral law no longer retained its supra-empirical necessity. Rather, empirical necessity itself became a new moral imperative, since its function was to create a certain type of good. While he was hardly a systematic

moral philosopher, we find in his thought glimmers of a modern con-
sequentialist ethics, where the goodness of ends trumps the goodness
of means. This would mark a significant departure from the deontological ethics of Christianity, where the goodness of an act is dependent on its conformity to universal moral rules. Virtuous behaviour is
thereby separated from its result, however harmful. Machiavelli,
like Bentham centuries later, wanted to define virtue in terms of
consequences.

Some might think it anachronistic to view Machiavelli as a founding
father of utilitarianism, a quintessentially liberal philosophy, indelibly
associated with nineteenth-century optimism. They would be wrong.
The mentality of the English shopkeeper – which Marx thought
Benthamism reflected – had its prototype in Italian urban life during
the Renaissance. The habit of calculation dominated everyday relationships. Time was seen as something precious, which had to be
'spent' carefully and not 'wasted'. The word *prudente* was common,
and a few writers developed a distinctively utilitarian approach to life.
Machiavelli may have been inspired by Lorenzo Valla's well-known
dialogue *On Pleasure*, where one speaker, representing the author,
defends an ethic of utility, with all actions based on calculations of
pleasure and pain.[190]

Certainly, Machiavelli is forever advising rulers to calculate the
practical costs and benefits of their actions. In pursuit of their goals,
they must be prepared to lie, to cheat, to break treaties, to use loyal
servants as scapegoats, and even to exterminate rivals. It has been
argued that Machiavelli's advice took the form of 'hypothetical imperatives' in the Kantian sense. With such imperatives, there is no question whether the end is morally good, but only what one must do in
order to attain it: 'If you want to achieve X, it is essential that you
should do Y'. Machiavelli is therefore not to be taken as necessarily
approving the postulated end.[191] One can find textual evidence to
support this view. Occasionally, he provides alternative courses, and,
indifferent to the object we desire, supplies us with a choice of
schemes and methods. When he says, for instance, that a new prince
who wishes to be absolute must change everything – despoiling the
rich, demolishing old cities and transporting the inhabitants to new
places – he adds:

> These modes are very cruel, and enemies to every way of life, not only
> Christian but human; and any man whatever should flee them and
> wish to live in private rather than as king with so much ruin to men.

Nonetheless, he appears quite happy to devise a useful maxim for the man 'who does not wish to take this first way of the good'.[192]

This evidence is taken from the *Discourses*. In *The Prince* as well, Machiavelli sometimes seems to adopt a conventional moral stance, just before offering 'technical' advice that contradicts it. He agrees in chapter 15 that it would be 'very praiseworthy' for a prince to possess all those qualities that are normally considered good. Likewise, in chapter 18, we are told that it is 'praiseworthy' for a prince to keep his word and govern 'by candour instead of craft'. But because these 'good' princes would be crushed in a world full of 'evil' men, Machiavelli sets out, with evident moral neutrality, to teach the satanic art of survival in unpropitious circumstances. Whether his pre-scriptions will be used for a good or evil purpose does not appear to figure in his calculations.[193]

While such passages support Croce's thesis, they are far from typical. More often than not Machiavelli forsakes the world of pure technique and asserts that certain courses of action are to be applauded because they promote the welfare of the community. Where the restoration of order and the safety of society are at stake, conventional vice might become political virtue, and conventional virtue might result in political ruin. In politics, it follows, we cannot draw a sharp line between moral virtue and moral vice: the two things often change place.

The prime example of this paradox – adduced by Machiavelli – is Cesare Borgia, whose ruthless methods were necessary to rid the Romagna of the plague of petty tyrants that had reduced the popula-tion to abject slavery. Borgia 'was considered cruel; yet his cruelty restored Romagna, uniting it in peace and loyalty'. He must therefore be judged kinder than the Florentines who, to avoid resorting to violent and repressive measures, allowed the warring factions in Pistoia to destroy the city's peace and prosperity. The prince who is prepared to take harsh action to keep his people loyal and united is infinitely more merciful (and, by implication, moral) than the prince who, 'through excessive kindness, allows disorders to arise from which murder and rapine ensue'. 'Disorders', Machiavelli continues, 'harm the entire citizenry, while the executions ordered by a prince harm only a few individuals.'[194] Spoken like a true utilitarian. Consider, too, the following statement: 'In all men's acts, and in those of princes most especially, it is the result that renders the verdict.' By ignoring the exigencies of statecraft, rulers who preach 'nothing but peace and faith' turn out to be 'the extreme enemy of both'.[195] In the *Discourses*,

Machiavelli makes the same point with characteristic elegance and economy. Wise men, he maintains, would never condemn the brutal acts of a ruler who endeavours 'to help not himself but the common good'. Quite the reverse, for 'when the deed accuses him, the effect excuses him; and when the effect is good ... it will always excuse the deed; for he who is violent to spoil, not he who is violent to mend, should be reproved.'[196]

A utilitarian interpretation of Machiavelli would seem to flow logically from his hostility to metaphysics. It can also make sense of his apparently contradictory attitudes concerning what is or is not morally 'praiseworthy'. He did indeed distinguish between public and private behaviour, but not quite in the way Croce thinks. It was basically a distinction between two different paths to happiness, the sole moral objective. In our personal interactions, Machiavelli implicitly concedes, we should adhere to conventional moral standards since the goodwill of those close to us can, by and large, be taken for granted. He himself was always loyal to his family and friends, and, by all accounts, cared deeply for their well-being. In this sphere, he could be described as a 'rule utilitarian', someone who thinks it obligatory to comply with moral rules that are socially useful, even when a particular act in compliance with the rules might, in certain circumstances, cause more harm than good. Although rule utilitarians are still consequentialists (rules are judged purely by reference to their ability to maximize happiness), their moral judgements will usually overlap with those of deontological moralists. This would explain why Machiavelli frequently uses terms like 'good' and 'evil' in a manner acceptable to Christians. Anyone who, in his private relationships, disobeys moral conventions which have stood the test of time threatens the delicate social balance and deserves nothing but reproach.

Political life, however, is a jungle. Here a fetishistic attachment to traditional moral rules will deliver the opposite of happiness. When Machiavelli makes statements to the effect that 'all men are bad', he is really referring to man as he functions politically – in a context where the natural ties of affection and sympathy are stretched to the breaking point. The ruler who acts as if he were surrounded by his loved ones, when he is in fact surrounded by predators, will come to grief, and probably destroy the stability of his state in the process. As a guardian of the public interest, he should behave like an 'act utilitarian', who will not recoil from acts of betrayal, deceit, injustice, cruelty, or the like if these are necessary to increase or preserve 'the greatest happiness of the greatest number' in the particular situation.[197]

Both 'rule' and 'act' utilitarianism (and let us stress that these are modern terms, which were never employed by Machiavelli) have the effect of bringing morality down to earth. What counts is not adherence to transcendent norms or divinely ordained purposes, but the maximization of empirically ascertainable well-being. And, of course, a preference for the observable and the concrete over the abstract and the imaginary is what lies at the core of Machiavelli's realism.

It almost goes without saying that the classical elitists were realists in the Machiavellian mould. Subsequent chapters will show how they shared the Florentine's low opinion of human nature as well as his assumption that elites will always rule, no matter what the constitution says. Politics is therefore about the management of power, and the job of the scientist is to reveal the processes and structures through which power is exercised. 'States are not run with prayer books,' wrote Mosca, deliberately echoing his Renaissance mentor.[198] Any ruler conducting himself solely in accordance with generally accepted moral principles is bound to fail. As Pareto puts it, such a ruler may be a 'perfect gentleman' but he is 'a no less perfect idiot'.[199] Yet the classical elitists agreed with Machiavelli that the environment of humanity is symbolically formed and ordered. Power always rests upon moral and political doctrines ('derivations' to Pareto; 'political formulas' to Mosca) that do not correspond to scientific truth. It would be mistaken, however, to dismiss these as 'mere quackeries aptly invented to trick the masses into obedience,'[200] for they answer to a profound need in man's social nature: the compulsion to seek refuge in an illusory world of absolutes. The classical elitists also denied the Enlightenment claim that humanity is capable of continuous and indefinite progress. As true heirs of Machiavelli, they argued that, deep down, the various periods of human civilization are 'very much alike'.[201] Pareto, in denying the 'myth of Progress', explicitly embraced the cyclical theory of history, using the Machiavellian imagery of 'lions' and 'foxes' to explain the successive phases. Government, as Machiavelli taught, is always by a mixture of force and fraud, but normally one or the other predominates. A regime led by 'lions' will prefer force; one led by 'foxes' will prefer fraud. The deficiencies of pure force and pure fraud as mechanisms of rule cause the two types of regime to succeed each other in infinitely repetitive cycles.[202]

The idea of utopia is therefore fatuous, not to mention dangerous. In Mosca's words, 'society will always be a wretched and disorderly affair'.[203] People will invariably be guided by passions and needs rather than some abstract, chimerical sense of 'justice'. The ineradicability of human selfishness and irrationality is precisely what renders utopian dreamers so pernicious. Should they ever gain the power to impose their vision, they would succeed only in destroying the 'natural' and time-honoured *modus vivendi* that allows frail, inward-looking individuals to live in productive harmony. Instead of utopia, we would end up with a Hobbesian 'war of all against all'. To quote Mosca again, 'any political system that assumes the existence of super-human or heroic virtues can result only in vice and corruption'.[204] Politics must be contextual, immersed in the given reality. Mosca, with Machiavelli, believes that the best we can hope for is a balanced pluralism, based on 'a multiplicity of political forces' that mutually restrain and check one another.[205] This is not to be confused with 'democracy', or rule by 'the people'. When 'political power originates from a single source', Mosca warns, it is 'liable to become oppressive'. The ruling class 'ought not to be monolithic and homogeneous', because – as Machiavelli was the first to understand – 'freedom to think, to observe, to judge men and things serenely and dispassionately' is the product of conflict and difference.[206] Sceptical as they were about 'universal truths', Mosca and Pareto thought that the triumph of a single absolute principle really amounted to the triumph of a single social force (class or group). Thus, while they never attempted to issue moral prescriptions, they broadly agreed with Machiavelli's relativistic perspective. Ethical precepts do not descend from heaven; they reflect human needs and human choices. Although Pareto did criticize utilitarianism, his quarrel was not with the basic idea of a prudential morality but with Bentham's misguided ambition to turn this morality into a scientific calculus.

Turning to Labriola and Gramsci, we encounter an immediate difficulty. Given that Marxists are almost universally regarded as utopian fantasists, how can we argue that two of their number continued the Machiavellian tradition of political realism? In reply, we can, once again, agree with Croce that the Machiavellian aspects of Marxism are unjustly ignored. For a start, what we might call 'analytical realism' has always been a staple of Marxist thought. Like Machiavelli (and the classical elitists), Marxists study human affairs primarily from the viewpoint of their effective reality, and only secondarily from the viewpoint of legal forms, ideological constructs and institutional mechanisms. They, too, presume a distinction between appearance and reality, between what *ought to* happen and what *actually* happens, though – unlike Machiavelli – they claim that a perfectly transparent society is attainable. Marxism is also a form of consequentialism: the pursuit of historically determined ends cannot be restricted by universally moral imperatives because the latter are deemed to be non-existent. Or, to put it in the simplest Machiavellian terms, the end justifies the means. It must be remembered, finally, that Marxists have always defined themselves as *anti*-utopian. No more than Machiavelli do they think that we can *impose* an ethical pattern on the torrential flow of history. However, Marx and his disciples steadfastly denied that the will-to-power was the key to human nature, or that man was unable to climb above the level of his baser self. They too readily assumed the infinite plasticity of human nature as well as the intrinsic rottenness of capitalism – assumptions that tended to make them absurdly optimistic about the communist ideal.

By comparison, our two Italian Marxists contemplated the future with a surprising degree of caution, even pessimism. Labriola, for his part, admitted that Marxist socialism 'still contains within itself some latent germs of a new utopianism'. Many Marxists, convinced as they are of the *moral* necessity of socialism, conflate this with *material* necessity. In other words, 'the future society of collectivist economic production ... *will come because it should come*'. These people, devotees of 'Madonna Evolution', think that history offers them 'a life insurance policy'. While we can plausibly predict the continued decline of capitalism and the eventual ascendancy of the proletariat, to go beyond that would be to substitute 'imagination' for reason.[207]

But it is Gramsci who emerges as the real Machiavellian. Extraordinarily, for a Marxist of his time, he expressed grave doubts about the viability of the communist future. The chief reason for his scepticism was not the fallibility of long-range prediction. Rather, he queried the conventional Marxist premise 'that all men are really equal and hence equally rational and moral, i.e. capable of accepting the law spontaneously, freely, and not through coercion'.[208] He goes so far as to say that the Machiavellian division between rulers and ruled, leaders and led, is a 'primordial and (given certain general conditions) irreducible fact' – indeed, the basis, the 'first element', of political science. The reference to 'certain general conditions' (the conditions of class society?) is slightly confusing. How can the fact in question be both 'primordial' (*primordiale*) and contingent? Essential to the 'science and art of politics' and yet dependent on 'certain general conditions'? A few sentences later Gramsci compounds the confusion by stating that the division between rulers and ruled also occurs within socially homogeneous groups, the implication being that even a 'classless' society could not eliminate elite domination. The 'technical' need for specialization and expertise, for the hierarchical organization of tasks, would not, he suggests, disappear with the class system.[209] Perhaps, then, the rulers/ruled distinction is not contingent after all. Gramsci's remarks on the future are fraught with ambiguity, but it is surely significant that – in one passage at any rate – he describes the coercion-free society of Marxist dreams as 'pure utopia'.[210] Gramsci, in fact, openly concurs with Machiavelli's 'realistic' approach to normative theory. In Machiavellian fashion, he poses a simplistic dichotomy between two ways of theorizing about what 'ought to be'. Such theorizing can be 'arbitrary or necessary', 'concrete will on the one hand or idle fancy, yearning, daydream on the other'. Machiavelli, we are informed, came down on the right side of the antithesis. A 'man of powerful passions', he nevertheless based his normative preferences 'on the terrain of effective reality'.[211] He realized that a unitarian and dictatorial state was needed to combat the forces of feudalism and particularism. Large-scale and internally cohesive states were a prerequisite of further economic development – something Machiavelli grasped intuitively.[212] Since Gramsci, like his 'bourgeois' predecessor, wanted to ground values and objectives in 'effective reality', his reservations about the more fanciful side of Marxist thought make perfect sense.

In general, Marxists see power politics as the servant of an ideological mission to change what exists. There is now widespread agreement that their scientific analysis was (and remains) clouded by wishful thinking. Even Labriola and Gramsci underestimated the productive power of capitalism, while, at the same time, greatly exaggerating the wonders of central planning. Hope triumphed over experience. In this respect as well, they resembled Machiavelli, who dreamt of impossible alliances for the purpose of driving the transalpine hordes out of Italy – a task that was not accomplished until some 350 years after he wrote. *Aspiring to* realism is one thing; *achieving* it quite another.


CONCLUSION

My main theme is that Machiavelli inaugurated a new way of understanding philosophy. Classical and medieval thinkers always looked at moral-political phenomena in the light of man's highest perfection, a goal that transcended particular societies or polities. Machiavelli's philosophizing, on the other hand, divorced politics from any kind of higher purpose, implanted in us by God or nature. Thanks largely to his efforts, much modern political reflection (especially in Italy) has adopted an empirical perspective, disdaining speculation about imagined republics or perfect justice and focusing instead on real wants and needs. The idea is to relieve man's suffering or to increase man's power over nature or to guide man towards a secure and (materially) prosperous future.

Both the classical elitists and the Marxist historicists felt entirely comfortable with this 'earthly' conception of political thought. What is more, their rejection of teleological abstraction caused them to converge – as we have seen – on five characteristically Machiavellian tenets:

1.  It is possible to construct a science of politics which will describe and correlate observable social facts, and on the basis of these, state more or less probable hypotheses about the future.

2.  The primary subject matter of political science is the struggle for power, in its diverse and concealed forms, between social groups or classes.

3.  The laws of political life cannot be discovered by an analysis that takes men's words and beliefs at their face value. Utterances, constitutions, declarations, laws, theories – all must be related to the whole complex of social and political phenomena in order to grasp their underlying meaning.

4.  There are no ethical 'truths' whose validity is completely independent of human choices or contextual particularities. Practice is central to the determination of how we ought to live. Any normative ideal or doctrine must be justified in terms of its ability to satisfy the material and psychic needs of actual (as opposed to idealized) people.

5.  Every known society has been ruled by varying combinations of force and fraud. Labriola and Gramsci, as Marxists, hoped for a society where pure reason could replace the respective talents of the 'lion' and the 'fox', but Pareto and Mosca unequivocally agreed with Machiavelli that there could be no substitutes for myth and violence as the dual linchpins of political stability.

Reflecting on the Machiavellian legacy, and on how it influenced thinkers at opposite poles of the left/right political spectrum, we might well ask if this spectrum does not serve to obscure more than it illuminates. Gramsci, for example, probably had more in common with Mosca than with a utopian socialist like, say, Fourier.[213] We might also pause to consider whether the Florentine's legacy was benign or malignant. Leo Strauss, the latest in a long line of Machiavelli-haters, blames him for instigating a 'stupendous contraction' of our moral horizon. Oblivious to universal truth and justice, Machiavelli encouraged 'a movement from excellence to vileness'.[214] The rights and wrongs of his moral scepticism and political realism are not our prime concern here. But it is worth pointing out that the most destructive regimes of the world have been those of men who have elevated their preferences to the pinnacle of moral imperatives and who have then confidently proceeded to impose those imperatives on others. Conversely, the most humane and liberal regimes in history have usually been run by Machiavellian 'foxes', the sort of people who rarely allow abstract moralism to interfere with political expediency. If the 'stupendous contraction' of our moral horizon promotes tolerance and pluralism, then perhaps it is no bad thing.

## NOTES

1.  N. Bobbio, 'Gramsci e la cultura politica italiana', *Belfagor*, XXXIII (30 September 1978), p. 597.
2.  So-called because it saw the spirit as existing concretely in the 'act' rather than in self-reflective consciousness.
3.  Bobbio, 'Gramsci e la cultura politica italiana', pp. 597–9.
4.  E. Jacobitti, *Revolutionary Humanism and Historicism in Modern Italy* (New Haven and London: Yale University Press, 1981), p. 6.
5.  Ibid., p. 52.
6.  E. Cassirer, *The Myth of the State* (New Haven: Yale University Press, 1946), pp. 153–6; L. Olschki, *Machiavelli the Scientist* (Berkeley: the Gillick Press, 1945), pp. 22–33; A. Norsa, *Il principio della forza nel pensiero politico di Niccolò Machiavelli* (Milan: Hoepli, 1938), p. 21.
7.  F. Chabod, *Machiavelli and the Renaissance*, trans. D. Moore (New York: Harper & Row, 1958), especially pp. 23, 78, 98–9.
8.  H. Mansfield, 'Machiavelli's Political Science', *The American Political Science Review*, 75 (1981), pp. 294–5.
9.  H. Butterfield, *The Statecraft of Machiavelli* (London: G. Bell & Sons, 1940), especially pp. 26–41, 114–32.
10. A.J. Parel, *The Machiavellian Cosmos* (New Haven and London: Yale University Press, 1992).
11. G. Prezzolini, *Machiavelli* (London: Robert Hale, 1967). This is a translation (by G. Savini) of *Machiavelli antricristo*, first published in Rome in 1954.
12. L. Strauss, *Thoughts on Machiavelli* (Chicago and London: University of Chicago Press, 1958), p. 9.

13. F. Alderisio, *Machiavelli: l'arte dello stato nell'azione e negli scritti* (Bologna: Cesare Zuffi-Editore, 1950), p. 190.
14. B. Croce, *Elementi di politica* (Bari: Laterza, 1925), pp. 59–67.
15. B. Fontana, *Hegemony and Power: on the Relation between Gramsci and Machiavelli* (Minneapolis and London: University of Minnesota Press, 1993).
16. Cassirer, *The Myth of the State*, p. 124.
17. R. Lodge, 'Machiavelli's *Il Principe*', *Transactions of the Royal Historical Society*, 4th series, XIII (1930), pp. 1–16. Reprinted in De Lamar Jensen (ed.), *Machiavelli: Cynic, Patriot, or Political Scientist?* (Boston: D.C. Heath, 1960). Quotation taken from p. 32 of Jensen's volume. For a similar viewpoint, see L.A. Burd's introduction to his own edition of *Il Principe* (Oxford: Clarendon Press, 1891).
18. Cassirer, *The Myth of the State*, pp. 124–5.
19. Ibid., p. 117.
20. See M. Praz, 'Machiavelli and the Elizabethans', *Proceedings of the British Academy*, 13 (1928), pp. 49–97.
21. F. Gilbert, 'The Composition and Structure of Machiavelli's *Discorsi*', *Journal of the History of Ideas*, 14 (1953), p. 156.
22. N. Machiavelli, *Discourses on Livy*, trans. by H.C. Mansfield and N. Tarcov (Chicago and London: University of Chicago Press, 1996), Book I, chapter 58, p. 117. Henceforth I shall use the abbreviated title, *Discourses*.
23. J.H. Geerken, 'Machiavelli Studies since 1969', *Journal of the History of Ideas*, 37 (1976), p. 357. This chronology, however, is not universally accepted. For a useful summary of the controversy surrounding the dating of *The Prince* and the *Discourses*, see E. Cochrane, 'Machiavelli: 1940–60', *Journal of Modern History*, 33 (1961), pp. 133–6. As Cochrane observes, the whole debate eventually became a 'great bore' (p. 135), whose main purpose, it seemed, was to display the subtle dialectical and philological skills of the various protagonists.
24. See H. Baron, 'Machiavelli: the Republican Citizen and the Author of "The Prince"', *The English Historical Review*, LXXVI (1961), p. 217.
25. *Discourses*, I, ch. 6, p. 23: 'But since all things of men are in motion and cannot stay steady, they must either rise or fall.' See, also, ibid., II, ch. 5.
26. Ibid., I, ch. 9.
27. Ibid., I, chs. 16 18, 34.
28. Butterfield, *The Statecraft of Machiavelli*, pp. 54–5.
29. Geerken, 'Machiavelli Studies Since 1969', p. 357. But, in a seminal article (see note 24 above), Hans Baron vigorously defended the opposing view. For him, the two works are substantially different, each with its own message, and express a development within the author's mind. Baron lays much stress on the fact that Machiavelli, after writing *The Prince*, formed close contacts with republican humanists and *literati* who met regularly for discussions in Cosimo Rucellai's gardens on the outskirts of Florence. These meetings, Baron believes, gave Machiavelli more faith in the civic energies of the people, a faith reflected in the *Discourses*. Baron is among the minority of scholars who insist that Machiavelli did not begin the *Discourses* until *after* he completed *The Prince*.

30. J. Burckhardt, *The Civilization of the Renaissance in Italy*, trans. S.G.C. Middlemore (London: Allen & Unwin, 1965). First published in 1860.
31. For an interesting contribution to the debate, see Chabod, *Machiavelli and the Renaissance*, ch. 4.
32. H. Baron, 'Towards a More Positive Evaluation of the Fifteenth Century Renaissance', *Journal of the History of Ideas*, IV (1943), p. 48.
33. E. Garin, *Italian Humanism: Philosophy and Civic Life in the Renaissance*, trans. P. Munz (Westport, Conn.: Greenwood, 1975), pp. 3–10.
34. Ibid., p. 13.
35. P.O. Kristeller, 'The Philosophy of Man in the Italian Renaissance', *Italica*, XXIV (1947), pp. 100–1.
36. P. Burke, *The Italian Renaissance: Culture and Society in Italy* (Cambridge: Polity Press, 1986), p. 198.
37. J. Hankins, 'Humanism and the Origins of Modern Political Thought', in J. Kraye (ed.), *The Cambridge Companion to Renaissance Humanism* (Cambridge and New York: Cambridge University Press, 1996), p. 123.
38. Ibid., pp. 124–33.
39. Ibid., p. 125.
40. M. Hulliung, *Citizen Machiavelli* (Princeton: Princeton University Press, 1983), p. 19.
41. Burke, *The Italian Renaissance*, pp. 193–4.
42. F. Gilbert, *Machiavelli and Guicciardini* (Princeton: Princeton University Press, 1965), p. 129.
43. F. Guicciardini, *Dialogo e discorsi del reggimento di Firenze*, ed. R. Palmarocchi (Bari: Laterza, 1932), p. 222.
44. A.H. Gilbert , *Machiavelli's 'Prince' and its Forerunners: 'The Prince' as a Typical Book de regimine principium* (Durham, N.C: Duke University Press, 1938).
45. F. Gilbert, 'The Humanist Concept of the Prince and "The Prince" of Machiavelli', *The Journal of Modern History*, XI (1939), pp. 449–83.
46. Ibid., pp. 459–60.
47. Ibid., pp. 460–1.
48. Ibid., pp. 462–8.
49. But Machiavelli does on occasion revert to the Christian sense of *virtù*. See, for example, *The Prince and Selected Discourses*, trans. D. Donno (New York: Bantam Books, 1966), ch. 8, p. 36. (Henceforth referred to as *The Prince*.) There are a number of English translations of *The Prince*. I prefer Donno's, though this is largely a matter of taste. Since the chapters of the work are very brief – three pages or so on average – readers using other translations will be able to follow my references by consulting the relevant chapters.
50. Croce, *Elementi di politica*, pp. 59–61.
51. Chabod, *Machiavelli and the Renaissance*, p. 116.
52. See, for example, chapter 3 of *The Prince*, pp. 14, 17.
53. Ibid., ch. 7, p. 29.
54. *Discourses*, II, Preface, p. 123.
55. *The Prince*, ch. 3, p. 18.
56. I. Berlin, 'The Originality of Machiavelli', in *Against the Current: Essays in the History of Ideas* (London: Hogarth Press, 1979), p. 37.

57. *Discourses*, I, ch. 2, pp. 11–13.
58. Berlin, 'The Originality of Machiavelli', pp. 67–8.
59. Jacobitti, *Revolutionary Humanism and Historicism in Modern Italy*, p. 5.
60. *Discourses*, I, ch. 2.
61. Alderisio, *Machiavelli: l'arte dello stato nell'azione e negli scritti*, p. 181.
62. Ibid., pp. 190, 186.
63. Ibid., pp. 195–6, 198, 200.
64. S. De Grazia, *Machiavelli in Hell* (Princeton: Princeton University Press, 1989), p. 31.
65. Ibid., pp. 119–20.
66. Ibid., pp. 69–70.
67. Ibid., p. 58.
68. Ibid., p. 89.
69. *Discourses*, I, ch. 12, p. 36.
70. *The Prince*, ch. 11, p. 44.
71. *Discourses*, I, ch. 11, p. 34.
72. Ibid., I, ch. 12, p. 37.
73. Ibid., I, ch. 12, p. 38.
74. Ibid., II, ch. 2, pp. 131–2.
75. *The Prince*, ch. 12, p. 47.
76. Canto VII, *Inferno*, J.D. Sinclair (trans.), *The Divine Comedy of Dante Alighieri*, Vol. I (New York: Oxford University Press, 1961), p. 103: 'He whose wisdom transcends all ... ordained for worldly splendours a general minister and guide who should in due time change vain wealth from race to race and from one to another blood, beyond the prevention of human wits, so that one race rules and another languishes according to her sentence which is hidden like the snake in the grass. Your wisdom cannot strive with her. She foresees, judges and maintains her kingdom, as the other heavenly powers do theirs. Her changes have no respite. Necessity makes her swift, so fast men come to take their turn. This is she who is so reviled by the very men that should give her praise, laying on her wrongful blame and ill repute. But she is blest and does not hear it.'
77. *The Prince*, ch. 25, p. 86.
78. Ibid., ch. 25, p. 84.
79. B. Croce, *Materialismo storico ed economia marxista* (Bari: Laterza, 1927), p. 112. First published in 1899.
80. Ibid., pp. xii-xiv. From the Preface to the 1917 edition.
81. A. Labriola, *Socialism and Philosophy*, trans. E. Untermann (St Louis, Mo.: Telos Press, 1980), pp. 84, 94–5 (Henceforth *SP*).
82. A Gramsci, *Selections from the Prison Notebooks*, trans. and eds. Q. Hoare and G. Nowell Smith (London: Lawrence and Wishart, 1971), pp. 348, 437. (Henceforth *SPN*).
83. Labriola, *SP*, pp. 95, 100.
84. *SPN*, p. 437.
85. Ibid., pp. 406, 407, 437; Labriola, *SP*, pp. 196, 201, 117, 128. However, as I point out in the chapter on Labriola (see pp. 73–4), he was not entirely consistent in his denial of historical inevitability. His usual position is that 'we do not know where history will end up' (ibid.,

p. 201); yet, in a few places, he claims that 'communism must inevitably happen by the immanent necessity of history' – or words to that effect. *Essays on the Materialist Conception of History*, trans. C.H. Kerr (Chicago, 1908), p. 244. It is probable that Labriola did not intend the words 'immanent necessity' to carry any metaphysical connotations. Socialism is therefore 'inevitable' only because the facts before our eyes point unequivocally in this direction. But it was certainly careless of him to lapse into conventional Marxist terminology when his main purpose was to attack the quasi-religious thinking that underlay the terminology.

86. SPN, p. 465.
87. Ibid., p. 341.
88. Ibid.
89. V. Pareto, *The Mind and Society* (Henceforth *MS*), trans. A. Bongiorno and A. Livingstone (London: Jonathan Cape, 1935), para. 6.
90. Ibid., paras 11, 19.
91. Ibid., paras 69, 506.
92. Ibid., para. 488.
93. Ibid., para. 51.
94. G. Mosca, *The Ruling Class* (Henceforth *RC*), trans. H.D. Kahn (New York: McGraw Hill, 1939), p. 125.
95. Ibid., p. 176.
96. Ibid., p. 128.
97. Gramsci, *SPN*, p. 368.
98. 'We have no knowledge whatever', declares Pareto, 'of what *must* or *ought to be*. We are looking strictly for what *is*.' *MS*, para. 28.
99. J. Burnham, *The Machiavellians: Defenders of Freedom* (Washington, DC: Gateway, 1943), p. 84.
100. Cassirer, *The Myth of the State*, p. 154.
101. Olschki, *Machiavelli the Scientist*, pp. 22–33.
102. Butterfield, *The Statecraft of Machiavelli*, p. 57.
103. Gilbert, *Machiavelli and Guicciardini*, p. 170.
104. See S. Anglo, *Machiavelli: a Dissection* (London: Paladin, 1971), ch. 9.
105. Chabod, *Machiavelli and the Renaissance*, p. 113.
106. *Discourses*, III, ch. 43, p. 302. See also ibid., I, ch. 39, pp. 83–4; and I, ch. 11, p. 36, where Machiavelli informs us that 'men are born, live, and die always in one and the same order'.
107. Butterfield, *The Statecraft of Machiavelli*, pp. 30–1.
108. F. Guicciardini, *Maxims and Reflections of a Renaissance Statesman*, trans. M. Domandi (New York, 1965), C, 110.
109. Ibid., B, 61; F. Guicciardini, 'Considerations on the "Discourses" of Machiavelli', in *Selected Writings*, trans. C. and M. Grayson (London: Oxford University Press, 1965), pp. 110–12.
110. Parel, *The Machiavellian Cosmos*, especially the 'Introduction' and 'Conclusion'.
111. Burnham, *The Machiavellians*, p. 38.
112. J. Kraft, 'Truth and Poetry in Machiavelli', *Journal of Modern History*, XXII (1951), pp. 109–10.
113. Butterfield, *The Statecraft of Machiavelli*, p. 126.

114. T. Kuhn, *The Copernican Revolution* (Cambridge, Mass.: Harvard University Press, 1957), p. 92.
115. *Discourses*, I, ch. 56.
116. Ibid., I, ch. 56, p. 114.
117. *The Prince*, ch. 18, p. 63.
118. In a passage from *The Art of War* quoted by Parel, *The Machiavellian Cosmos*, p. 62. Oddly, Parel cites this passage in support of his thesis that Machiavelli was a superstitious pagan, when in fact it suggests that he was neither superstitious nor a pagan.
119. S. Greer, *The Logic of Social Inquiry* (Chicago: Aldine Publishing Co., 1969), p. 178.
120. *Discourses*, I, chs. 26, 30; II, ch. 23.
121. Ibid., I, Preface, p. 123.
122. Ibid., I, Preface, p. 125.
123. Kraft, 'Truth and Poetry in Machiavelli', pp. 117–18.
124. Pareto, *MS*, para. 2532; Mosca, *RC*, p. 43.
125. J.R. Hale, *Machiavelli and Renaissance Italy* (London: English Universities Press, 1961), pp. 151–5.
126. See, for example, Butterfield, *The Statecraft of Machiavelli*, p. 71.
127. *The Prince*, ch. 4, pp. 21–3. See ch. 25 as well.
128. *Discourses*, III, ch. 9, p. 240.
129. Ibid., III, ch. 21, pp. 262–3.
130. *The Prince*, ch. 12, pp. 46–9. For another example of Machiavelli's readiness to consider inconvenient evidence, see ibid., ch. 19.
131. Hankins, 'Humanism and the Origins of Modern Political Thought', p. 121.
132. *The Prince*, ch. 20, p. 73.
133. Burnham, *The Machiavellians*, pp. 55–6.
134. *The Prince*, ch. 3, p. 18; *Discourses*, III, ch. 1, p. 209.
135. Baron, 'Towards a More Positive Evaluation of the Fifteenth Century Renaissance', pp. 37, 46.
136. Pareto, *MS*, para. 2410.
137. Ibid., para. 1975.
138. See, for example, ibid., paras 1158, 1704, 2166, 2262, 2535.
139. G. Mosca, 'Il "Principe" di Machiavelli quattro secoli dopo la morte del suo autore', in *Ciò che la storia potrebbe insegnare* (Milano: Guiffrè, 1958), pp. 708, 719. First published in 1927.
140. Mosca, *RC*, pp. 202–3.
141. Labriola, *SP*, p. 91.
142. Gramsci, *SPN*, p. 133.
143. Ibid., p. 134.
144. Ibid., p. 140.
145. Ibid., p. 446.
146. Ibid., p. 426.
147. Labriola, *SP*, p. 110.
148. Gramsci, *SPN*, p. 428.
149. Ibid., p. 412.
150. Mosca, *RC*, p. 6; Pareto, *MS*, para. 141. Interestingly enough, *both* writers use the words 'great complexity' in this context.

151. Pareto, *MS*, para. 101.
152. Mosca, *RC*, pp. 283–4.
153. Pareto, *MS*, para. 69.
154. Labriola, *SP*, p. 103.
155. Pareto, *MS*, paras 6, 1891.
156. Ibid., para. 1890.
157. Labriola, *SP*, p. 117.
158. Pareto, *MS*, paras 132, 138.
159. Labriola, *SP*, p. 110.
160. Mosca, *RC*, p. 439.
161. *The Prince*, ch. 15, p. 56.
162. Ibid., ch. 17, p. 60.
163. *Discourses*, I, ch. 3, p. 15.
164. Ibid., I, ch. 37, p. 78.
165. *The Prince*, chs. 3–5.
166. Ibid., ch. 18, pp. 62–3.
167. *Discourses*, II, chs. 4, 13, 19.
168. Ibid., II, ch. 17, p. 165.
169. Ibid., II, ch. 25, p. 190.
170. Ibid., I , ch. 6; II, ch. 19.
171. Ibid., I, ch. 16, p. 46.
172. Ibid., I, ch. 44, p. 92.
173. Ibid., II, chs. 17, 35, 55; III, ch. 8; *The Prince*, ch. 6.
174. *Discourses*, I, chs. 1, 11; *The Prince*, ch. 7.
175. Berlin, 'The Originality of Machiavelli', p. 57.
176. *Discourses*, II, ch. 2.
177. Ibid., I, ch. 20.
178. Ibid., I, chs. 29, 30.
179. Ibid., II, ch. 2; I, ch. 58.
180. Ibid., I, ch. 4, p. 16.
181. Ibid., I, chs. 3–5.
182. Ibid., I, ch. 2.
183. Chabod, *Machiavelli and the Renaissance*, pp. 164–5.
184. Croce, *Elementi di politica*, pp. 59–66.
185. Berlin, 'The Originality of Machiavelli', p. 45.
186. Ibid., pp. 46–50.
187. Hankins, 'Humanism and the Origins of Modern Political Thought', p. 136; Hulliung, *Citizen Machiavelli*, p. 8.
188. A.W.H. Adkins, *Moral Values and Political Behaviour in Ancient Greece* (New York, 1972).
189. A. MacIntyre, *A Short History of Ethics* (London: Routledge & Kegan Paul, 1967), pp. 5–7, 90.
190. Burke, *The Italian Renaissance*, pp. 198–200.
191. Cassirer, *The Myth of the State*, p. 154.
192. *Discourses*, I, ch. 26, pp. 61–2.
193. *The Prince,* ch. 15, p. 56; ch. 18, p. 62.
194. Ibid., ch. 17, p. 59.
195. Ibid., ch. 18, p. 64.
196. *Discourses*, I, ch. 9, p. 29.

197. For a useful, albeit brief, analysis of the distinction between rule and act utilitarianism, see W. Kymlicka, *Contemporary Political Philosophy: an Introduction* (Oxford: Clarendon Press, 1990), pp. 27–9.
198. Mosca, *RC*, pp. 193, 450.
199. Pareto, *MS*, para. 2459.
200. Mosca, *RC*, p. 71.
201. Ibid., p. 39.
202. Pareto, *MS*, para. 2178.
203. Mosca, *RC*, p. 457.
204. Ibid., p. 288.
205. Ibid., p. 292.
206. Ibid., p. 196; and G. Mosca, *Partiti e sindacati nella crisi del regime parlamentare* (Bari: Laterza, 1949), p. 35.
207. Labriola, *SP*, pp. 159–61, 117.
208. Gramsci, *SPN*, p. 263.
209. Ibid., p. 144.
210. Ibid., p. 263. In 'Gramsci's Patrimony' (reprinted in the present volume), I paid insufficient attention to this remark and wrote that, for Gramsci, 'the repressive function of the state would eventually "wither away" after a socialist revolution'. (see p. 112). The evidence I cited was solid, though less than conclusive. I am now of the opinion that Gramsci was in two minds about the prospects for a non-coercive society, and that his doubts outweighed his hopes.
211. Gramsci, *SPN*, p. 172.
212. Ibid., pp. 135–6.
213. For an inspired and scholarly analysis of the similarities between Gramsci and Mosca, see M.A. Finocchiaro, *Beyond Right and Left: Democratic Elitism in Mosca and Gramsci* (Yale University Press, forthcoming).
214. Strauss, *Thoughts on Machiavelli*, p. 295.

# 2 Antonio Labriola: a Forgotten Marxist Thinker

*I vow not to shut myself up in any system as though in a prison.*
*Antonio Labriola*

## I

Antonio Labriola, hailed by one historian as 'the great theorist of Italian Marxism and among the greatest teachers of European Marxism',[1] has suffered an unusual fate, so to speak, since his death three-quarters of a century ago: he has been simultaneously praised and neglected. For example, George Lichtheim, in his classic work *Marxism*, mentions Labriola twice *en passant* and does not discuss his thought *at all* – this despite Lichtheim's description of the Italian as 'a Marxist theoretician of some eminence'.[2] Similarly, David McLellan writes, in his widely read textbook *Marxism After Marx*, that 'Labriola was probably the best interpreter of Marx in any country during the years immediately following Engels' death'. McLellan then proceeds to devote precisely *one sentence* to what Labriola actually said.[3] Since 1968 or thereabouts, there has been a landslide of English language literature on Marxist theory and philosophers, and yet we can find only three articles,[4] and not a single book, about this 'great Marxist thinker'.[5] Even in Italy, where Marxology thrives and where the Gramsci industry has attained monumental proportions, Labriola has received little exegetical attention. Why are his writings held in such high regard? Why are they so perversely ignored? In what follows, I propose to answer these questions.

## II

It is sometimes said that Labriola 'was the first in his country to expound Marxism as a system',[6] but this is not quite accurate. The first well-known Italian Marxist thinker was one Achille Loria, an academic economist who enjoyed a certain vogue in the 1880s and 1890s and ranked as Labriola's *bête noire*. Loria's theory, like all positivist Marxism, combined Spencerian (or Darwinian) evolutionary history, inflexible economic determinism and boundless faith in a positivist science which would uncover the 'iron laws' of history. In this tidy world, human subjectivity was effectively abolished. What distinguished his formulation of Marxism was its *complete* lack of subtlety or nuance – which lack led Gramsci to dismiss his mentality as 'bizarre and degenerate'.[7] By 1890, with the general European reaction against positivism, a 'Hegelianized' version of Marxism appeared in Italy in competition with the 'vulgar' doctrine espoused by Loria and those of his ilk. Labriola, a professor of philosophy at the University of Rome, played the leading role in this reinterpretation of the Marxian canon. He had become a Marxist only in his late forties, after a long stint as a 'critical' Hegelian. But his conversion to Marxism was far from sudden. Starting out as a liberal democrat, sympathetic to Mazzini, he became, from 1873 onwards, increasingly disillusioned with Italian political life and radical in his proposed prescriptions. The stagnation of the liberal state, its apparent inability to realise the dream of a new secular culture, the Hegelian 'ethical state', eventually drove Labriola into the ranks of revolutionary socialism. As Croce recalled in his 1904 obituary of Labriola:

> Once he told me of having come to socialism through the critique of the idea of the State. When the ethical State, fantasized by German popularizers, turned out to be a utopia, and the antagonistic interests of the various classes appeared to him as the harsh but sole reality, he found himself in the arms of Marxism.[8]

In retrospect, it can be seen that Labriola's acquisition of Marxism and socialism was as much the result of his philosophical heritage as of his direct political experiences. From Hegel he learned to consider ideas as manifestations of particular eras rather than the subjective embodiment of ideal patterns. Needless to say, it is but a small step from this relativistic viewpoint to Marx's theory of ideology. But the young Labriola was not a Hegelian *tout court*. As Mario Tronti has pointed out, he lived for years 'with his soul divided between Hegel and Spinoza'.[9] The latter, with his assumption of 'man as natural power' or material creature, inspired the Italian by denying 'the metaphysical presupposition of the good as something substantial'.[10] Labriola also exhibited a predilection for Herbart, the empirical psychologist, who destroyed 'the myth of spiritual substance'[11] and encouraged him to trace the various forms of collective consciousness back to their concrete, or empirical, sources. Under the influence of Spinoza and Herbart, Labriola was able to *ground* his Hegelianism within the socio-historical dimension, thereby avoiding the empty universalism of the 'right' (orthodox) Hegelians. From abstract reconciliations within an *a priori* philosophical framework, the emphasis shifted to 'flesh and blood' human beings, engaged in real struggles and conflicts.

Labriola's best known Marxist work is *Essays on the Materialist Conception of History* (1896),[12] containing a general exposition of historical materialism as well as a discussion of *The Communist Manifesto*. *Essays* was soon translated into French and became a minor classic of Marxist literature. His underlying philosophical ideas (those expressed during his Marxist phase, that is) are presented in a collection of letters to Sorel, revised and published in 1897 under the title *Socialism and Philosophy*. The theoretical contribution made by Labriola resided in his devastating attack on the positivist deformations of Second International Marxism. His lonely crusade can be summarized in five basic points.

First, he set himself against a simple reductive reconstruction of historical and social events. Labriola's interpretation of history, like Marx's, is essentially economic: history is for him the development of human labour power and of the social conditions arising out of it. History, otherwise stated, is 'man producing himself', which means that social and historical phenomena are dependent upon the economic foundation.[13] Following Engels, however, Labriola emphasized that it is only 'in the final analysis', in the long run, that the underlying economic development can provide an explanation for the 'superstructure' of ideas and institutions.[14] Thus he rejected the crude thesis, maintained by influential positivists like Loria, that politics, culture and other 'superstructural' aspects of society were epiphenomena, mere reflections of the material base. He wished to underline the intermediate field of complex interactions between the economy, the socio-political structure, and the realm of ideas:

> The underlying economic structure is not a simple mechanism whence emerge, as immediate, automatic, and mechanical effects, institutions, laws, customs, thoughts, sentiments, ideologies. From this substructure to all the rest, the process of derivation and of mediation is very complicated, often subtle, tortuous, and not always legible.[15]

It follows that economic explanations are never sufficient. In particular, it is necessary to examine ideologies, which cannot be dismissed as 'simple artifice' or 'pure illusion'. States of mind, 'those forms of inner life to which we give the name of imagination, intellect, reason, thought, etc.', significantly affect the forms and rhythm of historical change and conservation. There is no fact in history, he asserts, which does not originate in economic conditions, but equally there is no historical fact which is not preceded, accompanied, and followed by 'determined forms of consciousness', whether they be 'superstitious or experimental, impulsive or self-controlled, fantastic or reasoning'.[16] These 'forms of consciousness', moreover, cannot simply be deduced from the order of economic facts. Labriola fulminates against Marxists who go by a shortcut from economic conditions to mental reflections, 'as though it were simply a matter of interpreting stenographic signs'.[17] He meant to study societies (and their evolution) in all their complexity. That events came about precisely as they did and that they took on certain forms, that they were clothed in certain vestments and painted in certain colours – these specific elements were not mere trifles to be ignored. Incredibly, for a Marxist of his generation, he even called attention to the role of 'accidents' and the 'element of chance' in the making of history.[18] True to his Hegelian upbringing, he always embraced the proposition that a given society or sequence of events must be understood in its unique individuality and not blindly regarded as an instance of a type. Genuine comprehension requires a grasp of the 'picturesque whole', not just the economic skeleton.[19]

The second major aspect of Labriola's reformulation of Marxism was his attack on the fatalism inherent in naturalistic materialism. It is absurd to view human history as a straightforward prolongation of nature. Historical materialism 'was not and is not designed to be the rebellion of the material man against the ideal man'.[20] Labriola is an ardent opponent of 'Darwinism, political and social', which he likens to an 'epidemic'. It is, he insists, impossible to extend to human history the principles and methods of investigation appropriate to the study and explanation of the material world.[21] For history is concerned with the artificial environment which human beings have produced and which reacts upon them. Social ties, it is true, evolve independently of human will, but men develop both actively and passively, shaping historical conditions and being shaped by them. Man is both subject and object of history, creator as well as creature in a process of continual reaction between cause and affect.[22] The economic interpretation of history, correctly construed, 'marks the end of naturalistic materialism'.[23] Historical materialism is revolutionary not because it declares the primacy of matter over mind, but because it builds theory around the concept of praxis, understood as the dialectical unity of being and consciousness. Therefore, 'there is no foundation for that opinion which tends to the negation of every volition ...'. Men, in Labriola's opinion, are not 'marionettes, whose threads are held and moved, no longer by providence but by economic categories'. All that has happened in history is 'the work of man', not of 'the logic of things'.[24]

The third basic feature of Labriola's polemic against the dogmatic sclerosis of official Marxism flows from the second: a denunciation of the 'fanatics' who attempt to turn historical materialism into 'a new philosophy of systematic history'.[25] According to Kolakowski, Labriola's Italian background is pertinent here:

> It was particularly hard for Italians, whether Marxist or not, to believe in a theory of uninterrupted historical progress, since the whole history of their country in modern times went to prove the contrary. After three centuries of regression and stagnation which followed the Counter-Reformation, the whole radical intelligentsia was imbued with a sense of the country's economic and cultural backwardness. The hopes aroused by the Risorgimento were not such as to encourage the conviction that progress was an inevitable consequence of 'historical laws', and Italian philosophers, including Marxists, tended to be more sensitive to the variety, dramatic complexity, and unexpectedness of the historical process.[26]

From this standpoint, Labriola instilled into Italian Marxism a sceptical attitude towards all-embracing explanations of 'universal' history. Progress, on his conception, 'is not suspended over the course of human events like a destiny or a fate, nor like a commandment'. In consequence, Marxism 'cannot represent the whole history of the human race in a unified perspective'; it cannot 'pretend to be the intellectual vision of a great plan or of a design', whereby all events – past, present and future – are fit into a universal, predetermined model.[27] History reveals no 'preconceived design', no 'hidden finality', no 'pre-established harmony'.[28] Those 'diseased' minds who worship at the feet of 'Madonna Evolution'[29] grotesquely distort the historical process:

> Hasn't the French excogitation of that sacramental scheme (slave economy, serfdom economy, salaried economy) been extended to the entire human species? We submit that whoever holds that formula in hand will not understand a single fact of 14th century

English life. And where could he possibly put good old Norway, which never had slaves or serfs? And how will he account for servitude in Germany beyond the Elbe right after the Reformation? And what will explain the singular fact that the European bourgeoisie inaugurated slavery in America with slaves deliberately imported just when the bourgeoisie was embarking on the liberal era?[30]

Only 'careless persons' wish to possess, once for all, summed up in a few propositions, the whole of knowledge, and to be able, with one single key, to penetrate all the secrets of life.[31] In his assault on the positivist Marxists – not just Loria but even more sophisticated thinkers like Plekhanov – whose comprehensive theoretical systems left practically nothing to contingency, making it possible to believe in the iron regularity of history, Labriola invoked the testimony of Marx and Engels, who – we are assured – 'never treated history as though she were a mare which they could straddle and trot around'.[32]

Marxism, then, is not a 'final' rationalization and schematization of history, but rather a '*method*' for understanding human affairs.[33] It must be flexible enough to encompass the variety of forces at work in history and take care not to reduce complicated social and historical processes to a small number of untouchable 'universal' categories. Man makes his history not in order to march along a line of predetermined progress, and not because he must obey the laws of some abstract (metaphysical, Labriola labels it) evolution. He does so in the endeavour to satisfy his needs, and it is for empirical observation to show how, *in each particular instance*, the means of satisfying these needs condition man's social relations and spiritual activity. It is a symptom of intellectual vulgarity to expect to find in the writings of Marx and Engels 'answers to all the questions which historical and social science may ever present in their vast and variegated experience, or a summary solution of the practical problems of all time and place'.[34] Labriola refused to regard socialism as a kind of church or sect that must have its fixed dogma or formula.[35] He took seriously the description of 'scientific socialism' as a 'critical' theory, in the sense that it deemed no truths everlasting, acknowledged that all established principles were provisional, and was prepared to jettison or revise its own ideas if experience should so require. One must confront the daily and the commonplace, adjust one's theory to the historical concrete. Historical materialism, it is obvious, 'demands of those who wish to profess it consciously and frankly a certain queer humility'.[36] The quest for absolute certainty is misconceived: Marxists who talk about universal and inexorable laws, totally independent of human intentions, about history moving along the rigid lines of dialectical necessity, have not freed themselves from 'the accursed metaphysical bacillus'.[37]

Which brings us to the fourth feature of Labriola's critique: his radical 'humanization' and 'historization' of knowledge. For him, Marxism is a philosophy of praxis: 'The nature of man, his historical making, is a practical process. And when I say *practical*, it implies the elimination of the vulgar distinction between theory and practice'.[38] Labriola's historicism leaves room for no cognitive values other than pragmatic ones: 'The main principle of critical cognition ... is this: It takes its departure from the practice of things, from the development of the labour process.'[39] Even science, according to Labriola, is a *practical* method of thought aimed at satisfying our material wants. Scientific knowledge, we are told, 'corresponds in quality, and is proportional in quantity, to the productivity of labour'. In other words, 'science depends on our needs'.[40] Labriola, it would appear, conceives of human intellectual activity, whether philosophy or science, as the derivation of practical behaviour, and not as the search for 'objective' truth. Since human thought is bound up with the historical process, with living experience, it cannot pretend to discover 'truths' independent of time and circumstance. Kolakowski rightly argues that Labriola's ascription of a functional character to all human knowledge echoes the young Marx but diverges from Engels' positivism (which was, of course, embraced by orthodox Marxism):

> For, if praxis signifies the whole of man's part in history, the value of intellectual production as an aspect of that whole is to be measured by the mind's ability to 'express' changing historical situations, and not by the correspondence between some 'objective' universe and the description of it.[41]

The philosophy of praxis, then, is not a scientific world-view in the sense in which Marxists employed the term; i.e. a world-view that corresponds to Reality 'in-itself' and unlocks the 'secrets' of the historical process.

Finally, Labriola was perhaps the only Second International thinker who, between Marx's death in 1883 and the Great War in 1914, called for an original and distinctive Marxist philosophy of life, or *Weltanschauung*. By philosophical activity, needless to say, he did not mean the intellectual pursuit of hidden essences, but the systematic reflection on the limits and forms of cognition, as well as on the relations of mankind to the rest of the knowable and known universe. In particular, philosophy had the task of analysing and clarifying concepts, or categories, recurring in specific acts of thought, such as unity, multiplicity, cause, effect, finite, infinite, and so forth.[42] In the long run, he hoped that 'science in its perfect state will have absorbed philosophy'. But this conformity of philosophy with science was an ideal outcome that remained 'mostly at the stage of mere desire' and could hardly be expected in the foreseeable future.[43] Meanwhile, philosophy was valuable, as both a cleansing agent and an aid to orientation in the world. In reducing the obstacles which 'the fantastic projections of the emotions, passions, fears and hopes pile in the way of free thought', philosophical reflection, properly conceived, 'serves, as Spinoza himself would say, to vanquish *imaginationem et ignorantium*' and impart unity or coherence to the results of our experience.[44] This Marxist philosophy, Labriola declares, must remain autonomous, free of both materialist and spiritualist encrustations. He hurls invective at those who attempt to fashion a synthesis between Marxism and some other philosophy – be it Darwinism or Kantianism or eighteenth-century materialism. What such 'synthesizers' fail to realize is that Marxism is inherently self-sufficient, carrying with it 'the conditions and expressions of its own philosophy'.[45]

III

Anyone remotely familiar with the work of Antonio Gramsci will by now have noticed the striking similarities between his own conceptual framework and that of Labriola: the critique of economic reductionism and naturalistic materialism, the forthright rejection of historical teleology, the notion that Marxism is a general and autonomous philosophy, a commitment to historicism, and a recognition of the non-objective nature of science and its basis in human need. By no means were these affinities fortuitous. Gramsci carefully read Labriola's works in 1916–17 and warmly recommended them to his friends.[46] Much later, in his *Prison Notebooks*, he referred to his predecessor as 'the only man who has attempted to build up the philosophy of praxis scientifically'.[47] In general, the *Notebooks* lavish praise on Italy's first major Marxist thinker. Indeed, Gramsci bemoans the widespread ignorance of his work, expressing the wish that it be brought back into circulation as part of the struggle for a superior proletarian culture.[48] Obviously, Gramsci's demolition of orthodox Marxism owes much to

Labriola; to be sure, many of the theoretical insights commonly attributed to Gramsci actually originated in the Neapolitan's historicist and anti-positivist version of Marxism. Why, then, has Labriola not received his due? Why do commentators on Gramsci almost uniformly underrate Labriola's contribution? Why is his *oeuvre* treated with little more than polite respect? Labriola, I noted at the beginning of this essay, is sometimes applauded as 'great', but this assessment is not universally shared. For a time, the *Essays on the Materialist Conception of History* enjoyed the status of a *minor* classic; no work by him, however, has been elevated to the rank of 'major classic'; none of his writings, in other terms, has achieved the lasting eminence of, say, the *Prison Notebooks* or Lukács' *History and Class Consciousness*. Why is this so?

Before attempting to answer the questions raised in the above paragraph, it might be useful to deal with a more general query: what qualities must a book possess if it is to become a 'classic' in philosophy or political theory? Few writers have made any attempt to grapple with this problem. A notable exception is Michael Levin, who, in an interesting article,[49] inquires into the obscure process whereby, from the great mass of literature that has been written throughout the ages on political theory, a select few books have been promoted to the status of 'classics'. The discussion focuses on John Locke's *Two Treatises of Civil Government*, in the hope that it can shed some light on how celebrated works managed to separate themselves from 'the now obscure volumes of old and forgotten polemic'.[50] The two most obvious criteria of selection, as Levin observes, are 'philosophical quality' and 'original content'. How does Locke rate in these two respects? According to the consensus among modern commentators, *Two Treatises* is neither a profound nor subtle work. So much for 'philosophical quality'. As regards originality, Levin quotes J.W. Gough, who wrote: 'Locke's characteristic arguments ... had long been commonplaces of political theory. They were part of the usual mental furniture of every "liberal" thinker of his age!'[51] If so, why did *Two Treatises* obtain a tremendous reputation and exercise great influence? An important part of the answer, concludes Levin,

> was surely that his theories were propounded in an environment well prepared and suited for their acceptance. Locke had the good fortune to express reasonably commonplace ideas at the right time, that is when circumstances made men particularly disposed to accept them. Furthermore, he presented his thought in a manner

that could be immediately understood by his readership. Peter Laslett has pointed out that 'the scholars of our own day have been confused by it, not the men of the eighteenth century' .... more than most other political theorists, Locke served a contemporary need.[52]

From this passage we can extract two basic reasons for the renown of Locke's *Two Treatises*: (1) despite some apparent inconsistencies, its overall message was 'immediately' evident; and (2) the volume appeared at an opportune moment, when the ideas it expressed (on property rights and resistance to arbitrary rule) were likely to find a large and receptive audience. Let us now apply these two criteria to Labriola's work.

First – clarity of content. For all his originality, Labriola frequently expressed his views in a vague and elusive manner, and some of his most suggestive ideas must be pieced together from incidental and elliptical remarks. Like Gramsci, he never produced a comprehensive, systematic treatise of Marxist theory. His *Essays on the Materialist Conception of History* did not pursue any issues in great depth, and their avowed purpose was merely to expound Marx's own ideas. Labriola's own assessment of the two essays was (excessively) modest: they were 'but rough sketches'.[53] His other important work, *Socialism and Philosophy*, consisted of letters, which – although revised for publication – abound with tantalizing hints, esoteric allusions, scattered observations, tentative suggestions, and sly asides. But, more important for our purposes, Labriola was not entirely consistent and often failed to take his undoubted insights to their logical conclusions. For example, whereas Gramsci, in keeping with his stress on human subjectivity, firmly denied the possibility of predicting the future, Labriola retained a notion of historical inevitability, at least regarding the genesis of the classless society. On Kolakowski's reading, however, Labriola 'avoids committing himself to the "historical necessity" of socialism'.[54] True, this conclusion would seem to follow logically from his contempt for '*Madonna Evolution*'; but he often wrote as if he considered the advent of the classless society, based on social ownership and collective administration, as certain, and held only that the exact forms it would take could not be predicted. To take an example, in one passage, he says of communism that it is not 'a hope, an aspiration', but a 'necessity'.[55] Elsewhere we learn that communism 'must inevitably happen by the immanent necessity of history'.[56] While these examples could be multiplied,[57] one more should suffice. Scientific socialism, he writes, 'affirms the coming of communist production, not as a postulate, nor as the aim of a free volition, but as the result of the *processus* immanent in history'. He then continues:

> ... the premise of this prevision is in the actual conditions of capitalist production ... a moment *will come*, when in one fashion or another, with the elimination in every form of private rent, interest, profit, the production will pass over to the collectivist association; that is to say, will become communistic.[58]

In one place, he even speaks of 'historical-social laws', without, however, elucidating their logical and epistemological status.[59] On the question of free will, Labriola equivocates. Notwithstanding his oft-repeated aversion for fatalism, he states time and time again that 'social being' *determines* 'consciousness',[60] and, in numerous passages, takes pains to gainsay that the historical process is the product of 'acts of free and voluntary thought'.[61]

Also difficult to reconcile with Labriola's humanistic formulations is his attitude to Engels, which is one of enormous respect bordering on reverence. As for the *Anti-Dühring*, it is an 'exquisite work', containing 'in a nutshell the whole philosophy required for the thinkers of socialism'.[62] Labriola once complained about John Stuart Mill's vacillation on theoretical issues, noting that the Englishman was 'always suspended between the yes and the no in matters of importance'.[63] This complaint could equally well be lodged against Labriola himself. Because his theoretical innovations were blurred by inconsistencies, many of his contemporaries took him for a fairly standard, if somewhat eccentric, orthodox Marxist. Plekhanov, of all people, actually wrote a favourable review of *Essays on the Materialist Conception of History* in *Novoje Slovo*, the journal of the 'legal' Marxists. Although the Russian was critical of certain 'distortions on the idealist side', his general estimate of the book was quite high, and he even expressed his 'full agreement' with it on 'most' matters.[64] Lenin too, found much to admire in the essays, and, in a letter dated 23 December 1897, urged his sister Anna to translate at least one of them into Russian.[65]

How is this tension between the two strands in Labriola's thought to be explained? Remember, he was squaring off against two very different adversaries. While he plainly wished to save Marxism from its vulgarizers by accentuating human creativity, he was also keenly aware of the danger of lapsing into an idealism which loses its essential links with material reality. He therefore combated those who assumed that ideas 'fall from heaven' as fiercely as those who reduced ideas to their 'economic determinants'. What he never managed to do, unfortunately, was to blend the materialist and spiritualist elements of his thought into one, coherent whole. Right up to his death in 1904, he was beset by 'lingering theoretical doubts concerning many fundamental questions'.[66] Labriola may have ridiculed the positivists as 'embarrassing guests' at the Marxist party,[67] but in the end we must doubt whether he himself succeeded in transcending the limitations of the positivist perspective. Evidently, his message did not emerge with great clarity, and he therefore fails to meet one of the criteria isolated by Levin.

Let us now turn to the other precondition of 'greatness': the existence of a receptive (and sizable) audience. In this connection, it must be said that Labriola's ideas – in so far as they were heterodox – were not expressed at an opportune moment. In the 1890s, the Second International, together with the positivist Marxism that formed its 'official' doctrine, were thriving. The industrial proletariat throughout Europe was increasing in numbers and power, and Kautsky's brand of evolutionary determinism presented itself as an altogether fitting expression of the optimism of the time. Those who, in the manner of Labriola, raised doubts about the 'official' interpretation of Marxism were swimming against the proverbial tide – even in Italy, where the cultural revolt against positivism did spread to socialist circles. Serious and widespread disenchantment with the familiar banalities of orthodox Marxism barely surfaced, within the European movement, until after Labriola's death. A number of factors are relevant here: the growth of outright reformism within the Western working class, the outbreak of the First World War (revealing as it did the fragility of proletarian internationalism), the failure of the socialist revolution to spread outside Russia, the crushing defeat of the post-war rebellions in Germany and Hungary, and the subsequent rise of popular right-wing movements. This series of psychological and physical defeats led to grave doubts about the theoretical foundation of revolutionary action. Hence the stage was set for thinkers like Lukács and Gramsci *more thoroughly* to 'Hegelianize' the Marxist inheritance. But by this time, Labriola's texts had been more or less forgotten. They had, in Faenza's picturesque phrase, been 'relegated to the attic'.[68]

In trying to sort out why Labriola has enjoyed such a limited fortune, we must also consider his role (or lack thereof) in the political struggles of his day. He was not a 'man of action' but a publicist and theoretician, who remained aloof from the Italian Socialist Party and even refused to attend its founding Congress – this at a time when all other leading Marxist thinkers, such as Kautsky and Plekhanov, were closely integrated into the political life of their national parties and held official positions in them. Why did Labriola choose to stand outside? To him, the PSI leaders, in particular Filippo Turati, were amateurish thinkers, inferior products of the positivist pseudo-culture he so detested. Turati and his friends, it is true, expressed a highly confused theoretical vision, lacking in rigour and utterly irritating to a thinker of Labriola's stature. In addition Labriola was disgusted with the organizational principles upon which the party was founded. Turati believed in the necessity of concessions to political expediency. Given the backward condition of Italian society, with its relatively small (and geographically restricted) industrial base, he fought for a heterogeneous organization, encompassing a broad spectrum of views and groups. Labriola, on the other hand, favoured the German model of a homogeneous *proletarian* party based on a well-defined pro-gramme. There were, then, sound political and ideological reasons for his decision to spurn the neophyte party and call down imprecations on the heads of its leaders. But we must also take account of Labriola's personality. He was, by temperament, a 'man-of-words', a thinker – a *professorissimo* as Anna Kulischioff described him.[69] Once, in a fit of exasperation, Turati denounced him as 'a German, an ideo-logue, unaware of life, and a lover of a logical line'.[70] As one commen-tator puts it, 'It is not difficult to understand how *this* Labriola, so caustic ... would create a vacuum around himself.'[71] Isolated from political life, the distant and imperious *professorissimo* even seemed to frighten off potential disciples. As a man, Labriola inspired awe mingled with hostility, and he could never benefit from the prestige which – in the pre-war era – accrued to those 'men-of-words' who could combine theory with practice.

All in all, we can see why Labriola's diatribes against what he called 'the epidemic spread of positivism'[72] did not find a large and enthusi-astic audience. The ideas he articulated were (in a sense) too far ahead of their time, and, for reasons of temperament and politics, he repelled many who might otherwise have followed him and spread his word. His work – notwithstanding its originality – would seem to meet neither of the criteria suggested by Levin.

IV

Labriola, it seems, exerted no deep or widespread influence, even in his native land.[73] Many who read his texts either failed to comprehend their true message, or else deliberately chose to ignore it. Many more did not bother to read them at all. A spectacular exception was Gramsci, who wished to rescue Labriola from near-oblivion. Ironically, however, Gramsci's own exalted position has only reinforced the tendency to pay little attention to his haughty predecessor. For the latter's theoretical contribution was resurrected and developed by Gramsci in a way that makes Labriola seem redundant. In the interests of historical accuracy, I am bound to point out that he – not Gramsci – was the first to interpret Marxism as a philosophy of historical praxis, thus stressing the humanistic, relativistic aspects of the doctrine and opposing the scientistic ideology that dominated orthodox Marxism. He – not Gramsci (or Lukács) – is the real founder of 'Hegelian' Marxism.

## NOTES

1.  G. Arfè, *Storia del socialismo italiano (1892–1926)* (Turin, 1965), p. 9.
2.  George Lichtheim, *Marxism* (London, 1964), pp. 281, 294.
3.  David McLellan, *Marxism after Marx* (London, 1979), pp. 20–1.
4.  The best account of Labriola in English is L. Kolakowski, 'Antonio Labriola: an Attempt at an Open Orthodoxy', in *Main Currents of Marxism*, Vol. 2, trans. P.S. Falla (Oxford, 1978), pp. 175–92. See, also, E. Jacobitti, 'Labriola, Croce and Italian Marxism', *Journal of the History of Ideas*, 36 (April–May 1975), 297–318; and P. Piccone, 'Labriola and the Roots of Eurocommunism', *Berkeley Journal of Sociology*, XXII (Winter 1977–8), 3–43.
5.  E. Jacobitti, 'Hegemony Before Gramsci: the Case of Benedetto Croce', *The Journal of Modern History*, 52 (March 1980), 78.
6.  Kolakowski, 'Antonio Labriola: an Attempt at an Open Orthodoxy', p. 175.
7.  A. Gramsci, *Gli intellettuali e l' organizzazione della cultura*, Collected Works, Vol. 3 (Turin, 1949), p. 169.
8.  Cited in Piccone, 'Labriola and the Roots of Eurocommunism', p. 15.
9.  'Tra materialismo dialettico e filosofia della prassi: Gramsci e Labriola', in A. Caracciolo e G. Scalia, eds., *La città futura* (Milan, 1959), p. 147.
10. A. Labriola, *Scritti varii di filosofia e politica*, ed. B. Croce (Bari, 1906), p. 86.
11. A. Labriola, *Socialism and Philosophy*, trans. E. Untermann (St. Louis, Mo., 1980), p. 100.
12. A. Labriola, *Essays on the Materialist Conception of History*, trans. C.H. Kerr (Chicago, 1908).
13. See, for example, *Socialism and Philosophy*, pp. 94–5; *Essays on the Materialist Conception of History*, p. 201; and 'Storia, filosofia della storia, sociologia e materialismo storico' in A. Labriola, *Saggi sul materialismo storico*, eds. V. Gerratana and A. Guerra (Rome, 1964), p. 339.

14. *Essays on the Materialist Conception of History*, p. 111.
15. Ibid., p. 152.
16. Ibid., pp. 108, 111, 113, 121.
17. *Socialism and Philosophy*, p. 99.
18. *Essays on the Materialist Conception of History*, pp. 153–4.
19. Ibid., pp. 109–11, 230.
20. Ibid., pp. 104, 120.
21. Ibid., p. 114.
22. Ibid., pp. 120–4, 211.
23. *Socialism and Philosophy*, p. 95.
24. *Essays on the Materialist Conception of History*, pp. 124, 228.
25. Ibid., p. 127.
26. Kolakowski, 'Antonio Labriola: an Attempt at an Open Orthodoxy', p. 177.
27. *Essays on the Materialist Conception of History*, p. 135. See, also, *Socialism and Philosophy*, p. 133.
28. *Essays on the Materialist Conception of History*, p. 239.
29. *Socialism and Philosophy*, p. 117.
30. A. Labriola, 'From One Century to Another', included in *Socialism and Philosophy*, p. 220.
31. *Essays on the Materialist Conception of History*, p. 204. See, also, *Socialism and Philosophy*, p. 110.
32. *Socialism and Philosophy*, p. 81.
33. *Essays on the Materialist Conception of History*, p. 135,
34. *Socialism and Philosophy*, pp. 71, 74.
35. Ibid., p. 83.
36. Ibid., p. 63.
37. Ibid., p. 166.
38. Ibid., p. 84.
39. Ibid., p. 110.
40. Ibid., p. 99.
41. Kolakowski, 'Antonio Labriola: an Attempt at an Open Orthodoxy', p. 191.
42. *Socialism and Philosophy*, pp. 98, 104.
43. Ibid., p. 105.
44. Ibid., p. 114.
45. Ibid., pp. 76, 118–19.
46. For detailed documentation, see W.L. Adamson, *Hegemony and Revolution: Antonio Gramsci's Political and Cultural Theory* (Berkeley, 1980), p. 252, note 72; and A. Davidson, *Antonio Gramsci: Towards an Intellectual Biography* (London, 1977), pp. 104–6.
47. Antonio Gramsci, *Selections from the Prison Notebooks*, ed. and trans. Quintin Hoare and Geoffrey Nowell Smith (London, 1971), p. 387.
48. Ibid., pp. 386–390.
49. Michael Levin, 'What Makes a Classic in Political Theory?', *Political Science Quarterly*, 88 (September 1973), 462–76.
50. Ibid., 463.
51. Ibid., p. 464.
52. Ibid., 466.

53. A. Labriola, *Socialism and Philosophy*, p. 61.
54. Kolakowski, 'Antonio Labriola: an Attempt at an Open Orthodoxy', p. 190.
55. *Essays on the Materialist Conception of History*, p. 16.
56. Ibid., p. 244.
57. Ibid., p. 26; *Socialism and Philosophy*, pp. 160–1.
58. *Essays on the Materialist Conception of History*, p. 190 (my emphasis).
59. Ibid., p. 156.
60. Ibid., pp. 49, 112–13, 123, 156, 159, 201.
61. Ibid., pp. 203, 121–4, 206–7.
62. *Socialism and Philosophy*, p. 72. On page 90, Engels' volume is described as 'the unexcelled book in the literature of socialism'.
63. Ibid., p. 78.
64. G.V. Plekhanov, 'The Materialist Conception of History', *Fundamental Problems of Marxism*, trans. J. Katzer, ed. J.S. Allen (New York, 1969), pp. 117, 124, 132.
65. Lenin and Plekhanov read the French edition. Lenin's letter is reprinted in *Rinascita*, Vol. X, 3 (March 1954), p. 184.
66. Piccone, 'Labriola and the Roots of Eurocommunism', 40.
67. *Essays on the Materialist Conception of History*, p. 17.
68. L. Faenza, 'Labriola e Gramsci', *Mondo Operaio*, VII (4 December 1954), 16.
69. Arfè, *Storia del socialismo italiano*, p. 83.
70. Cited in Piccone, 'Labriola and the Roots of Eurocommunism', p. 23.
71. Ibid., p. 27.
72. *Socialism and Philosophy*, p. 91.
73. V. Gerratana, *Ricerche di storia del marxismo* (Rome, 1972), p. 149.

# 3 Gramsci's Patrimony

## I INTRODUCTION

No Marxist thinker, apart from Marx himself, is so universally respected and admired as Antonio Gramsci, one of the originators of what Merleau-Ponty called 'Western Marxism', a tradition including Lukács, Korsch, Sartre and Frankfurt School theorists such as Adorno and Marcuse. In their different ways, these thinkers all attacked Marxist positivism for its determinism and its objective materialist theory of history. Marxism, they thought, would have to admit the importance of human agency, of creative human action, of the 'subjective factor'. Disenchantment with the deterministic modes of analysis championed by classical Marxists began to gather momentum by the turn of the century. Economic depressions had come and gone without producing a general systemic collapse; rather than increased misery, the working classes were experiencing higher living standards and shorter working hours as the capitalist economy expanded; socialist parties, reflecting the demands of their constituents, became less and less revolutionary and more and more concerned with the melioration of conditions within the framework of capitalism. This stabilization of the bourgeois regime evoked grave disquiet within the Marxist community, bound together as it was by the firm belief that capitalism would crumble under the weight of its inherent contradictions. The outbreak of war in 1914, and the subsequent disintegration of proletarian internationalism, further nourished the suspicion that the European masses had ceased to be a revolutionary force. With the ignominious defeats of the post-war rebellions in Germany and Hungary, and the rapid rise of popular right-wing movements, it became progressively difficult to cling to the optimistic Marxist assumption that 'history is on our side'.

The intellectual grounding of classical Marxism was further undermined by developments in the sphere of science. Einstein's special theory of relativity, published in 1905, both epitomized and promoted the breakdown of the traditional paradigm of science, which 'premised an out-there world consisting of a kind of "substance" anterior to any attributes assigned to it'.[1] If observations were no longer seen simply as reflecting an immanently unfolding order but as depending on the standpoint chosen by the observer, then science could no longer be a source of certainty. The new philosophy of science, as Gouldner writes, 'took a romantic turn away from a mirror image epistemology toward a mind-as-lamp epistemology; mechanical models came under attack'.[2] But 'mirror image epistemology' formed the basis of Marx's materialism, which entailed an impulse to assimilate and reduce social relations to the natural sciences. As the old model of science buckled, classical Marxism found itself deprived of a solid intellectual foundation. The 'crisis of science' merged with the 'crisis of Marxism' and the scene was set for the emergence of 'humanistic' or 'critical' Marxism, asserting the centrality of human choice and consciousness.

It is against this background of events and trends that we must view Gramsci's contribution. Gramsci – it should be stated at the outset – bequeathed no 'finished' intellectual legacy. Before 1926, when Mussolini's regime finally felt secure enough to place him behind bars, he was a professional politician and first-class journalist, not a composer of systematic treatises. After building up a formidable reputation with the Socialist Party (PSI), he co-founded the Italian Communist Party (PCI) in 1921. His service to the organization was impressive: in 1922 he went to Moscow as the PCI's representative on the Executive Committee of the Comintern; in 1924 he was elected to parliament and soon became Secretary-General of the Party. Through sheer force of intellect, the shy and retiring country boy from backward Sardinia had become a leading political figure. He was tried in 1928 and condemned to imprisonment for twenty years and four months. He died in 1937, shortly after being released from prison for reasons of poor health. In a remark which would prove ironic, the Fascist prosecutor declared at Gramsci's trial: 'We must prevent this brain from functioning for twenty years.' This did not happen. The last years of Gramsci's life were years of intense mental activity, pursued with the aid of only a few books and under the duress of prison conditions in which his always precarious health steadily deteriorated. The result was the *Prison Notebooks* (*Quaderni del carcere*), a profound, monumental, tormented, labyrinthine work, consisting of unfinished essays and notes, often elliptical and barely comprehensible. Gramsci, it can be seen, articulated his ideas and doctrines on different planes of expression. His pre-prison work was, for the most part, the ephemeral outpouring of the political diatribist and pamphleteer. Even when dealing with minor or transient issues, he brought a capacious intellect and powerful imagination to the task; but the articles and editorials published before 1926 do not comprise a significant

body of theory. In the *Notebooks* we see a more considered exploration of doctrine, set within the framework of a view of things as a
whole. These notes and comments constitute 'one of the most original
contributions to twentieth-century Marxism',[3] and it is upon these that
my discussion shall concentrate. The reader should bear in mind,
however, that the *Notebooks* are incomplete and tentative. Written for
self-clarification, and never intended for publication in their present
form, they pose excruciating problems for anyone anxious to disen-
gage an unambiguous, well-rounded message. For this reason, the
weight to be placed on particular formulations in these notes is a
subject of dispute, and we must be careful, as Gramsci himself
warned, not to infer too much from 'casual affirmations and isolated
aphorisms'.[4] There is, moreover, sharp disagreement about the question of continuity in the development of his thought. Are the
*Notebooks* a natural outgrowth of his writings as a young man? Or do
they represent a radical intellectual change? It is a mistake, I submit,
to ignore his evolution as a thinker and treat the whole of his work as
a single, homogeneous bloc. In my exposition and evaluation of
Gramsci's patrimony, the discontinuity of his thought, its progression
through different phases, will be highlighted.

## II   GRAMSCI AND IDEALISM

Before 1918, Gramsci's writings revealed no significant debt to Marx
and reposed instead on an idealism and a preoccupation with culture
inspired, above all, by Benedetto Croce, the neo-Hegelian philosopher, who dominated Italian intellectual life in the early years of this
century. Gramsci cut his intellectual eye-teeth on the works of the
man he described as 'a sort of lay pope',[5] and, in the *Notebooks*, he
conceded that he had once been 'rather Crocean in tendency'.[6]
Radiating influence from his beloved Naples, Croce was a major
figure in Italy's cultural 'rejuvenation movement', which attacked positivism as both a philosophy and a style of life without a spiritual
dimension. Central to this movement – a remarkably 'broad church',
including conservatives, radicals, nationalists, socialists and syndical-
ists – was a passionate moralism, rooted in the conviction that human
beings are responsible for their own actions and make their own
history. This revolt against 'scientism' and materialism (in every
sense), though not confined to Italy, was particularly pervasive in that
country, due to the relative feebleness of the indigenous positivist

tradition. The prevailing intellectual currents of the Risorgimento had been idealist and specifically Hegelian, and this supremacy had been only partially eroded by the positivist tides of the late nineteenth century.

Voluntarism, culturalism, moral fervour – these permeate the articles written by the young Gramsci for Socialist publications like *Avanti!* and *Il Grido del Popolo*. To be more specific, we find the following, closely linked themes:

1. a belief that human civilization develops through a process of thought, through cultural diffusion and the penetration of ideas;
2. a 'creative' revolutionary posture, according to which men can transcend themselves through critical reflection and a determination to seize history;
3. a quasi-existentialist emphasis on individual moral responsibility – for one's character, destiny, behaviour, etc.;
4. the goal of building an integrated and autonomous proletarian culture that would transform the working masses from oppressed and dehumanized victims of capitalism into revitalized collective architects of a noble, classless future.

In an important article, entitled 'Socialism and Culture', Gramsci blends all these themes together, proclaiming that, 'above all, man is mind', a historical creature who forms his personality through 'intelligent reflection' and transforms his society through 'an intense labour of criticism'. Culture, moreover, is not a matter of 'encyclopaedic knowledge'. It is 'discipline of one's inner self ... the attainment of a higher awareness'. To achieve this 'higher awareness' means 'to know oneself ... to be master of oneself, to distinguish oneself, to free oneself from a state of chaos'.[7] In *La Città futura*, a short treatise published in newspaper format by the Socialist Youth Federation on 11 February 1917, Gramsci denounces 'positivist fatalism', an 'arid mysticism with no outburst of suffering passion', and ardently appeals to *'the tenacious will of man'*. We are capable of great deeds and heroic sacrifices, if only we can overcome our indifference and lethargy (our 'spiritual failure') and accept responsibility for our actions.[8] The Sorelian resonances in these early writings are not fortuitous. By 1916 Gramsci was drawing inspiration from the romantic socialist sector of the French intelligentsia: not just Sorel but also *letterati* such as Romain Rolland and Charles Péguy, all of whom were united by an intense faith in conscious will-power, a mystical, almost religious conception of socialism, and a burning desire to renovate the 'consciousness' of the masses through education and culture.[9]

Gramsci's idealist leanings culminated in a famous article, 'The Revolution Against "Capital"', which first appeared in *Avanti!* on 24 November 1917. The October Revolution was 'against' *Capital*, Gramsci argued, in so far as Marx's *magnum opus* defended the thesis of unilinear evolutionary determinism: 'Events have exploded the critical schema determining how the history of Russia would unfold according to the canons of historical materialism. The Bolsheviks reject Karl Marx.' While Lenin and his comrades are not dogmatic 'Marxists', they nevertheless embrace the 'eternal' part of Marxist thought, 'which represents the continuation of German and Italian idealism, and which in the case of Marx was contaminated by positivist and naturalist encrustations'. The dominant factor in history is 'not raw economic facts, but man', who 'moulds objective reality' in whatever way his will determines.[10]

By 1918, however, Gramsci's perspective appears to alter, and we witness a growing concern with the material conditions that prevent men from imposing their will on events. The domain of ideas, of spirit, he now tells us, is anchored 'in the economy, in practical activity, in systems and relations of production and exchange'.[11] In October of that year, Gramsci could still state that 'Marxism is based on philosophical idealism',[12] but overtly idealist concepts and language no longer enjoyed pride of place in his writing; and by 1919 they seemed to disappear altogether, being replaced by conventional Marxist assertions about the centrality of economic phenomena in the determination of human behaviour. Wholly typical, for example, in his pronouncement that any change in the 'objective conditions for the production of material wealth' is bound to produce 'a corresponding change in the totality of relations that regulate and inform human society and a change in the degree of men's awareness'.[13] Why did Gramsci virtually abandon a mode of thought and inquiry bounded by the horizon of idealist philosophy? We can only speculate, but an important factor may have been his reading of Antonio Labriola, Italy's earliest theoretical Marxist, who was the first Second International thinker to (mildly) 'Hegelianize' Marxism, to purge the doctrine of its cruder positivist elements and reinterpret it as a 'philosophy of praxis', recognizing human subjectivity. That Gramsci, in 1916 or 1917, read and admired Labriola is a matter of historical record.[14] From him, the youthful Sardinian revolutionary learned that it was possible to reject vulgar materialism and at the same time acknowledge the priority of objective economic forces, which restrict human freedom. Partly (if not wholly) because of the influence of this vastly underrated Neopolitan Marxist, Gramsci wrote *finis* to the philosophical style of his youth.

Although the erosion of his idealism began while he was still a young militant, Gramsci did not properly 'settle his accounts' with his 'erstwhile philosophical conscience' until after his imprisonment, when he sketched the preliminary outlines of an 'Anti-Croce'.[15] Croce was to be dialectically surpassed, just as Marx had surpassed Hegel. As an idealist, Croce followed Hegel in asserting that the substance of the universe is homogeneous with and identical to that which composes ideas and mind. Yet the Italian was not uncritical in his embrace of Hegel. He, Croce, like Marx, repudiated the metaphysical trappings of Hegel's 'World Spirit': the only real history was *human* history; the only real spirit was the spirit of *man*. Bowing to what is particular and contingent in historical development, Croce dismissed, as a theological remnant, Hegel's *a priori* concept of history as the progress of 'Spirit' along a logically necessary path towards pre-ordained goals. For Croce, there is no 'cunning of reason' immanent within the sequence of events and determining its overall direction. By the same token, there is no universal conception of ultimate truth, corresponding to an ideal model outside the human mind. Our values, our beliefs, our ideas express nothing but our historically conditioned needs and choices. 'Truth', like history, is the creation of man's evolving spirit – there is no extra-human reality to which we are subordinate.

Even in his 'Anti-Croce', Gramsci retained admiration for certain contributions made by his former teacher. Firstly, he endorsed Croce's rejection of 'universal history', understood as an effort to unify, in one single cause, the total social/historical process. Secondly, he believed that Croce was correct to deny the existence of a transcendent realm of truth, beyond the spirit of man, and to relate all philosophical thought to 'problems posed by the historical process'.[16] Croce's philosophy was valuable, thirdly, because it drew attention to 'the importance of facts of culture and thought in the historical process'.[17] In a nutshell, speculative philosophy *à la* Croce, with its stress on creative human activity, provided the 'premise' for a 'renewal' of the 'philosophy of praxis' (i.e. Marxism), then suffering – so Gramsci thought – from the deformations of positivism, mechanicism, and economism.[18] In criticizing these 'degenerate forms',[19] he never – as we shall see presently – forgot that Marxism, as Marx himself said, was the heir of classical German philosophy, of idealism, which discovered that man produces himself throughout history.

The trouble with speculative philosophy, however, is that it reduces man to an abstract 'universal' man, defined in terms of self-consciousness or pure spiritual activity. History is thus 'spiritualized', viewed as an externalization of thought, and the social reality of empirical, 'flesh and blood' human beings is correspondingly obscured. Croce's defect, Gramsci explains, is to invert the real relation of thought to the world: he fails to see that the driving force behind historical change is not self-consciousness but natural human energies in the form of labour, understood as physical commerce with nature.[20] What Croce enunciated was a 'pure conceptual dialectic', a 'history of concepts', unconnected with any concrete historical unfolding.[21] Nevertheless, Gramsci hailed the blending of idealist tendencies with Marxism as most significant for making the latter a potent force, as well as for bringing out the philosophical potential of Marxism, over and against the preoccupation with economics and, as a consequence, fatalistic economic determinism.

## III   CRITIQUE OF POSITIVISM AND MATERIALISM

By the 1890s Marxism was firmly established as but one form of the reigning cult of positivism. Lying at the core of positivism was an earnest belief that human society could be described, analysed, and represented by the language of the mathematical and physical sciences. Marx, bewitched by this outlook, attempted to create a human science in principle analogous to that which tells us about the behaviour of 'bees and beavers', and his followers took this to mean that we could explain socio-cultural phenomena with criteria, concepts, and techniques derived from the natural sciences. Inspired by the advance of physics and chemistry, they were convinced that social processes could be studied in the same completely objective way as natural phenomena, human behaviour being subject to universal laws of change in the same way as, say, geological formations. Indeed, 'man' himself was interpreted naturalistically, with all spiritual phenomena being explained by material ones – cellular and molecular structures and motions. What is now codified as dialectical materialism, it must be remembered, was formulated under the influence of Darwin's discoveries and in the intellectual atmosphere of Darwinism. The dominant trend of opinion among Marxists was to treat human history as a prolongation and a special case of natural history, to presume that the universal laws of nature apply, in specific forms, to the destiny of humankind. It was accepted, needless to say, that people, in contrast to animals or insects, behaved according to conscious intentions – but their intentions (and actions) were seen to conform to the 'objective' laws of human behaviour, which were independent of whether men understood them or not. The notion that man's purposes are autonomous ultimates controlling his life and his history was, according to the classical Marxists, a pernicious illusion. We can study human purposes just as we study the purposes (drives and reactions) of primates or any other living organisms. We must see ourselves and others, and their and our actions, objectively, as natural objects and events.

In keeping with his idealist past, the Gramsci of the *Notebooks* sharply rejected this passive materialism: 'Man does not enter into relations with the natural world just by being himself part of the natural world, but actively, by means of work and technique. Further: these relations are not mechanical: they are active and conscious.'[22] Marxism, Gramsci insists, 'cannot be reduced to a naturalistic "anthropology"'.[23] So far from believing that human history was a particular application of the general laws of nature, Gramsci conceived nature, as we know it, as an extension of man, an organ of practical activity. His hostility to the 'reduction of historical materialism to traditional metaphysical materialism'[24] is most clearly observed in his scathing, extended prison critique of Bukharin's well-known and influential *Theory of Historical Materialism*. Attacking the Bolshevik theorist, Gramsci argues that there is no point in inquiring about the universe 'in itself':

It might seem that there can exist an extra-historical and extra-human objectivity. But who is the judge of such objectivity? Who is able to put himself in this kind of 'standpoint of the cosmos in itself' and what could such a standpoint mean? ... Objective always means 'humanly objective' which can be held to correspond exactly to 'historically subjective': in other words, objective would mean 'universal subjective' ... The idea of 'objective' in metaphysical materialism would appear to mean an objectivity that exists even apart from man; but when one affirms that a reality would exist even if man did not, one is either speaking metaphorically or one is falling into a form of mysticism. We know reality only in relation to man, and since man is historical becoming, knowledge and reality are also a becoming and so is objectivity.[25]

Gramsci, it is essential to recognize, nowhere denied the existence of what Marx called the 'natural substratum'. Man did not create nature and it is not a subjective mental image: 'abstract natural forces' exist even before man becomes aware of them, and humankind cannot evade the determination of nature and its 'objective, intractable laws'.[26] The object of our knowledge, however, is not nature 'in itself' but our active contact with it. The external reality we confront is not a pure objective datum; it 'does not exist on its own, in and for itself, but only in an historical relationship with the men who modify it'.[27] Man's relation with nature is always dialectical: man shapes it as it shapes him; there is no understanding one without the other. Nature is nothing to us ('historical nothingness')[28] until it becomes the object of historically defined human purposes. And, in Gramsci's view, nothing that enters into relationship with man remains simply non-human. The orthodox Marxists are mistaken, Gramsci holds, in their belief that thought reflects the real, factual attributes and relationships of nature itself, considered in the abstract, independent of man's cognitive activity. We can conceive of no 'standpoint of the cosmos in itself' from which the subject can apprehend 'extra-human reality' in order then to replicate it in his own mind.

In taking issue with the 'contemplative' notion of reality, which leaves no room for the unity of theory and practice or the subject's creative role, Gramsci echoes the doctrines put forward by the 'early' Marx. While the *Paris Manuscripts* were published too late for the Sardinian to read them, he claimed to derive his position from the *Theses on Feuerbach*, which, in his opinion, 'show precisely the extent to which Marx had got beyond the philosophical position of vulgar materialism'.[29] The *Theses* deride all previous materialism for treating the material world as given and completely precedent to consciousness, for failing to perceive the reciprocal interaction between mental activity and the realm of 'things'. This insight, Gramsci points out, has been overlooked by those Marxists who, after the fashion of Bukharin, regard historical materialism as 'traditional materialism slightly revised and corrected'.[30]

Gramsci was certainly influenced by the idealist assumption that mind permeates nature and thus gives it significance and form. He did not, however, repudiate materialism as such, for what he sought was, to quote him, '"materialism" perfected by the work of speculative philosophy'.[31] The materialist interpretation of consciousness, according to him, has nothing to do with physiological reductionism; it is simply that knowledge and all things mental – emotions, ideals, imaginings –

are the products of social life. By the term 'materialism', he means the dependence of consciousness on concrete conditions and *not* the metaphysical primacy of matter over mind. 'Matter as such ... is not our subject but how it is socially and historically organized for production.'[32] In denying the validity of naturalistic materialism, then, Gramsci is by no means endorsing those forms of idealism which regard actually existing things as mere reflexes, reproductions, imitations, illustrations, or results of so-called *a priori* thought. He never fell victim to the illusion that because all reality is *mediated* by thought, it is therefore also *constituted* by thought.[33] As his 'Anti-Croce' makes plain, Gramsci's objective is not a regression to idealism, but a transcendence of the sterile dichotomy between idealism and materialism.

Gramsci concludes, against Bukharin and others of his ilk, that a science of men treated purely as natural entities, on a par with rivers and plants and stones, rests on a cardinal error.[34] Those who uphold a single logic of explanation, who believe that the same scheme of concepts can be used to encompass human actions as well as natural processes and events, take no account of the *creativity* and *spontaneity* which distinguish the human species from the physical world. Since the domain of mind or will or feeling is neither subordinated to natural determinism nor wholly amenable to quantitative treatment, the rules and laws of physics and the other natural sciences do not apply to it.

## IV CRITIQUE OF ECONOMISM

Gramsci's stress on human subjectivity led him to oppose any form of 'economism', which – on his account – involves: (*a*) 'the claim, presented as an essential postulate of historical materialism, that every fluctuation of politics and ideology can be presented and expounded as an immediate expression of the structure',[35] and (*b*) 'the iron conviction that there exist objective laws of historical development similar in kind to natural laws, together with a belief in a predetermined teleology like that of a religion'.[36] Orthodox Marxists, viewing human society as merely an extension of organic nature, advocated a rigidly deterministic interpretation of social phenomena, which purported to demonstrate that the links between different aspects of social life and successive phases of historical development were matters of objective necessity, transcending human will. Though some were less dogmatic

than others, the 'scientific' Marxists exhibited a monistic faith in 'productive forces' as the all-sufficient motive power in history: these
thinkers adhered, as a rule, to a mechanistic model of the substruc-
ture/superstructure relationship, which tended to move directly from
economic (or technological) cause to political or cultural effect.
History was reduced to a sequence of modes of production, an objective process of evolution, apart from us and our doing, and subject to
inescapable laws. Socialism, on this conception, is vouchsafed by the
impersonal dynamic of economic and historical development; it is not
simply a vastly better society than capitalism, nor is it a mere hope or
aspiration; it is a necessary outcome, arising from the maturation of
capitalism's insoluble contradictions. Despite its professed hostility to
the abstract systems of the German ideologists, orthodox Marxism
enchained man in a preconceived historical dialectic as effectively as
orthodox Hegelianism had done. Indeed, the economic and historical
determinism displayed by the scientific Marxists derived from the
Hegelian tendency, which they inherited from Marx, to make deductions about social conditions from abstract, *a priori* dialectical
schemata, with insufficient regard to actual facts.

Gramsci protested against the notion that laws of social life impose
themselves on individuals with the same inexorable necessity as an
earth-quake or tornado. Underlying his critique of 'economism' was
an attempt to restore consciousness – the social actor's decisions, ini-
tiatives, and frame of reference – to the heart of Marxism. Like all
Marxists, he divided the socio-cultural world of objects and events into
two basic structures – the economic infrastructure (or base) and the
political/ideological superstructure; but Gramsci did not interpret the
base/superstructure distinction as a linear, mechanical relationship
between source and reflection or cause and effect. Far from being a
realm of 'mere illusion', the superstructure is 'a reality ... objective
and operative'.[37] The nexus of relationships linking ideas and political
activity to material imperatives is rarely, if ever, specifiable in terms of
a unilateral causal derivation from one level to the other.[38]

How does the relative autonomy of the superstructure manifest
itself? One important point underlined by Gramsci is that ideologies
are hardly inessential or ineffective in the historical process; they are,
on the contrary, substantial and active elements in social development, because 'men acquire knowledge of their social position and
therefore of their tasks on the terrain of ideologies'.[39] He also argues
that political activity is not merely accessory to socio-economic activity
but contains values independent of its role in subserving a particular

order of society. Consider this extraordinary (for a Third International Communist) statement:

Politics becomes permanent action and gives birth to permanent organisations precisely in so far as it identifies itself with economics. But it is also *distinct from it*, which is why one may speak separately of economics and politics, and speak of 'political passion' as of an immediate impulse to action which is born on the 'permanent and organic' terrain of economic life but which *transcends it*.[40]

As Adamson points out,[41] the inspiration behind this passage 'derives less from Marx than from a reading of Machiavelli', who asserted the autonomy of politics and – as we shall see more clearly in later pages – exerted a profound influence on Gramsci's thought. Politics, Gramsci was saying, is (semi-) autonomous because it manifests its own principles and tendencies distinct from those of economics. For example, it is 'not sufficiently borne in mind', he writes, 'that many political acts are due to internal necessities of an organisational character, that is they are tied to the need to give coherence to a party, a group, a society'.[42]

Because Gramsci regarded the relationship between 'base' and 'superstructure' as 'necessarily interactive and reciprocal',[43] it is superficially plausible to argue that he advanced, in Adamson's words, 'an organicist conception of mediations within a totality', an image within which 'the concepts of "primary" and "secondary" make little sense'.[44] Adamson's language may be slightly eccentric, but his message – that Gramsci posited a straightforward interactionism, wherein everything influences everything else in ways that cannot be calculated or specified – is commonly assumed to be true. It is, however, false. Still further from the truth is the argument submitted by Norberto Bobbio, who contends, in an influential essay, that Gramsci was *reversing* the Marxian primacy of base over superstructure, thus making the latter 'primary' and the former 'secondary'.[45] That Gramsci (after 1918) endorsed the economic interpretation of history, inasmuch as he believed that the economic factor is the fundamental factor on which other aspects of life are dependent, can be amply documented. Evidence from his pre-prison writings has already been presented, but the *Notebooks*, too, are littered with affirmations of the predominance of economic conditions. Recall that, for him, 'Politics becomes permanent action and gives birth to permanent organisations *precisely in so far as it identifies itself with economics*'.[46] For the most part, Gramsci does not distinguish among the various elements of the 'base' and attributes explanatory priority to 'econ-omics',[47] the 'economic factor',[48] the 'economy',[49] 'economic phe-nomena',[50] 'material preconditions',[51] and 'economic necessity'.[52] Elsewhere, however, the pre-eminence of the productive forces is plainly singled out. He informs us, for example, that the cultural and moral life of a nation 'corresponds to the needs of the productive forces for development',[53] and, further, that these 'material forces of production' constitute the 'active and propulsive force' of history.[54] It is impossible to escape the conclusion that Gramsci agreed with Marx and Engels about the material mode of existence being the *primum agens*. But where does this leave the idea of 'interaction'? In Gramsci's eyes, although economic and non-economic factors interact, a larger proportion of the causal impetus comes from the productive sphere. Such a conception may be arbitrary and untenable (how does one divide the interacting processes and determine which played the larger role?), but there can be no doubt that he adhered to it. While wishing to avoid reductionist formulae, he nevertheless maintained that men's opinions, customs, and institutions are predominantly affected by the prevailing system of production. This system is 'historically subjective', the result of past human creativity, but it assumes an 'objective' form and structures collective choices. To paraphrase the renowned epigram, men have made their social world – that is, their civilization and institutions – but not out of 'whole cloth', not out of infinitely mal-leable material; the 'objective' realm, nature and pre-existent social forms, limits our margin of creativity.

Marx and Engels also recognized the two-way, mutual influence of different social regions on one another – rigid economic determinists they were not. However, their position differs from Gramsci's in one crucial respect. For them, although the various elements of the super-structure 'exercise their influence upon the course of historical strug-gles and in many cases preponderate in determining their *form*', economic variables are 'finally decisive'.[55] In the 'last analysis', the superstructure must conform to immanent structural imperatives. Thus, according to Marx and Engels, the revolutionary consciousness of the proletariat will, *of necessity*, issue from the development of capitalist society, burdened as it is by ever-worsening contradictions. Capitalism, through the operation of its own blind, impersonal, and necessary economic laws, is destined to give rise to socialism. Like Bernstein before him, Gramsci departs from classical Marxism in rejecting the theory of historical necessity. This is not to say that he denies Marx's analysis of the structural weaknesses of capitalism. On the contrary (and here he diverges from Bernstein), this analysis remains for him an essential presupposition: throughout his career he takes it for granted that there is a derangement in the functioning of the capitalist economic base, with its 'deficiencies and incapacity', its 'incurable structural contradictions'.[56] But this derangement is only a *necessary* condition of socialism, *not a sufficient* one. History, then, comprises a field of possibilities, open, within strict limits, to creative intervention. Since the flow of events is not irrevocably determined by economic factors, cultural and political activity is *ultimately* decisive.[57]

But – it might be asked – how can a decadent system, beset by internal economic contradictions, *not* collapse? To Gramsci, neither mass poverty nor anarchic production nor a falling profit rate is devastating enough to ensure the demise of capitalism, still less the emergence of socialism. An unhealthy society, like an unhealthy human being, can survive – though not thrive. In the absence of a strong and imaginative political/ideological challenge, a stagnant form of capitalism can last indefinitely. So, while Gramsci holds that the conditions of material existence constitute the source of superstructural changes, he cannot accurately be described as an economic *determinist*. The 'base' may be crying out for socialism, but its pleas, however, loud and desperate, need not incite men to action. Gramsci could find no grounds for the conviction that mankind is necessarily evolving towards a final messianic kingdom. Once ideas and values and political actions are given causal significance, scientific prediction of future events becomes impossible, for such superstructural elements defy quantification. Determinism, in any prognostic sense, is incompatible with the 'essence' of human existence, which is creativity. Those who attempt to predict 'what will be' are misled by the supposition of a basic homogeneity between the science of nature and the study of society. While the former furnishes us with the ability to foresee the evolution of natural processes, the latter, contrary to the beliefs of the orthodox Marxists, can supply us with no foreknowledge of humankind's evolution and ultimate destiny.[58]

Gramsci's emphasis on the creative historical role of human effort and purpose led him to attack those who transformed historical materialism into a 'universal history', whereby all events are fit into a pre-determined model. Man, in Gramsci's account, is not merely a sub-category of the historical dialectic. Behind history there is no 'invisible hand' which manipulates people and things, but only a capacity for choice, for knowledge, for action. If blind necessity appears to rule, if history appears to be nothing but an immense natural phenomenon, a volcanic eruption, this is because of mass passivity, which prevents individuals and human groups from forging their intelligence and will, collective or individual, for shaping the objective processes they confront.[59] Gramsci firmly repudiates the conception which makes men and women into – to quote Labriola – 'marionettes whose strings are pulled no longer by Providence but by economic categories'.[60] History, as surely as perceptual objects, exists in relationship with human agents; it is not the unfolding of natural law but the autogenesis of man, the product of collective human action – which explains why Marxism, on Gramsci's understanding, is 'absolute humanism.'[61] Marxist fatalism – described by the Sardinian as a primitive, quasi-religious faith, comparable to Christian theories of predestination – must be buried 'with all due honours'.[62]

His contempt for doctrinaire schemas, designed to encompass the whole of historical development, stemmed only in part from his stress on human agency. As we have seen, he accentuated Marxism's continuity with the idealist tradition, and from this derives the idea that each and every society exhibits unique, complex characteristics, which resist summary in the form of precise and simple axioms. (Although Hegel, with his preconceived dialectic, betrayed the implications of this insight.) A Marxian doctrine which granted history an inexorable logic and coherent meaning could not be realistically reconciled with actual historical events and processes, for history is characterized by – in Gramsci's words – 'infinite variety and multiplicity'.[63] He upheld the specific and the unique over the repetitive and the universal, the concrete and particular over the abstract and general. A 'mechanical formula' cannot adequately explain any *particular* historical phenomenon, for a given historical event is a confluence of manifold circumstances and conflicts.[64] This respect for historical specificity caused Gramsci to distrust abstract mental constructs, disjoined from empirical actuality and common experience. If, as he says, 'reality produces a wealth of the most bizarre combinations', then it is up to the theoretician to find proof of his theory in this untidiness. Against those who remain encamped on the plane of rarefied theory, Gramsci insists that the validity of a theoretical formulation derives only from its contact with the data of the real world.[65]

History, according to his view, is law-like only in a highly restricted sense. The interrelations of social actors and institutions *do* 'operate with a certain regularity and automatism', and these statistical regularities ('laws of tendency' in Gramsci's terminology) can be isolated through systematic and careful observation. But there can be no 'question of "discovering" a metaphysical law of "determinism", or even of establishing a "general" law of causality'. Devoid of a 'speculative halo', 'laws of tendency' have no unalterable and final validity and on no account conflict with free will. It is simply that the sum total of free and conscious human acts forms a pattern of statistical correlations and results in mass phenomena which are not consciously willed by anyone.[66] Gramsci credits David Ricardo with discovering the concept of 'law of tendency' – an idea purified of 'the mechanical aspect of the law of causality of the natural sciences' – and claims that this discovery made it possible for Marx (though not his epigones) to 'go beyond' the 'speculative logic' embodied in Hegel's notion of dialectical necessity. Thus, Ricardo's contribution to the philosophy of praxis lies not solely in his labour theory of value, but in his 'whole way of thinking', in his realistic integration of the experimental method into the study of human events and social phenomena.[67]

In denying that history is driven forward by dialectical necessity, Gramsci was explicitly directing his critique at 'scientific' Marxists like Bukharin, but his arguments also apply to Lukács, his fellow Marxist humanist, whose work he more or less ignored. Although the Hungarian comprehended the historically creative role of self-conscious human praxis and denounced the idea of mechanical, causal necessity, he nevertheless considered history as the immanent realization of the human 'essence', an objectively necessary process, impelled by the historical dialectic and fated to have a happy ending.[68] This 'essentialist' or 'teleological' approach was every bit as alien to Gramsci as was Bukharin's 'sociological' approach, with its misguided attempt to derive the impersonal 'laws of evolution of human society in such a way as to "predict" that the oak tree will develop out of the acorn'.[69] Both assumed that history revealed a 'logic', which could be grasped through an act of intellectual cognition; whereas Gramsci, viewing the social world as a fluid process, eschewed the notion of historical closure.

According to him, Bukharin's supposition that history is predictable 'favours mental laziness and a superficiality in political programmes'. What the orthodox Marxists fail to realize is that 'laws can be employed in the science and art of politics only so long as the great masses of the population remain ... essentially passive', but the purpose of political action is 'precisely to arouse the masses from passivity', to break the mould of traditional patterns of behaviour.[70] Because mechanical determinism lulls both leaders and masses into a false sense of security and optimism, the conceptual machinery of orthodox Marxism poses an obstacle to the pursuit of effective politics. If socialist revolution is inevitable, if salvation comes through grace and not works, why not wait complacently for the wonderful event to happen?

Since, for Gramsci, the revolution is not guaranteed by 'history' itself, the future hinges upon the awareness, vigour and commitment of the proletariat. Clearly, none of this will be forthcoming unless the revolutionary forces are inspired by a vision of what 'ought-to-be'. The classical Marxist did not tell the proletariat what it *ought* to do, but showed it what it would be *forced* to do, by its own character and situation, by its location in 'history'. Tolstoy's question, 'What shall we do and how shall we live?' was ridiculed as the irrelevant legacy of a pre-scientific epoch. Once the assumption of determinism is removed, however, the dimension of 'ought' comes to the fore, and the ethical questions scorned by 'scientific socialism' take on crucial importance. Never deviating from his youthful tendency to portray socialism as, essentially, a doctrine of regeneration and redemption, Gramsci, in the *Notebooks*, called for 'intellectual and moral reform'.[71] The fundamental goals of his Marxism were to preserve and develop human culture, to construct what Engels once called 'a really human morality', and to restore men and women to life in an integrated community. The socialization of the means of production, together with an equitable distribution, were but the first steps towards 'the creation of a new integral culture, having the mass character of the Protestant Reformation and the French Enlightenment as well as the classical character of the cultures of Ancient Greece and the Italian Renaissance, a culture which ... synthesizes Maximilien Robespierre and Immanuel Kant'.[72] Under the spell of people like Bukharin, a purveyor of obscurantist hocus-pocus, Marxism had become 'prejudice' and 'superstition', bereft of intellectual refinement, indifferent to long-standing cultural concerns, and 'absolutely inadequate to combat the ideologies of the educated classes'.[73] It was imperative to raise the intellectual level of the doctrine, and this endeavour would require the rehabilitation of philosophy. Once again breaking sharply with Marxist orthodoxy, Gramsci inveighed against the scientistic belief that philosophy would, in the fullness of time, be superseded by the positive sciences of nature and history. Philosophy must not be *extinguished*; it must be *brought down to earth* – hence the synthesis of Robespierre and Kant – and made to yield norms and values for practical action. What must be abandoned is the *traditional conception* of philosophy, as a science seeking its own aims in a Mount Olympus of pure speculation, isolated from the concrete history of humankind.[74]

The objective, therefore, is 'a philosophy that produces an attendant morality',[75] but whence does this morality originate? Did Gramsci follow the neo-Kantians in proclaiming the existence of a transcendent morality, valid universally, eternally, and immutably? Certainly not. After the manner of Marx (and Croce), he argues that our cherished purposes and values reflect nothing but the contingencies of our historical situation. Conscience, Reason – these are not ahistorical faculties confronting man as the voice of an inner essence: they are, on the contrary, *human* functions and activities, products of the continuous interaction between changing men and their changing environment.[76] Gramsci's 'man' is not an abstraction, defined in terms of metaphysical and speculative co-ordinates. Rather, human nature is a vacuum filled by society, or more precisely, a set of quiescent capacities excited into action by the 'totality of historically determined social relations'.[77] Since there is no 'man-in-general', there can be no 'morality-in-general', for universal ethical truths are derivable only from an abstract, unchanging human nature. Far from being a Kantian moral imperative, based on a timeless model, the 'ought-to-be' is, properly conceived, a projection of forms and principles inherent in existing actuality. In the absence of forces that make for its realization, an ideal is nothing but 'idle fancy, yearning, day-dream'. Marxists should pursue goals that are 'necessary', 'concrete', and 'realistic'; i.e., implicit in the extant equilibrium of forces. Gramsci feels that, in this respect, we can learn from Machiavelli, the realist thinker *par excellence*, who combined concern for what 'ought-to-be' with an appreciation of the limits imposed by 'the terrain of effective reality'.[78]

## V   MARXISM AS ABSOLUTE HISTORICISM

For Gramsci, then, Marxism is neither a positive science nor a theory of 'man', or 'human nature'. Marxism is 'historicism', a view whose essence has been neatly and eloquently summarized by Leszek Kolakowski:

> that the meaning and 'rationality' of all human behaviour and every product of human activity, including works of the mind such as philosophy and science, is manifested only in relation to the 'global' historical processes of which they are part. In other words, the 'truth' of philosophy or science is 'truth' in a socially pragmatic sense: what is true is that which, in a particular historical situation, expresses the real developmental trend of that situation.[79]

Historicism, or 'immanentism',[80] was, in Gramsci's opinion, the quintessence of Marxism, which is why it was a 'philosophy of praxis'. In common with other sets of ideas, it must be understood in terms of its function and origin: anyone who speaks of a 'science of Marxism', taken as a doctrine that 'reflects' reality as it is, regardless of whether we know it or not, 'falls headlong into dogmatism'.[81] For there can exist no 'extra-historical and extra-human objectivity'.[82] There is no such thing as mere knowing, in which we passively apprehend the nature of a purely 'given' object. All knowing is bound up with doing and everything we know has in some measure been modified by our agency. Knowledge is not, *pace* the 'scientific' Marxists, the simple reflection of a pre-existing reality. On the contrary, theoretical knowledge and practical activity are two sides of the same coin (unity of theory and practice). The implications of this humanist epistemology are as follows: (*a*) there are no 'extra-historical' or 'extra-human' truths, which are true no matter whether or when they are known; (*b*) intellectual activity can never exceed the bounds of historical praxis; and (*c*) thought is always evaluated in terms of its social embodiment, and never in terms of its intrinsic properties; the criterion of validity is located in neither an autonomous realm of experience (as it was for the positivists) nor a pure domain of 'reason' (as it was for the rationalists).

Thus, according to Gramsci, a doctrine or philosophy or vision of life proves its rationality and 'truth' not by conforming to some fixed standard, or 'objective' reality, beyond the reach of human volition, but by becoming 'concretely – i.e. historically and socially – universal'.[83] The point is formulated more prosaically in the following passage:

> Mass adhesion or non-adhesion to an ideology is the real critical test of the rationality and historicity of modes of thinking ... constructions which respond to the demands of a complex organic period of history always impose themselves and prevail in the end.[84]

An ideology demonstrates its 'rationality and historicity', otherwise phrased, only when it 'becomes actual and lives historically',[85] i.e., penetrates deeply into men's practical lives. The only legitimate warrant for declaring one standpoint superior to another is 'practice', or – to be more exact – 'success'.

To deny that truth is truth, regardless of whether it is known or believed, to assert that the rightness of an idea is confirmed by the fact that it prevails historically, and to declare that any political or philosophical statement which convinces no one has no validity – all this is foreign to orthodox Marxism and irreconcilable with the usual view of truth. And yet Gramsci (perhaps perversely) disclaims the imputation of relativism:

> To think of a philosophical affirmation as true in a particular histor-
> ical period (that is, as the necessary and inseparable expression of a
> … particular praxis) but as superseded and rendered 'vain' in a suc-
> ceeding period, without however falling into scepticism and moral
> and ideological relativism, … is quite an arduous and difficult
> mental operation.[86]

In what sense is he *not* a relativist? There are, on his conception, no *absolute* truths, for everything changes; but there are *objective* (under-stood as 'historically subjective' or 'humanly objective') truths, which despite being relative to particular eras, are nevertheless valid, or rational, or 'true' within this framework. That is, 'true' = 'true in the conditions of its time'. Thus, for Gramsci (and here he differs from Mannheim) the analysis of the social location of ideas does not preclude an assessment of their truth value.

In his reduction of all mental products to a practical/historical func-tion, Gramsci refuses to distinguish sharply between science and other forms of cerebral activity: 'All science is tied to needs, to life, to the activity of man … in reality, even science is a superstructure.'[87] Orthodox Marxists took the opposite view, that the scientific explana-tion of the universe accumulates historically as the advance of truth in the conventional sense, and that science, unlike theological systems or political beliefs, is thus *not* part of the superstructure. They believed, accordingly, that Marxism itself, as a 'scientific' theory, could be valid-ated 'objectively'; i.e., independently of the fact that it served a politi-cal purpose as the intellectual weapon of the proletariat. But, to Gramsci, Marxism, no less than science, is superstructural: 'non-definitive' and 'perishable', 'an expression of historical contradic-tions'.[88] The philosophy of praxis, he maintains, should by no means be reified or canonized; it is one scheme of ideas among others – the most fruitful perhaps, but one that still has to demonstrate its utility (and therefore rationality) in actual contact with events. He even sug-gests that Marxism could extinguish itself in the process of its realiza-tion. For if people learn to control rationally their reciprocal exchanges and to bend necessity to their collective will, then historical materialism, the subordination of humankind to economic forces, may become 'false'; i.e. inoperative.[89]

Gramsci was well aware that his relativization of Marxism, however justified by a close reading of Marx himself, went against the grain of current thinking. The prevailing perspective was represented by Bukharin, who interpreted the doctrine as 'a dogmatic system of eternal and absolute truths', resting on a 'metaphysics of "matter"'.[90] Gramsci's alternative was 'absolute historicism' (his phrase), or the 'absolute secularization and earthliness of thought, an absolute humanism of history'.[91] His was a 'modest', or 'chastened' Marxism, freed from an autonomous dialectic of history and stripped of rationalist as well as determinist guarantees. The functional and historical view of knowledge can find some support in Marx. In the second thesis on Feuerbach, for example, he states: 'The question whether human thinking can pretend to objective truth is not a theoretical but a *practical* question. Man must prove the truth, i.e. the reality and power, the "this-sidedness" of his thinking, in practice.'[92] But Gramsci's 'absolute historicism' is also (perhaps mainly) rooted in his study of Croce, who – as we have seen – set himself squarely against the notion of a supra-human or meta-historical reality. For Croce, modern philosophy had commenced with Machiavelli and Vico, whose respective attacks on abstract Christian and Cartesian theories presupposed a worldly humanism as distinct from 'theologizing philosophy', whether that philosophy was religious or secular, whether it worshipped a Divine Creator or impersonal nature. The most fertile philosophical tradition of post-mediaeval Italy is anti-metaphysical, expressing a healthy scepticism towards all-embracing schemes and systems; and Gramsci's 'modest' Marxism, a body of ideas purged of prophetic and universalistic claims, is very much an outgrowth of this tradition.

Belief in the efficacy of human will and consciousness, aversion for 'final' solutions and the pretensions of Marxist 'science' – these philosophical commitments constitute the foundation for Gramsci's political thinking in general and his renowned concept of hegemony in particular. Eric Hobsbawm once characterized him as 'a political theorist, perhaps the only major Marxist thinker who can be so described'.[93] In the remainder of this essay, I shall give substance to Hobsbawm's interpretation, and then conclude with an assessment of Gramsci's contribution to our understanding of history and society.

## VI   HEGEMONY AND REVOLUTION

The impact of Croce is quite evident in Gramsci's theory of 'hegemony', which was set out – albeit unsystematically – in the *Prison
Notebooks*. The theory, one of the most significant contributions to
twentieth-century Marxist thought, is founded on a simple premise:
that modern man is not ruled by force alone, but also by ideas.
Physical domination is not enough; there is a need for spiritual
supremacy as well.[94] Those who obey must, to some degree, share the
values and standards of their 'superiors', and *consent* to their own subordination. Hegemony therefore signifies the control of social life (by
a group or a class) through cultural, as opposed to physical, means.

The term 'hegemony' certainly had a place in Marxist discourse
before Gramsci's adoption of it. *Gegemoniya* was one of the most frequently used slogans of the Russian Social-Democrats in their turn-of-
the-century polemics. It was introduced by Plekhanov, Axelrod, Lenin
and others in their dispute with the 'economists' over the issue of
'spontaneity' *versus* political action. In brief, *gegemoniya* referred to
the primacy of the proletariat in the struggle against Tsarist absolutism, due to the political impotence of all other classes. After the
October Revolution the term was often used in the external docu-
ments of the Comintern, which regularly enjoined the Western proletariat to eschew narrow 'corporatism' and exercise hegemony, or
leadership, over the other exploited groups (mainly the peasantry)
that were its class allies in the fight against capitalism. 'Hegemony', in
this early usage, applied to the attitude of the proletariat *vis-à-vis*
other, potentially revolutionary classes. Gramsci extended the
concept, defining it as a mechanism of rule applicable to any set of
social relations where one group or class holds sway. Moreover, his
equation of hegemony with *cultural* ascendancy is completely absent
from the original usage, which referred simply to *political* leadership
within a system of alliances.

Gramsci was a historical materialist, for whom a system of beliefs
arises within a specific mode of production and in some sense reflects
it. Nevertheless, the theory of hegemony calls to mind the Hegelian
principle that a given society embodies a 'spirit' or 'idea', whose locus
is the psychological structure within its inhabitants. Here lies the key
to capitalism's vexatious powers of endurance, says Gramsci. Why
have the workers not filled the elevated role assigned to them by
Marxist theory? Because they (or most of them) are in thrall to the

dominant *Weltanschauung*. Classical Marxism never dreamed of giving such weight to non-economic factors like ideology and culture. True, Marx and Engels observed that 'In every epoch the ideas of the ruling class are the ruling ideas', but they never adopted a fully-fledged theory of ideological incorporation, and the notion of class struggle, at the cultural as well as at the economic and political levels, plays a central part in their work. Classical Marxism rested upon a 'conflict' model of society, from which even Lenin did not depart. While trade unionism, he believed, can canalize and possibly temper the chronic confrontation between oppressors and oppressed, it cannot transform a society torn apart by class division into anything resembling an integrated whole. For Lenin, as for all Marxists before Gramsci, every state is a dictatorship, based upon force and coercion.

Gramsci had no wish to deny the obvious: he understood that every state is *ultimately* a 'dictatorship', inasmuch as it will clamp down on those who reject its authority or seriously challenge its foundations. But, for him, all talk of the 'dictatorship of the bourgeoisie', while rhetorically and psychologically pleasing, was analytically useless and practically dangerous, for it blurred important distinctions between different forms of rule. Gramsci recognized that Western societies exhibited a great deal of internal cohesion and that this stability could not stem solely, or even mainly, from fear. Bourgeois spiritual despotism, the moral and cultural integration of the masses into a system operating against their interests, rendered physical despotism unnecessary in all but the most extreme circumstances.

This upgrading of the factor of cultural leadership required a reappraisal of the Marxist concept of 'superstructure', which could no longer be interpreted as a pale reflection of the socio-economic infrastructure. Gramsci divided the superstructure into two major 'levels', which he labelled 'civil society' and 'political society'. The former consists of 'the ensemble of organisms commonly called "private"' – parties, schools, universities, the mass media, trade unions, Churches – which shape social and political consciousness. The ruling class is able to clutter the minds of the masses with mystifications and distortions (i.e., establish its hegemony) because it controls this apparatus of transmission.[95] Political society, on the other hand, is composed of all those public institutions – the courts, the police, parliament, the army, the bureaucracy, the government – which exercise 'direct domination' or 'command'.[96] Political society is, according to some *Notebook* passages, synonymous with the state.[97] Elsewhere, however, Gramsci adheres to a broad definition of the state, comprehending all institutions which, whether formally public or private, enable the dominant social group to rule. Note the following succinct formulation: 'State = political society + civil society, in other words hegemony protected by the armour of coercion'.[98] The 'armour of coercion' serves to discipline those who do not 'consent'.

If, as Gramsci says, the bourgeoisie can generally count on the 'spontaneous consent' of the masses, if it gains political legitimacy by weaving its own cultural outlook into the social fabric, then how can forms of oppositional, alternative thought (such as Marxism) ever manage to flourish? Do we not have here an early version of Marcuse's 'one-dimensional man', doomed to a life of illusion within a closed universe of discourse? In fact, Gramsci maintains that hegemonic situations differ in intensity, and the degree of variation is rooted in the dynamics of historical development. In a paradigm case, which we can call *integral* hegemony, mass affiliation to the extant system would approach unqualified commitment. Such a situation, however, can persist only when the ruling class performs a progressive function in the productive process, when it 'really causes the whole society to move forward'. But in modern capitalist society, Gramsci thinks, bourgeois economic dominance has become outmoded, for it limits further development of the productive forces. Consequently, the 'ideological bloc' shows signs of decay.[99] In some of his most intriguing (and overlooked) notebook entries, he focuses on the superficiality of mass consent within the capitalist system by drawing attention to the frequent incompatibility between a person's conscious thoughts and the unconscious values implicit in his actions. This 'contradiction', we are told, expresses 'profounder' contradictions:

> the contrast between thought and action ... signifies that the social group in question may indeed have its own conception of the world, even if only embryonic; a conception which manifests itself in action, but occasionally and in flashes – when, that is, the group is acting as an organic totality. But this same group has, for reasons of submission and intellectual subordination, adopted a conception which is not its own but is borrowed from another group; and it affirms this conception verbally and believes itself to be following it.[100]

A few pages later he continues:

> The active man-in-the-mass has a practical activity, but has no clear theoretical consciousness of his practical activity. ...One might almost say that he has two theoretical consciousnesses (or one

*contradictory consciousness*): one which is implicit in his activity ...
and one, superficially explicit or verbal, which he has inherited from
the past and uncritically absorbed.[101]

The common man, in this account, evinces a 'contradictory consciousness': on an abstract plane, he endorses the prevailing world-vision (if
in a naive, commonsensical form); on the situational or practical level,
however, he reveals not outright dissent, but a reduced commitment, as
evidenced in strikes, factory sit-ins, riots, crime, etc. – manifestations of
discontent which occur 'occasionally and in flashes', and suggest the
existence of an incipient revolutionary mentality. Because of the
ambivalence and inconsistency in mass consciousness, bourgeois hegemony is a *decadent* hegemony, powerful enough to ensure 'passivity'
and 'submission',[102] but none the less vulnerable, out of harmony with
the true needs and inclinations of the people. Conflict lurks just
beneath the calm surface of social life.

The theory of hegemony carries important implications for strategy
and enabled Gramsci to modernize the classical Marxist–Leninist
approach to revolution. He lamented the fact that many Marxists, in
their eager quest for the economic laws of history, had lost all sense of
the crucial *political* dimension in human affairs. As a student of
Machiavelli, he wanted to revive the art and science of politics, which
Marxists had blindly dismissed as epiphenomenal and therefore
unworthy of serious attention. In particular, he sought to devise analytical tools and complex courses of action to cope with the *geistige*
superiority of the Western bourgeoisie. Marxist–Leninists took as
their point of departure the presupposition that the foundation of
social order was force, not consensus. As a result, they conceived the
struggle for socialism in pure paramilitary terms: to the concentrated
violence of the bourgeois state, they would counterpose the concentrated violence of the revolutionary party. The attainment of power
was construed as a technical problem, a matter of effectively deploy-
ing one's legions for a military style assault on the apparatus of coercion. Gramsci acknowledged that the paramilitary approach was valid
in the case of Russia in 1917, but this was a special case: 'In Russia the
State was everything, civil society was primordial and gelatinous; in
the West, there was a proper relation between State and civil society,
and when the State trembled a sturdy structure of civil society was at
once revealed.'[103] The Tsarist regime lacked highly developed mechanisms of cultural organization, and, consequently, the people were in
no way integrated into the regime's framework of values. Social order

was founded on ignorance, apathy, and repression, not on voluntary consent. Thus, in analysing the revolutionary process, we must distinguish between 'modern States' and 'backward countries' and vary our strategy accordingly.[104] In order to illustrate this point, Gramsci draws a parallel between politics and war:

> The superstructures of civil society are like the trench-systems of modern warfare. In war it would sometimes happen that a fierce artillery attack seemed to have destroyed the enemy's entire defensive system, whereas in fact it had only destroyed the outer perimeter; and at the moment of their advance and attack the assailants would find themselves confronted by a line of defence which was still effective. The same thing happens in politics.[105]

Continuing the military analogy, and borrowing terminology from military science, he argues that a lightning 'war of movement', a rapid frontal assault on the state apparatus, was sufficient in the conditions of Russia, a 'backward country', without a secondary 'line of [cultural] defence'. But in the West, the state ('the outer perimeter') is supported by a powerful system of 'fortresses and earthworks'[106] (i.e., civil society), which serve to absorb and contain discontent. What is needed, then, is a protracted siege, or 'war of position', which focuses on the destruction of the 'fortresses and earthworks' lying behind the 'outer perimeter'. The Bolshevik coup, Gramsci reluctantly concludes, cannot provide the model for revolution in advanced capitalist countries, where circumstances demand a radically different approach, one centred on the gradual subversion of the multiple organs of ideological dissemination. The revolutionary forces must aim to scrape away the whole system of bourgeois attitudes, prohibitions, myths, and values, thus rendering 'the ruled intellectually independent of the rulers'. In so doing, we 'destroy one hegemony and create another', and this cultural transformation is a 'necessary phase', an indispensable precondition, of successful political revolution in the West.[107] Even if we suppose that a Jacobin vanguard, by some chance or other, could seize the state apparatus by a *coup d'état*, they could not introduce a proper socialist system. The result would be a political abortion, destroyed by a hostile, uncomprehending populace, its vision clouded by the haze of bourgeois ideology.

What Gramsci was saying, in contrast to the evolutionary Marxists, was that revolution was more likely to occur in underdeveloped societies than in developed ones, not because the workers in the latter had been 'bought off' by the profits of imperialism (a phenomenon in which Gramsci showed little interest) but because, in the normal course of development, they had been intellectually and morally integrated into the prevailing order. In underdeveloped countries, on the other hand, the agencies of socialization are 'primordial and gelatinous': the masses do not experience reality through the conceptual categories of the dominant class. Once the 'outer perimeter', the state, is taken, the triumphant revolutionaries need not trouble their heads about an inner line of defence.

Did the 'war of position' amount to a 'parliamentary road' to socialism? Was Gramsci's theory an early version of Eurocommunism, that bold and curious doctrine which aspires to combine full-blooded socialism with multi-party competition and the 'rules of the [parliamentary] game'? Certainly Togliatti and subsequent PCI leaders have claimed Gramsci as their source of inspiration. Other commentators have even gone so far as to argue that the *Notebooks* enunciate a quasi-liberal or social-democratic vision of the transition to socialism.[108] While the evidence is ambiguous, it would seem to be misleading to project Gramsci as an apostle of the 'Via Italiana', let alone the brand of socialism espoused by Mitterrand and other reformists.

It is sometimes assumed that Gramsci's majoritarian revolution, based on mass consent, necessarily entails a respect for political traditions and constitutional procedures. Gramsci himself thought otherwise. For one thing, he expressed nothing but contempt for the parliamentary system, regarding it as hopelessly elitist.[109] And nowhere does he say that the 'war of movement' is *irrelevant* in the West. Whereas once the military element was 'the whole' story, it is now only 'partial' – but nevertheless essential to ultimate victory.[110] As he writes, 'The decisive element in every situation is the permanently organised and long-prepared *force* which can be put in to the field when it is judged that a situation is favourable.'[111] When the 'situation is favourable', when the 'war of position' has been won, the assault on the state apparatus, the 'war of movement', finally takes place. Under the watchful eye of the prison censor, Gramsci refrained from devoting much space to armed struggle, but he never questioned its necessity. Moreover, he held fast to a goal of *total* social transformation, involving nothing less than the radical recomposition of society. Against Croce, for example, he defends the force of negativity in history: progress does not take the form of 'reformist evolution'; it is discontinuous and invariably destructive.[112]

The *Notebooks* do extol the virtues of flexibility as regards strategy and tactics. Gramsci poured scorn on those who displayed a 'rigid aversion on principle' to compromises or class alliances, who confused 'politics, real action, with theoretical disquisition'.[113] In defiance of the 'purists', he insisted that strategy be adapted 'to real men, formed in specific historical relations, with specific feelings, outlooks'.[114] Implicit here is a critique of dogmatic 'internationalism' and a defence of the *national* character of revolutions. But hostility to dogmatism does not equal revisionism. Gramsci's theory, we may safely conclude, was neither Muscovite nor Eurocommunist nor social-democratic in content. Still, commentators like Salvadori, who hold that the current PCI line has 'nothing in common with the ideas of Antonio Gramsci',[115] go too far. One could even maintain that the 'Via Italiana' is a logical deduction from his premises, given the change in historical circumstances.

## VII PROLETARIAN ORGANIZATION AND THE FUTURE SOCIETY

Gramsci's views on the organization of the mass movement were not all of one piece. In order to bring his shifts of emphasis and direction into relief, it is useful to isolate three distinct phases in his career: (1) the *biennio rosso* of 1919–20, when he co-edited *L'Ordine Nuovo*, a weekly newspaper distinguished by its advocacy of factory councils; (2) the years of 1921 to 1926, from the founding of the PCI to Gramsci's arrest; and (3) the period of his confinement, during which he composed the *Notebooks*.

The dramatic months of Italy's *biennio rosso* witnessed unprecedented labour unrest and (especially in Turin) the setting up of workers' councils. Gramsci, the most eloquent spokesman of the *Ordine Nuovo* group, developed the theoretical foundations of the *consigli di fabbrica* in a series of articles. At this stage he had not yet developed his concept of hegemony and was therefore optimistic about the imminence of revolution in Italy, a country he frequently compared to Kerensky's Russia. Indeed, the major inspiration for the workers' soviets came from Lenin and the Russian experience. (Gramsci sincerely believed that the slogan, 'All power to the Soviets', was in line with Russian reality.) The councils, for him, provided the 'model of the proletarian state', which would, so to speak, take its pattern from the shop floor. Let us briefly list the main features of the councils, according to the *Ordine Nuovo* vision. They would be, first, independent of traditional working-class institutions, and unlike these institutions, representative of *all* the wage-earners in a given plant, regardless of political allegiance, through a mechanism of mandatory democracy. Second, the councils would attempt, in the proximate future, to establish a system of 'dual power' in the factory. And, third, they would serve two basic educative functions: (1) to prepare the workers for a seizure of power in the factory by inculcating technical and managerial skills; (2) to foster in the workers 'a producer's mentality', allowing a self-realization that overcomes the false dichotomy of 'economic man' and 'citizen'.[116]

What role did Gramsci envisage for the party and the trade unions? These institutions, having arisen as affirmations of 'capitalist free competition', and developing under the formidable pressures and compulsions inherent in this competition, 'do not and cannot embrace the whole spectrum of teeming revolutionary forces that capitalism throws up'.[117] The *raison d'être* of the councils, on the other hand, lies not in the peculiarities of the bourgeois regime, but in 'something permanent', in 'the labour-process' itself. For this reason, they can transcend the logic of capitalist society and become the principal organs of liberation.[118] As for the party, its role should be limited to promoting the formation of councils, providing them with organizational assistance and theoretical advice, and generally clearing obstacles from their revolutionary path. What we have here is a model for 'revolution from below'.

Despite Gramsci's hopes, the series of strikes, factory occupations, and riots which punctuated the *biennio rosso* petered out in the autumn of 1920. Given the equivocal attitude of the PSI, no other outcome was possible. A disillusioned Gramsci concluded that the absence of rigorous political organization and tutelage had contributed greatly to the failure of the revolutionary upsurge. Along with other opponents of 'reformism', he proceeded to participate in the founding of the PCI, whose first leader was the ferociously uncompromising Amadeo Bordiga. Gramsci had become something of a Jacobin, proclaiming that 'Revolution is like war; it must be minutely prepared by a working-class general staff'.[119] Although he still favoured the formation of councils, he now saw them as instruments employed by the Communist Party for obtaining consent to the proletarian dictatorship. And by 1926, the year of his arrest, councils had entirely disappeared from his discourse. (They receive no discussion whatsoever in the *Notebooks*.)

Because of his opposition to the 'United Front' strategy, Bordiga came into sharp conflict with the Comintern in the early 1920s.

Although initially supporting his leader, Gramsci became increasingly uneasy about Bordiga's defiance of Moscow – especially after Mussolini's 'march on Rome'. Without the material and moral support of the Comintern, the Party, he feared, could lose all influence and even be annihilated. In August of 1924, he managed to replace Bordiga as General Secretary – with the blessing and encouragement of the International. Gramsci attacked the Neapolitan not just for his inflexibility *vis-à-vis* Moscow's directives, but also for placing excessive faith in a small, insulated nucleus of professional revolutionaries, whose actions would be governed by 'correct' theory. The Party, complained Gramsci, had become a sect, 'suspended in the air', theoretically pure but detached from the masses.[120] Tactics, he believed, should be 'flexible', thus enabling the Party to maintain contact with 'the broadest layers of the working population'.[121] While rejecting the sectarian approach of Bordiga, Gramsci (as leader) harboured a monolithic image of the Party, in which minority dissent was viewed as 'extremely dangerous'.[122] Curiously, he did not believe that his goal of multiplying the Party's links with the masses required full freedom of discussion. In his effort to 'Bolshevize' the PCI, his chief obstacle was the so-called *Comitato d'intesa*, a group of dissidents, led by the deposed Bordiga. By a strange twist of fate, the sectarian purist became the champion of free debate. Gramsci, for his part, feared that the Party would end up like the PSI, 'where unity was shattered into an infinity of disconnected fragments by the continuous clash of factions'. In a Bolshevik organization, he informs us, 'iron proletarian discipline must reign', which means that factions cannot be tolerated.[123] In the *Notebooks*, Gramsci shifts his ground, turning decisively towards a critique of authoritarian leadership wherever it appears. Without doubt this change was due, in the main, to his increasing alienation from Stalin's Russia, which – as we shall see – comes in for some thinly veiled criticism.

In order to understand the theory of the party developed in the *Notebooks*, it is first necessary to consider Gramsci's discussion of intellectuals and their role in the organization of culture – which role he regarded as significant. Still, he hoped to shatter the illusion of the autonomous, 'free-floating' intellectual, who elaborates a classless cultural patrimony while remaining above sordid practical interests. Every social class owing its existence to the performance of an essential economic function 'organically' creates 'one or more strata of intellectuals', who 'give it homogeneity and an awareness of its own function'. For example: 'The capitalist entrepreneur creates alongside himself the industrial technician, the specialist in political economy, the organisers of a new culture, of a new legal system, etc.'[124] Gramsci used the term, 'intellectual', in a wide sense, to include all those who exercise directive or high-level technical capacities in society, 'whether in the field of production, or in that of culture, or in that of political administration'.[125] The category of intellectuals thus embraces not only 'thinkers', but managers, civil servants, political leaders, clerics, technocrats, and so on. Within this general category, he distinguishes between 'organic' and 'traditional' intellectuals. The former are directly related to the productive and political structure, and are intimately tied to the class they represent, giving it 'homogeneity and an awareness of its own function'. The 'traditional' group comprises: (*a*) creative artists, pure scientists, men of letters, 'detached' scholars, all of whom are traditionally regarded as intellectuals, and (*b*) the vestiges of 'organic' intellectuals from previous social formations (e.g., ecclesiastics).[126] While these traditional intellectuals see themselves as 'autonomous', even they serve one or another social class – if only indirectly.

Intellectuals of all types are, of course, in the forefront of the battle for hegemony. Gramsci often describes the Communist Party as a 'collective intellectual', emerging 'organically' from the proletariat, whose experience it 'expresses'. In his *Notebooks* he builds his theory of the Party around an analogy with Machiavelli's *The Prince*, which – like Gramsci's Party – was intended to arouse the Italian people. The Party, in Gramsci's idiom, becomes the 'modern Prince'. This metaphor is not simply a rhetorical or literary device. For Machiavellian themes are deeply instilled in Gramsci's political thought. 'Politics', according to Machiavelli, could not be deduced from the principles of ethics or theology or metaphysics; it was an independent realm, with its own rules and norms. Likewise, Gramsci defended the autonomy (or at least *relative* autonomy) of politics, but against a new breed of metaphysicians – the economic reductionists, who analysed political activity in terms of categories and assumptions that conceptualized it out of existence. He also admired Machiavelli's view of politics as an 'art', combining the qualities of the 'fox' and the 'lion', aiming to adapt creative political initiative to the objective situation, in all its complexity. But, on Gramsci's interpretation, the protagonist of *The Prince* is not the Prince himself, understood as a creative figure who gives shape to an unformed, pliable material (the people). No, the true protagonist of *The Prince* is the 'collective will', the will to mobilize and unify Italy, which finds in a historical 'personality' its interpreter and guide. Just as Machiavelli's *Condottiere* is the expression of an embryonic collective will, so the 'modern Prince', the Communist Party, is 'the active operative expression' of the emergent proletarian culture. The Party must function as an organ of 'intellectual and moral reform', leading the assault on civil society and supervising the formation of a revolutionary 'collective will'.[127]

How will the 'modern Prince' be organized? Gramsci proposed a three-level structure. At the bottom, we have a 'mass element, composed of ordinary, average men, whose participation takes the form of discipline and loyalty, rather than any creative spirit or organisational ability'. At the summit, there is the 'principal cohesive element', endowed with 'the power of innovation'. The third or 'intermediate element' maintains contact between the other two, 'not only physically but also morally and intellectually'.[128] The 'modern Prince', with its rank-and-file of 'average' people, seems to cast its net wider than does Lenin's exclusive vanguard party. But there is another, perhaps more important, difference between Gramsci and his Bolshevik predecessor. For Lenin, the truly proletarian (i.e., scientific) consciousness is elaborated independently of the actual proletariat, and the political organization which possesses that consciousness is entitled to regard itself as embodying the 'will of history', whatever the empirical working class thinks of the matter. Scientific truth is 'discovered' through a process of intellectual labour, and then 'injected' into the working population, who, like Plato's cave-dwellers, inhabit a world of appearance and illusion. In Gramsci's perspective (and in this he follows Marx), the 'authentic' proletarian consciousness is an articulation of 'the spontaneous philosophy of the multitude',[129] for reality should not be expected to conform to an 'abstract schema'.[130] Remember, to him, the validity of any theory derives only from its practical effectiveness. While refraining from any explicit attack on Lenin, Gramsci ridicules the notion that the Party (or its leader) is an 'infallible bearer of truth', 'enlightened by reason'.[131] What is needed is an 'active and reciprocal' relationship between leaders and led, in which 'every teacher is always a pupil and every pupil a teacher'.[132]

After his imprisonment in 1926, he came to perceive the close connection between unimpeded debate within the Party and the type of 'dialectical' mass/elite relationship he desired. Himself the victim of political oppression, he no longer spoke of stamping out 'factions'. His concern, in the *Notebooks*, was to liberate political discussion from the fetters of dogma and administrative fiat. This concern is evident in his contrast of 'bureaucratic' and 'democratic' centralism. The former he denigrates as a type of 'fetishism', where the party becomes 'a phantasmagoric entity ... a species of autonomous divinity',[133] where the leadership degenerates into 'a narrow clique', perpetuating 'its selfish privileges by controlling or even by stifling the birth of oppositional forces'. The inevitable result is not 'unity' but 'a stagnant swamp, on the surface calm and "mute"'. 'Democratic' centralism is, by contrast, 'a "centralism" in movement – i.e. a continual adaptation of the organisation to the real movement, a matching of thrusts form below with orders from above'.[134] Although Gramsci did not actually say so, this attack on 'bureaucratic centralism' was almost certainly aimed against Stalin's Russia. Consider, also, the following observation:

> when the impetus of progress is not tightly linked to a vast local economic development ... but is instead the reflection of international developments which transmit their ideological currents to the periphery – currents born on the basis of the productive development of the more advanced countries – then the group which is the bearer of the new ideas is *not the economic group* [the proletariat] *but the intellectual stratum* [party], *and the conception of the state advocated by them changes aspect; it is conceived of as something in itself, as a rational absolute.*[135]

Bureaucratic absolutism, then, meets with Gramsci's disapproval. But, like all communists, he was convinced that the parliamentary system of government could not provide the model for the society of the future. Neither did he think, in the *Notebooks* at any rate, that workers' councils furnished the answer. What, then, was his alternative? A form of 'self-government', or radical participatory democracy, where (1) all citizens are actively involved in the formulation *and* implementation of policy, and (2) the barrier between legislative and executive functions is broken down.[136] What Gramsci says about this system of 'self-government' is all very general, but it does seem to coincide with Marx's own views – and like the founders of the 'philosophy of praxis', Gramsci believed that the repressive function of the state would eventually 'wither away' after a socialist revolution. As he defines it, this process of diminution means that the state is gradually 'absorbed by civil society', with the end product being a truly communist, 'regulated society' (Gramsci's phrase).[137] Whether the system of 'self-government' is to emerge before or after (or before *and* after) the advent of 'regulated society' remains unclear.

Stateless or not, Gramsci's future society would be highly disciplined and based on 'productivism', or the ordering of the factors of production in accordance with the principle of optimality.[138] He saw no conflict between discipline and freedom, provided that the former stemmed from rational and 'democratic' authority; i.e., authority which aims at the advancement of the *whole* people and derives from specialized, technical knowledge, as distinct from arbitrary 'will'.[139] There was a puritanical streak in Gramsci: as much as any Victorian capitalist, he was repelled by idleness, profligacy and improvidence. The rationalization and mechanization of industrial labour was, in his eyes, an irreversible and – when freed from its undemocratic, capitalist shell – beneficial process. Other Marxist humanists, such as Lukács and Adorno, advocated a cultural revitalization which would constitute a romanticized opposition to the mechanization of the modern world. Gramsci, on the other hand, never used the language of alienation and 'human essence', and therefore regarded the repression or sublimation of natural instincts, in the cause of improved industrial output, as both healthy and progressive.

Many commentators have denounced Gramsci for creating a 'blueprint for an explicitly "totalitarian" culture organized from above'.[140] True, he sometimes defended a 'totalitarian' (his word) politics in which party members find in this allegiance 'all the satisfactions they previously found in a multiplicity of organizations' and which seeks to 'destroy all other organizations or to incorporate them in a system of which the party is the sole regulator'.[141] It is well to note, however, that the word 'totalitarian', in Gramsci's time, did not have the connotation of arbitrary despotism. Also, his anti-sectarianism, his fulminations against 'bureaucratic centralism', his advocacy of popular participation, his coded but more or less transparent attacks on Stalin, his denial that the Party is an infallible bearer of truth – all these suggest that he favoured a dynamic, democratic movement from below incompatible with any image of authoritarian control from above. Yet, the Party/Prince is, in Gramsci's doctrine, the revolutionary church, the sole organ of human salvation, which claims unlimited jurisdiction over all the manifestations of individual and collective life. If there is to be a free interplay of various ideas and interests, it will somehow have to take place within a single structure. The Party can tolerate dissent, but not its institutionalization.

## VIII  ASSESSMENT

The Swedish Marxist Goran Therborn has observed that the history of Marxism has in no sense been a success story:

> Fundamental aspects of Marxist theory have been called into ques-
> tion both by its historic defeats, so far, in North America and
> Western Europe, and by the aftermath of its successes – Stalinism,
> the Sino-Soviet split, the present social and political condition of
> that third of the world claiming to be governed by Marxist theory.
> These and other contradictory and often unexpected developments
> ... make it possible to speak also of a crisis of Marxism.[142]

In Gramsci, we can find explanations – often implicit and ill-defined – for these 'contradictory' and 'unexpected developments', as well as ideas and strategies which might enable Marxists to avoid failure and disappointment in the future. His work, in other words, can be read as an extended comment on the long-standing 'crisis of Marxism'. How valid are his diagnosis and his prescription(s)?

Gramsci, as I have shown throughout these pages, articulated an anti-determinist but none the less Marxist historicism, which elevated the evidence of actual historical development over *a priori* axioms, and which refused to reduce man to a undimensional scheme and espe-cially to the *homo economicus* of Marx. The Sardinian's heterodoxy resulted in three important innovations: (1) the theory of hegemony, (2) the 'war of position' strategy, and (3) the 'absolute' historicization of Marxism. I shall now consider these innovations and their possible bearing on the 'crisis' mentioned by Therborn.

Gramsci's unusual interest in superstructural questions of ideology and politics has found favour among modern Marxists. In particular, the causal efficacy of 'bourgeois' culture has been stressed by recent Marxist writers who wish to account for the perplexing survival of cap-italism, despite its periodic crises and exploitative nature. A wide range of theorists, from Marcuse and Habermas to Althusser and Poulantzas, follow Gramsci in arguing that the coherence of late cap-italist society is to be explained primarily by the ideological incorpora-tion of the labour force. Is this explanation correct? On the question of mass beliefs, the information available is somewhat limited. Yet a fair number of studies have been conducted in the USA; and in Britain at least the attitudes of the working class have been invest-igated in some depth. There are, of course, methodological difficulties in measuring people's beliefs, but the data emerging from interview surveys as well as studies based on other techniques, such as participant observation, are broadly in agreement.[143] Workers will, it appears, generally concur with most elements of the dominant ideology, especially when these are presented as abstract principles; but will often accept deviant values when they themselves are directly involved or when these values are expressed in terms of everyday reality. The available evidence, then, does seem to lend empirical support to Gramsci's concept of 'contradictory consciousness'. In so far as prevailing ideological beliefs reflect the situation and interests of the powerful and the privileged, they are of dubious appropriateness for subordinate groups, whose life conditions will constrain them to modify, or occasionally ignore, their commitment to the reigning value framework. Bourgeois hegemony is far from absolute, but it *is* powerful enough – at the very least – to impede the development of radical alternatives; for, as Gramsci points out, it 'influences moral conduct and the direction of will' and reduces the workers to 'political passivity'.[144] Without doubt, other factors play their part in the maintenance of order and stability – the perpetual shadow of state violence, what Marx called 'the dull compulsion of economic relations', perhaps even some form of social inertia. But, as Gramsci was the first Marxist to recognize, such factors are of secondary importance in the highly developed societies of the West, where there usually exists widespread agreement on fundamental values. Indeed, it is difficult to see how social peace could ever endure in the absence of consensus. As recent history indicates (Iran, Zimbabwe, Poland, El Salvador, Nicaragua), people who deny the legitimacy of their rulers *do* – even in 'backward' countries – rise up against them.

What Gramsci says about the extent and function of value integration, in advanced capitalist countries, is perceptive and probably accurate. But the question remains: *why* does consensus exist? For Gramsci, it is the result, essentially, of ideological indoctrination: the masses, in this view, are caught up in a web of illusion, spun by the bourgeoisie, with its monopoly of cultural production. While this explanation cannot be dismissed, it is incomplete at best. He never took seriously the possibility that the mass of workers might endorse the capitalist *status quo* because they actually enjoy a real economic stake in it. In his opinion, this system was irredeemably unhealthy, incapable of 'buying off' more than a narrow 'aristocracy' of labour.[145] But, for the vast majority of the population, capitalism *does* 'deliver the goods', and there can be little doubt that this steady stream of rewards helps to secure the loyalty of ordinary people. Whatever its inherent weaknesses, the capitalist economy has proved much more resilient and efficient than Gramsci ever imagined. It has massively increased the sum total of wealth, with the consequence that the condition of the working population has improved dramatically – notwithstanding continuing (and unjustifiable) inequalities in the distribution of this wealth. His image of capitalism is simply outmoded; it is, in essence, the traditional picture of a grossly inefficient system of production, ruled over by bloated financiers and tycoons, ruthlessly exploiting a downtrodden workforce. About mass consumerism or the welfare state, Gramsci's doctrine is (necessarily) silent. He was an innovator, but also a child of his time.

Turning to his theory of revolution, one might well ask whether the 'war of position', as described by him, might not turn out to be a labour of Sisyphus. In his favour, it must be said that the persistence of conflict between the generalized value system and particular experiences and actions indicates the potential for a radicalization of consciousness – which potential has been partially realized in Italy and (perhaps) France. But how far can a Marxist movement go in establishing the nucleus of anti-capitalist culture *prior* to the overturning of the 'bourgeois' state? Is civil society independently conquerable? The distinction between civil society and political society may be analytically clear, but in practice the two spheres are interwoven. And Gramsci recognized this. For example, he calls attention to how the modern state manipulates the newly emergent mass media, radio and the yellow press, in order to mould public opinion.[146] He also takes note of increasing state control of educational institutions – libraries, schools, etc. – which formerly lay within the province of private initiative.[147] A paradox thus lies at the heart of Gramsci's theory of revolution. On the one hand, he argued that in advanced Western countries, the key to political power resided in the hegemonic control of civil society; the idea of a seizure of power in a Bolshevik-style coup had become a pernicious fantasy. On the other hand, his texts imply that the conditions for the independent conquest of civil society, prior to the assault on the military command posts of the state, have passed into history. As modernization proceeds, civil society, Gramsci admits, is more and more open to manipulation by the political powers-that-be. If this is so, however, the formation of an alternative hegemony will meet with serious, if not insurmountable, obstacles.

Another limitation of Gramsci's proposed strategy is its insistence on the need for a revolutionary upheaval – a clean break with the bourgeois, parliamentary past. In the comfortable societies of the West, appeals to overthrow the liberal regime, by fire and sword if necessary, simply fall on deaf ears. Whatever its relevance in Gramsci's own era, insurrectionary violence is now quite out-of-date – in the West. Still, the 'war of position', with its focus on flexibility, consent, prudence, compromise, free debate and culture, is the not so distant ancestor of contemporary Eurocommunism. The practitioners of this diluted form of Marxism have taken some of Gramsci's most interesting ideas and realistically applied them to present circumstances. Berlinguer and Carillo can plausibly claim to be following the spirit, though not the letter, of Gramsci's teachings.

Let us now examine Gramsci's chief philosophical innovation: his interpretation of Marxism as 'absolute historicism'. Our discussion here falls into two parts: (1) a consideration of the theoretical cogency of 'absolute historicism', and (2) an exploration of the implications of this doctrine for Gramsci's vision of the revolutionary process.

Marxists who think of themselves as 'scientists' producing 'objective' truth are discomfited by Gramsci's notion that Marxism – no less than liberalism or idealism or Confucianism – is a social and historical product, shaped as much by concrete human needs as by reason and research. Louis Althusser, to take one example, dismisses historicism as an unfortunate Hegelian residue, obscuring the radical nature of Marx's conceptual breakthrough. One need not, however, share the scientific pretensions of Althusser and other Marxists in order to raise fundamental doubts about Gramsci's formulation of 'absolute historicism'. By what means do we determine that a world-view enjoys 'mass adhesion'?[148] That it is 'accepted by the many and accepted permanently'?[149] That it has become 'concretely – i.e. historically and socially – universal'?[150] That it is 'actual and lives historically'?[151] Gramsci affords us no instructions. Indeed, he complicates matters by conceding that 'arbitrary constructions', or false ideologies, 'sometimes, through a combination of immediately favourable circumstances ... manage to enjoy popularity of a kind'.[152] But let us suppose, for the sake of argument, that I can persuade myself that a certain world-view meets the above, extremely vague, criteria. Can I therefore conclude that it is true? The word 'true' represents for us a different idea from that represented by phrases like 'accepted by the many'. The question of the truth of a proposition or belief or doctrine is logically distinct from the question of its popularity. Do we decide philosophical questions by putting them to the vote? The fact that a world-view wins 'mass adhesion' does not obviate the need for a separate rational-empirical evaluation of its descriptive and prescriptive claims, *even if we accept that all doctrines are products of historical development*, i.e., grow out of a specific social context. Of course, such a critical appraisal can take us only so far: all visions of the world are irreducibly value-laden, and there is no rational way of resolving fundamental conflicts between values. In the final analysis, neither logic nor factual evidence can tell us whether, say, socialism is morally superior to capitalism. Within these confines, however, the application of logical rules and empirical methods can bear fruit. It is possible, for example, to demonstrate inconsistencies between different components of a doctrine or to show that it rests upon mistaken empirical beliefs or errors in probabilistic reasoning. Reflect on the case of Marxism, which of course includes a body of economic theory. In order to assess the worth of this theory, we do not ask if it has become enshrined in 'common sense'. Rather, we consider whether it provides the most convincing account of economic data, whether it enables us to predict or control events. Perhaps Gramsci would accept this point: after all, he firmly believed that the validity of logical and empirical procedures transcended particular historical determinants.[153] But his formulation of absolute historicism fails to incorporate a role for these procedures.

There is also the question whether a social critic, like Gramsci, can adopt 'absolute historicism' and still remain consistent. For example, he often writes as if it is self-evidently true that an active, self-autonomous, theoretically self-conscious human being is superior to a passive, uncritical and obedient one. But does this evaluation not rely on an unacknowledged, non-historical factor belonging to the permanent, unchanging idea of humanity – on *universal* human values? Would a consistent historicist be moved to revolutionary outrage? Implicit in Gramsci's thinking, the argument runs, is an 'Archimedean point', outside history, on which his critique of bourgeois society is based. Indeed, without such an Archimedean point, how could we declare that Nazism was, is and always will be an evil, 'false' doctrine – no matter what sort of popularity it enjoys? Had the Nazis won the war, as well as the souls of the European masses, and had Gramsci lived to witness these events, would he – in accordance with the rules of 'absolute historicism' – have pronounced Nazism to be a 'true' world-view?

His conception of 'absolute historicism' does not, then, withstand examination: it is muddled and intellectually untenable. Yet its consequences for his political thought can only be described as salutary. For it inclined him towards a healthy scepticism – nothing is certain, everything is liable to revision, and the attainment of any truth in which we can rest securely is impossible. Like the pragmatists, whose theory of truth resembled his own, Gramsci expressed opposition to a number of inveterate habits dear to philosophers and Marxists: verbal solutions, *a priori* reasoning, closed systems, a craving for absolutes, the pretence of finality in truth. Instead, he favoured concreteness and empirical reality. Unlike his successors in the 'Western Marxist' tradition, he was careful not to pour the world into a mould of self-contained theory. All philosophical or doctrinal tenets, said Gramsci, should be treated as rough 'working hypotheses' and jettisoned if they fail the test of concrete experience. No one could pretend to be in possession of absolute truth – about humankind, society or history. This 'modest' Marxism would appear to avoid the authoritarian implications of so-called 'scientific' Marxism, which manifestly *did* believe that it had unlocked the secrets of the universe. The very idea of a science of man, which identifies the determinants of human behaviour, seems to conflict with a democratic concept of society. If the course society takes is an outcome whose determinants are encompassed by an applied science of this kind, beyond the ken of most, there is no room for collective decision. The 'bearers of science', those who are blessed with expert knowledge of society's immutable laws, would be justified in taking charge. In Marxist practice, these 'experts' are invariably the professional revolutionaries, who claim the prerogative of guiding historical development in the interest of truth itself. But if, as Gramsci believed, the vanguard is *not* the repository of infallible truth, then there can be no authoritative imposition of a pre-fixed schema on the inert masses. The way is thus open for rule *by* the people rather than over them. Marxism, it is fair to observe, has been a travesty in practice, mainly (if not entirely) because of its arrogant assumption that revolutionary 'scientists' enjoy access to hidden truths. And Gramsci, with his humanist alternative, dimly perceived this. He wanted an active movement of real workers, not of professional revolutionaries manipulating a passive population. There can be no doubt, moreover, that the democratic elements in his political thought are organically related to his democratic conception of truth.

Yet, his libertarianism was hedged about with qualifications. His Italian critics have argued that a truly open society – what they call a 'pluralist' society – presupposes 'the free circulation of all social energies (ideas, values, interests, etc.)'. Gramsci's 'modern Prince', by contrast, concentrates all power in the hands of a single 'command' structure, which – continue the critics – cannot tolerate 'competition, rivals, alternative projects', since its mission is to create a 'compact, homogeneous, and perfectly harmonious society'.[154] Gramsci, it must

be conceded, was no 'pluralist', since he opposed the institutionalization of dissent. However, dissent *was* to be permitted, albeit within a
one-party, or 'totalitarian', framework. To assume that all legitimate
interests can be embraced by a single, essentially homogeneous, political organization (the Party/Prince) is to take a narrow view of what
constitutes a legitimate interest. Still, Gramsci seeks a unity that is
*real*, not imposed. Unity, as he understands it, is to be distinguished
from uniformity, for the former is, in principle, compatible with divergence of opinion. The collective will would emerge out of vigorous
discussion, and it would never demand uncritical worship. In his view,
it would be a truly collective will, not the arbitrary will of a single
'*capo*' or narrow elite, claiming a monopoly of scientific truth.

What, then, is our verdict? Gramsci's *Notebooks* certainly furnish
the nucleus of a more humane and democratic form of communism,
differing in vital respects from the Leninist version. Whether this
Gramscian alternative could ever be realized in practice, without
degenerating into a dictatorship of the party vanguard, remains moot.
Though a defender of free inquiry, Gramsci shared the messianic
vision common to all Marxists – the vision of universal harmony. But
in no society of any complexity will all people wish to play the same
tune. The only feasible technique of preventing social cacophony is
despotism. Gramsci, we may conclude, cut a contradictory figure, torn
between the 'totalitarian' arbitration of the Party/Prince and a sincere
commitment to democratic procedures. He was pulled in opposing
directions by his messianic aspiration, on the one hand, and his philosophical relativism, on the other.

For those who seek a 'third way', which overcomes the limitations of
both social-democracy and 'actually existing socialism', Gramsci offers
a source of inspiration. His was a consistently humanist (and humane)
Marxism, opting for free will over determinism, culture and creativity
over crude materialism, the real world of flesh and blood individuals
over self-sufficient speculation and self-justifying theorems, free
debate and mass participation over bureaucratic imposition. There is
a rich legacy here, and it still needs exploration.

## NOTES

1.  Alvin W. Gouldner, *The Two Marxisms: Contradictions and Anomalies
    in the Development of Theory* (London: Macmillan, 1980), p. 127.
2.  Gouldner, *The Two Marxisms*, p. 130.

3. Leszek Kolakowski, 'Antonio Gramsci: Communist Revisionism', in *Main Currents of Marxism*, Vol. III (Oxford: Clarendon Press, 1978), p. 226.

4. *Selections from the Prison Notebooks of Antonio Gramsci* (hereafter abbreviated to *SPN*), ed. and trans. Quintin Hoare and Geoffrey Nowell Smith (London: Lawrence and Wishart, 1971), p. 384. Whenever possible, quotations form Gramsci's writings will be taken from existing English translations. Much of his work, however, has not yet been translated.

5. *Il materialismo storico e la filosofia di Benedetto Croce* (hereafter *MS*), Volume I, *Quaderni del carcere* (Turin: Einaudi, 1948), p. 250.

6. *MS*, p. 199.

7. In *Il Grido del Popolo*, 29 January 1916; Antonio Gramsci, *Selections from Political Writings (1910–1920)* (hereafter *SPW I*), trans. and ed. Quintin Hoare and John Mathews (London: Lawrence and Wishart, 1977), pp. 11–13.

8. *History, Philosophy and Culture in the Young Gramsci* (hereafter *HPC*), ed. Pedro Cavalcanti and Paul Piccone (St Louis: Telos Press, 1975), pp. 41–2.

9. See Walter L. Adamson, *Hegemony and Revolution: Antonio Gramsci's Political and Cultural Theory* (Berkeley: University of California Press, 1980), pp. 33–4, 253.

10. *SPW I*, pp. 34–5.

11. 'Our Marx', *Il Grido del Popolo*, 4 May 1918; *HPC*, p. 10.

12. 'Mysteries of Poetry and Culture', *Il Grido del Popolo*, 19 October 1918; *HPC*, p. 18.

13. 'The Conquest of the State', *L'Ordine Nuovo*, 12 July 1919; *SPW I*, p. 75.

14. In an article of 29 January 1918 ('Achille Loria e il socialismo', in *Avanti!*), Gramsci referred to Labriola in glowing terms. The article is reprinted in *Scritti giovanili, 1914–1918* (Turin: Einaudi, 1958), pp. 162–3. On 5 January 1918, he published a short excerpt from Labriola's main work, *Essays on the Materialist Conception of History*, in *Il Grido del Popolo*. Much later, in the *Notebooks*, Gramsci praises Labriola as 'the only man who has attempted to build up the philosophy of praxis [Marxism] scientifically' (*SPN*, p. 387).

15. *MS*, p. 200.

16. *MS*, pp. 179–80.

17. *MS*, pp. 201–2.

18. *MS*, p. 199.

19. *SPN*, p. 371.

20. *MS*, p. 233.

21. *SPN*, p. 356; *MS*, pp. 215–17, 190–1, 204, 237.

22. *SPN*, p. 352.

23. *SPN*, p. 355.

24. *SPN*, p. 455.

25. *SPN*, pp 445–6.

26. *SPN*, pp. 467, 34.

27. *SPN*, p. 346.

28. *SPN*, p. 467.

29.  *SPN*, p. 375.
30.  *SPN*, p. 456.
31.  *SPN*, p. 371.
32.  *SPN*, p. 465.
33.  *SPN*, p. 345; *MS*, pp. 55–6.
34.  *SPN*, pp. 426, 438–9, 442; *MS*, p. 56.
35.  *SPN*, p. 407.
36.  *SPN*, p. 168.
37.  *MS*, pp. 236–7.
38.  *MS*, p. 230.
39.  *MS*, p. 237.
40.  *SPN*, pp. 139–40, my emphasis.
41.  *Hegemony and Revolution*, p. 203.
42.  *SPN*, p. 408.
43.  *MS*, p. 230.
44.  *Hegemony and Revolution*, p. 218.
45.  'Gramsci e la concezione della società civile', *Gramsci e la cultura contemporanea*, Vol. I, ed. Pietro Rossi (Rome: Editori Riuniti, 1969), p. 88.
46.  *SPN*, p. 139, my emphasis.
47.  *SPN*.
48.  *SPN*, p. 168.
49.  *MS*, p. 233.
50.  *SPN*, p. 168.
51.  *SPN*, p. 194.
52.  *SPN*, p. 161.
53.  *SPN*, p. 258.
54.  *SPN*, p. 466; see, also, pp. 180–1, 432 and *Passato e presente* (hereafter *PP*), Vol. 6, *Quaderni del carcere* (Turin: Einaudi, 1951), p. 201.
55.  Engels's letter to J. Bloch, 21 September 1890; K. Marx and F. Engels, *Selected Correspondence* (New York: International Publishers, 1942), p. 475.
56.  'Political Capacity', *Avanti!*, 24 September 1920 (*SPW I*, p. 348); and *SPN*, p. 178. See, also *MS*, pp. 211–15, 272–3.
57.  *SPN*, p. 184.
58.  *SPN*, pp. 437–8.
59.  'Against Pessimism', *L'Ordine Nuovo*, 15 March 1924; *Antonio Gramsci, Selections from Political Writings (1921–1926)* (hereafter *SPW II*), trans. ed. Quintin Hoare (London: Lawrence and Wishart, 1978), p. 213.
60.  Antonio Labriola, *Essays on the Materialist Conception of History*, trans. C.H. Kerr (Chicago: Charles H. Kerr, 1908), p. 124. Labriola, too, criticized those who interpret Marxism as a 'final' rationalization and schematization of history: 'our doctrine cannot serve to represent the whole history of the human race in a unified perspective ... Our doctrine does not pretend to be the intellectual vision of a great plan or of a design' (*Essays on the Materialist Conception of History*, p. 135). Yet he also wrote that communism 'must inevitably happen by the immanent necessity of history' (p. 244). On this point, then, Gramsci parted company with his mentor.

61. *SPN*, p. 465.
62. *SPN*, pp. 336- 7, 342.
63. *SPN*, p. 428.
64. *SPN*; see also, *Letterature e vita nazionale*, Vol. 5, *Quaderni del carcere* (Turin: Einaudi, 1950), p. 6.
65. *SPN*, pp. 200–1.
66. *SPN*, pp. 410–12, 428.
67. Letter from prison to his sister-in-law, 30 May 1932; *Letters from Prison by Antonio Gramsci*, selected and translated by Lynne Lawner (New York: Harper and Row, 1973), pp. 239–41.
68. Georg Lukács, *History and Class Consciousness*, trans. R. Livingstone (Cambridge, Mass.: MIT Press, 1971), pp. 177–8, 197–8.
69. *SPN*, p. 426.
70. *SPN*, pp. 428–9.
71. *SPN*, p. 133.
72. *MS*, pp. 199–200.
73. *SPN*, pp. 396, 393.
74. *MS*, p. 232.
75. *MS*.
76. *SPN*, pp. 201, 404–7; *PP*, p. 201.
77. *SPN*, pp. 133, 360, 355.
78. *SPN*, pp. 172–3.
79. 'Antonio Gramsci: Communist Revisionism', p. 228.
80. *SPN*, pp. 371, 417.
81. *SPN*, p. 436.
82. *SPN*, p. 445.
83. *SPN*, p. 348.
84. *SPN*, p. 341.
85. *SPN*, p. 369.
86. *SPN*, p. 436.
87. *MS*, pp. 55–6.
88. *SPN*, pp. 138, 405.
89. *SPN*, p. 407.
90. *SPN*, pp. 406–7.
91. *SPN*, p. 465.
92. *Karl Marx, Selected Writings in Sociology and Social Philosophy*, ed. T.B. Bottomore and Maximilien Rubel (Harmondsworth, Middlesex: Penguin, 1961), p. 82.
93. 'The Great Gramsci', *New York Review of Books* (4 April 1974), p. 41.
94. *SPN*, p. 57.
95. *SPN*, p. 12.
96. *SPN*.
97. *SPN*, pp. 226, 227–8, 238, 243.
98. *SPN*, p. 263; see pp. 239, 244 as well.
99. *SPN*, pp. 60–1.
100. *SPN*, pp. 326–7.
101. *SPN*, p. 333, my emphasis.
102. *SPN*, pp. 333, 327.
103. *SPN*, p. 238.

124     *The Machiavellian Legacy*

104. *SPN*, p. 243.
105. *SPN*, p. 235.
106. *SPN*, p. 238.
107. *MS*, p. 236; *SPN*, p. 57.
108. See, e.g. Giuseppe Tamburrano, *Antonio Gramsci: la vita, il pensiero, l'azione* (Bari: Laterza 1963), pp. 257–9, 267, 284–97.
109. *SPN*, pp. 192–3, 221; *MS*, p. 159; *PP*, p. 158.
110. *SPN*, p. 243.
111. *SPN*, p. 185, my emphasis.
112. *MS*, pp. 184, 219–22.
113. *SPN*, pp. 167–8, 198.
114. *SPN*, p. 198; see pp. 84–5 as well.
115. Massimo Salvadori, 'Gramsci and the PCI: two Conceptions of Hegemony' in *Gramsci and Marxist Theory*, ed. Chantal Mouffe (London: Routledge and Kegan Paul, 1979), p. 257.
116. 'Workers' Democracy' (21 June 1919) in *SPW I*, pp. 65–8; 'The Conquest of the State' (12 July 1919) in *SPW I*, pp. 73–8; 'Unions and Councils' (11 October 1919) in *SPW I*, pp. 98–102.
117. 'The Conquest of the State', *SPW I*, pp. 74–5; 'The Factory Council' (5 June 1920) in *SPW I*, pp. 260–1.
118. 'Unions and Councils', *SPW I*, p. 100.
119. 'Political Capacity' (24 September 1920), *SPW I*, p. 348.
120. Letter to Togliatti (9 February 1924) in *SPW II*, pp. 197–8.
121. 'Lyons Theses' (January 1926) in *SPW II*, p. 360.
122. Handwritten notes, in *SPW II*, p. 154.
123. PCI statement (1925), in *SPW II*, p. 290; 'Lyons Theses', *SPW II*, pp. 364–5.
124. *SPN*, p. 5.
125. *SPN*, p. 97.
126. *SPN*, pp. 6–7.
127. *SPN*, pp. 125–33.
128. *SPN*, pp. 152–3.
129. *SPN*, p. 421.
130. *SPN*, p. 200.
131. *Note sul Machiavelli, sulla politica, e sullo stato moderno* (hereafter *Mach.*) Vol. 4, *Quaderni del carcere* (Turin: Einaudi, 1949), p. 113.
132. *SPN*, p. 350.
133. *Mach.*, p. 157.
134. *SPN*, pp. 188–90.
135. *SPN*, pp. 116–17, my emphasis.
136. *SPN*, pp. 40, 186, 193–4.
137. *SPN*, pp. 260, 263, 382.
138. *Mach.*, pp. 150–1.
139. *PP*, p. 65.
140. Thomas R. Bates, 'Antonio Gramsci and the Bolshevization of the PCI', *Journal of Contemporary History*, XI (July 1976), p. 116.
141. *Mach.*, p. 134.
142. Goran Theborn, *Science, Class and Society* (London: New Left Books, 1976), p. 38.

143. There is no space here to give details of the various findings. For such details, see my *Gramsci's Political Thought* (Oxford: Clarendon Press, 1981), Chapter 7.
144. *SPN*, p. 333.
145. *SPN*, p. 311.
146. *PP*, p. 158.
147. *Gli intellettuali e l'organizzazione della cultura*, Vol. 2, *Quaderni del carcere* (Turin: Einaudi, 1949), p. 124.
148. *SPN*, p. 341.
149. *SPN*, p. 346.
150. *SPN*, p. 348.
151. *SPN*, p. 369.
152. *SPN*, p. 341.
153. Unlike most Marxists of his time, Gramsci defended the merits of formal logic. See *PP*, pp. 162–3; and *MS*, pp. 59–62.
154. Interview with Luciano Pellicani, *Il Popolo*, 20 February 1977; reprinted in *Oltre Gramsci*, edited by Corrado Belci (Rome: Cinque Lune, 1977), pp. 138–9. The quotations are taken from Pellicani, but he speaks for many who reject Gramsci's patrimony. See, also, L. Pellicani, *Gramsci e la questione comunista* (Florence: Vallecchi, 1976).

# 4 Mosca Revisited

Notwithstanding his status as a pioneer of modern political science (with his *The Ruling Class*, English edition 1939, hereafter *RC*), Gaetano Mosca has never been a fashionable thinker. Democrats dislike him for ridiculing their vision of human relationships as 'a great conglomerate of dreams and falsehoods', 'not in the slightest degree justified by the facts' (*RC*: 421, 326). Some commentators even hold him partly responsible for the advent of fascism in Italy (Mannheim 1936: 119). Did he not – for all his verbal opposition to *Il Duce* – attempt to revive ancient ideas of social hierarchy and to erect obstacles to the spread of democratic notions? Did he not sit comfortably in the Italian Senate during the darkest days of Mussolini's regime? A furious C.J. Friedrich resorts to the *argumentum ad hominem* by referring to 'the deferential peasants on estates of large landowners in Sicily where Mosca's cradle stood' (Friedrich 1950: 264f). How could the offspring of such a backward and corrupt society possibly appreciate the finer points of liberal democracy?

But the democratic ideal was only one of the 'collective illusions' that Mosca sought to dispel. Socialism, especially in its Marxist variant, was for him an 'intellectual malady', typified by 'chimerical fancies' as dangerous as they are absurd (*RC*: 325ff). The carriers of this 'malady' understandably reciprocate by deriding or (more often) ignoring their persecutor, a Mediterranean Prince of Darkness who had the effrontery to preach that 'equality is contrary to the nature of things'. No matter whether the economy remains capitalistic or becomes the plaything of equalitarian levellers, there will always be a ruling class, and therefore exploitation. So says Mosca. As for peace and fraternity, those other lofty goals of socialism, he was similarly dismissive, informing us that 'the human being's need for hating' forms 'the basic state of the human psyche' (*RC*: 470ff). The Sicilian, dwelling as he did on the incurably bad nature of man, held out no hope for a future of sweetness and light. Whether a political system is labelled democratic or not, whether it is socialist or capitalist in its economic organization, it will necessarily exhibit a demonstrable and inescapable fact of human existence: subjection. J.H. Meisel aptly describes Mosca's elitist analysis as 'a new dismal science aimed at the naive optimism of eighteenth-century enlightenment' (Meisel 1958: 10).

Despite the catastrophic events of this century, optimism (naive or otherwise) remains the dominant mode of thought in Western civilization – where a dismal scientist like Mosca can expect a dismal reception.

Hostility to his conclusions is reinforced by contempt for his methodology. On the one hand, he appears to embrace crude positivism. According to Mosca, disciplined observation of facts, after the pattern of physics or chemistry, will yield the constant laws that determine 'the behaviour of the human masses' (*RC*: 40, 337). By the turn of the century, a revolt against such scientific pretensions was already gathering momentum, and Benedetto Croce spoke for many when he argued that the infinite profusion of social and historical data needed to be filtered through a prior theoretical framework, governed by the values and interests of the observer. It is ridiculous to worship the 'facts', since these are, to a large extent, our own creation (Croce 1923: 377). Antonio Gramsci, a Marxist of idealist hue, made essentially the same point when he rebuked Mosca for assembling facts 'higgledy piggledy' rather than – in true dialectical fashion – ordering them in accordance with a (prefabricated?) structural analysis of class relations (Gramsci 1971: 176). He is, on this criticism, a blinkered empiricist, lost in a maze of raw data, foolishly seeking refuge in the methods of natural science. Others, however, accuse him of allowing his ideological preferences to deflect him from the path of detached scientific inquiry. Even a sympathetic commentator like Meisel concludes that the iron law of oligarchy is more political myth than scientific finding (Meisel 1958: 5). Less charitably, Geraint Parry maintains that, when we peel away the 'scientific clothing', Mosca's elitism 'is revealed as ideology – a political theory for the middle class' (Parry 1969: 42). The suggestion here is that the Sicilian does not so much worship as abuse the facts.

The most common methodological criticism – levelled by Robert Dahl at *all* elitists – is that Mosca (and his disciples) never specify 'clear criteria according to which the theory could be disproved' (Dahl 1971: 126). Gramsci, in this vein, expresses puzzlement at his 'elastic and variable' terminology (Gramsci 1949: 140), while Friedrich chides him for smuggling in the unproven (and implicit) assumption that the ruling class constitutes a compact body, conscious of its role and functioning in concert. Without this assumption, Friedrich insists, we are left with the statement that the ruling class is composed of the people who rule: 'the argument remains tautological' (Friedrich 1950: 257–8). The testability of Mosca's propositions is also called into question by

Tom Bottomore, who wonders whether the theory is founded upon anything more than the 'trivial observation that in most known societies of the past there has been a clear distinction between the rulers and the ruled' (Bottomore 1966: 115).

The picture that emerges is one of a methodologically naive reactionary, a strange anachronism, whose writings are of historical interest only. This, it seems to me, captures the prevailing view of Mosca, especially in the English-speaking world, where he receives little scholarly attention. I wish to challenge this view and argue that his ideas are much more subtle and penetrating than is generally supposed. And while he was, in some sense, a reactionary, I would suggest that radicals and even socialists could, with profit, incorporate some of his insights into their own thinking. At the very least, a dialogue with Mosca could encourage these reformers to examine their cosy assumptions. As Norberto Bobbio, no friend of Mosca's politics, reminds us, political thought has perhaps drawn more nourishment from the uncomfortable observations of conservatives than from the visionary constructs of radicals, 'who – with their gaze fixed on the future – are often unaware of the ground beneath their feet' (Bobbio 1977: 217). In presenting my case, I shall look at three crucial elements of Mosca's thought: (1) his 'historical method', (2) his critique of the democratic ideal, and (3) his demolition of Marxian socialism.

As already mentioned, Mosca's methodology is widely reckoned to be wrong in principle and improperly applied in practice. Let us consider the validity of this harsh verdict. Mosca opens his master work, *The Ruling Class* (original edition 1896; 2nd vol. 1923), by contrasting the successes of the natural sciences in explaining physical phenomena by subsuming them under general laws with the failure to achieve equivalent success in political science. He is perfectly aware that this asymmetry is due, in no small measure, to the different nature of the material studied. While he does claim that scientific objectivity is possible in the social studies, he acknowledges that it is difficult to attain. Two main reasons are cited: 'the great complexity' of human interaction, together with the 'divers prejudices' that prevent social analysts from looking dispassionately upon religious or political doctrines and movements (*RC*: 6, 40f). Imposing though these obstacles may be, they are not, to Mosca, insurmountable. Of course, history presents us with a bewildering variety of civilizations, unamenable at first glance to the generalizing requirements of scientific discourse. But Mosca remains convinced that 'underneath superficial differences in customs and habits human beings are psychologically very much alike the world over'. Moreover, 'anyone who has read history at all deeply reaches a similar conclusion with regard to the various periods of human civilization'. People of past ages 'were very much like us' (*RC*: 39). Beneath surface diversity, invariant psychological (and therefore organizational) necessities govern the life of all nations.

In our relativistic era, it is easy to criticize anyone who insists upon the uniformity of human nature and of resultant social patterns. Listen, for example, to Geraint Parry:

> Mosca ... ignores the fact of historical development not only in material terms but also in human experience and thought. To most historians since the mid-eighteenth century it has been the dissimilarity of past action and thinking which has seemed the most striking feature of human history ... Mosca's use of the term 'the historical method' to describe his practice of adducing instances of his general law from societies as varied as China, Russia, Italy and Britain and periods as far apart as the fifth century BC and the nineteenth century AD would seem a misnomer. (Parry 1969: 36)

Whether Parry and 'most historians' are correct depends on the level of abstraction at which we pitch our analysis. Even Vico, the founder of the historicist perspective, conceded that we could abstract what is common to various phases of culture – parallels and correspondences of psychological and social structure common to individuals remote from one another in time and space, race and outlook. Accordingly, he refers to 'uniform ideas originating among entire peoples unknown to each other', ideas transcending 'variations of detail'; to 'the universal and eternal principles ... on which all nations were founded and still preserve themselves'; and to 'the human necessities or utilities of social life', upon which the science of human affairs can be established (Vico 1961: paras. 144–5, 333, 347). Exactly what these uniformities are, and whether they are more significant than the obvious dissimilarities, are matters of unresolvable dispute. There is no compelling reason to *assume* that Mosca was wrong to speak of 'the constant laws or tendencies that determine the political organization of human societies' (*RC*: 6).

It is also noteworthy that Mosca, unlike Marx, makes modest claims for the predictive capacity of social science. He distinguishes between negative and positive prediction (*RC*: 283, 463). The former, the claim that certain things 'cannot and never will happen' because of 'the laws that regulate the social nature of man', is precisely the kind of 'prediction' (if that is the appropriate word) that Moschian social science endeavours to provide. The latter, the claim that certain things *will* happen (e.g. capitalism will collapse, socialism will rise from the rubble), is not possible, mainly because of what Mosca calls 'chance', the 'chain of circumstances that escape human control and foresight' (*RC*: 39). In other words, Mosca accepts that the social scientist cannot, except in the most limited conditions, conduct the sort of controlled experiments where – because of the exclusion of 'chance' – distinct causal sequences are isolated and identified (*RC*: 337).

But even negative 'predictions' are impossible if social scientists cannot aspire to the objectivity of natural scientists, who experience no difficulty in maintaining emotional detachment from the impersonal forces of nature that constitute their object of study. 'Man can much more easily study the phenomena of physics, chemistry or botany', Mosca admits, 'than he can his own instincts and his own passions'. There is a natural human tendency to view social facts from 'a subjective, one-sided and limited point of view that is inevitably productive of erroneous results'. The only safeguard, says Mosca, is rigorous intellectual training, which enables one 'to lift one's judgement above the beliefs and opinions which are current in one's time or peculiar to the social or national type to which one belongs'. And this lack of bias comes 'with a broad and thorough knowledge of history, not, certainly, of the history of a single period or a single nation but – so far as we possibly can – the history of mankind as a whole' (*RC*: 40ff). Through historical study, we can free our minds from the constraints imposed by our own cultural conditioning and – without discarding our own values – approach those of others in a scientific spirit. Mosca recognizes that objective social scientists will always be a rare breed; but, unless we assume that reality is entirely in the mind of the beholder, he is surely right to believe that disinterested social analysis is possible, not to mention desirable.

True, his inductive method wrongly posited a sharp dividing line between the subject which contemplates and the object which is contemplated. According to this model, the observer passively registers facts independent of his consciousness and draws the obvious conclusions. But it is now widely assumed that social and even natural science involve selective abstraction, relying on theoretical assumptions not derivable from the observations they are invoked to explain. The investigator can still, however, frame hypotheses so that they are in principle capable of empirical disconfirmation. The validity of a scientific hypothesis does not depend on the values or prejudices of the observer. What counts, ultimately, is whether the hypothesis squares with the available data. It should go without saying that hypotheses in the social sciences will normally lack the formal precision of natural scientific ones. And given the 'great complexity' (Mosca's words) of social interaction, evidence will rarely be discrete or determinate enough to eliminate the need for judgement and interpretation. Yet we can aim for the empirical rigour, if not the mathematical certainty, of the physical sciences.

But even if Mosca's 'historical method' is fundamentally sound, what about his attempt to apply it? The scholarly consensus seems to be that the Sicilian was inconsistent in his terminology, vague in his formulation of concepts, and impressionistic in his selection of evidence. While there is a great deal of truth in these accusations, some of Mosca's critics make the erroneous assumption (wrongly attributed to Mosca himself) that social science can indeed achieve the precision of the physical sciences. Robert Dahl is an obvious offender in this respect. For him, the ruling elite model, as propounded by Mosca and others, has no 'operational meaning'; it is 'quasi-metaphysical' (Dahl 1971: 133, 126). If the thesis is to be empirically tested, certain conditions must obtain. In particular, there must be 'a fair sample of cases involving key political decisions in which the preferences of the hypothetical ruling elite run counter to those of any other likely group that might be suggested'. For if a political system displays complete consensus, there is no conceivable way of determining whether a ruling elite exists (Dahl 1971: 131, 134). But (and here is where Dahl's critique falls down) the most successful ruling elite is one that exerts such influence over the 'ruled' that they willingly adhere to its norms and goals. Dahl's rigorous 'scientism' debars him from examining the (necessarily intangible) ideological context of political decision-making, a context Mosca deals with in his discussion of 'political formulas'. '[R]uling classes', he observed, 'do not justify their power exclusively by de facto possession of it, but try to find a moral and legal basis for it, representing it as the logical and necessary consequence of doctrines and beliefs that are generally recognized and accepted' (*RC*: 70). For Mosca, these political formulas, though they justify the power of the elite, are not 'mere quackeries aptly invented to trick the masses into obedience'. On the contrary, 'they answer a real need in man's social nature', the need, common to both rulers and ruled, to feel that the established order is based not on force but on 'moral principle'. Mosca thus concurs with Marxists in uncovering the asymmetric power dimension behind authority over belief, and in debunking liberal illusions, but he rightly generalises the attack, seeing ideological control as an inevitable feature of all societies, not least those purporting to be socialist. He speculates that 'great superstitions' – the Divine Right of kings, the 'will of the people', common ownership of the means of production, and so on – contribute powerfully to consolidating political organizations and unifying peoples or even whole civilizations (*RC*: 71). While he was perhaps wrong to regard all such formulas as illusory, it seems hard to deny that they shape the social and political preferences of the 'ruled'. Systems of belief are neither irrelevant to the determination of power relationships nor responsive to the strict methodological injunctions of Robert Dahl.[1]

Does this mean that we must turn a blind eye to what is commonly seen as Mosca's impressionistic treatment of historical evidence? Mosca was heir to the 'realist' tradition of Machiavelli; and like his illustrious forerunner, he is censured for erecting grand theorems upon few examples, many of them ambiguous. His conclusions, it tends to be assumed, owed more to political prejudice than to a systematic sifting of historical sources. To many observers, the perfect congruence between his 'empirical findings' and his ideological preferences is no accident. We must be careful, however, to judge Mosca's various theses on their merits. As Robert Michels once remarked, the 'iron law of oligarchy' is 'beyond Good and Evil'. Either it is an empirical truth or it is not. Neither its practical consequences nor the political predilections of those who claim to discover it are strictly relevant.

Having said this, we must concede that Mosca's approach to empirical research was not as rigorous as it might have been. His hypotheses *are* ill-defined, and his work abounds in *ex-cathedra* pronouncements masquerading as scientific discoveries.[2] Still, the reader of his *magnum opus* is bound to be impressed by the dazzling erudition displayed throughout. In common with Marx, Mosca is hoist with his own petard. Were it not for his scientific ambitions the charge of methodological crudeness would carry much less conviction. One doubts whether his treatment of evidence is any more impressionistic or one-sided than that of most other historians or political analysts who choose to deal with grand themes. Though lacking in the patience (or narrowness of interests?) to implement his scientific methodology, he undoubtedly possessed an empirical caste of mind. The principal target of his fury was what Popper has called 'essentialism', *a priori* certainty directly revealed to reason or intuition about the unalterable development of men in pursuit of goals bestowed by God or nature. Mosca, like Machiavelli – like all the best Italian thinkers, genuinely sought to free himself from theological or metaphysical preconceptions, to embody *spregiudicatezza*, the gift of looking at issues without prejudice. Political principles, according to the canons of Italian 'realism', should be derived from *verità effettuale*, not from doctrinaire abstractions that fit truth into an intellectual straitjacket. The question remains: were Mosca's attacks on the 'myths' of democracy and socialism actually rooted in factual reality or did he unwittingly substitute one set of *a priori* convictions for another? What we are not entitled to say is that his less than scientific approach necessarily renders his conclusions wrong. Let us look, first, at his critique of democracy.

The main intention of *The Ruling Class* was to refute the myth, as the author saw it, of popular sovereighty:

> Among the constant facts and tendencies that are to be found in all political organisms, one is so obvious that it is apparent to the most casual eye. In all societies ... two classes of people appear – a class that rules and a class that is ruled. The first class, always the less numerous, performs all political functions, monopolizes power and enjoys the advantages that power brings, whereas the second, the more numerous class, is directed and controlled by the first, in a manner that is now more or less legal, now more or less arbitrary and violent. (*RC*: 50)

Mosca is not simply saying that the minority makes decisions and the majority obeys – this would be an uninformative truism. His argument is that the dominant minority cannot be controlled by the majority, whatever democratic mechanisms are employed. We must, in other words, distinguish between *de jure* authority and *de facto* authority – between formal political structure and informal political power. The key to elite control lay for Mosca in a minority's capacity for organization:

> A hundred men acting uniformly in concert, with a common understanding, will triumph over a thousand men who are not in accord and can therefore be dealt with one by one. Meanwhile it will be easier for the former to act in concert and have a mutual understanding simply because they are a hundred and not a thousand.

The minority will weld itself into a cohesive and active force, whereas the majority will remain a large aggregation of individuals – apathetic, inward-looking, devoid of common purpose (*RC*: 53)

Mosca was adamant that free-elections could not alter the universal reality of domination and submission – and he took special pains to explain why:

When we say that the voters 'choose' their representatives, we are using a language that is very inexact. The truth is that the representative *has himself elected* by the voters, and, if that phrase should seem too inflexible and too harsh to fit some cases, we might qualify it by saying that *his friends have him elected*.

His 'friends' are the party bosses who, assisted by their minions, choose candidates, direct campaigns, manipulate public opinion and therefore control the parliamentary process. Mosca points out that the sheer size of the electorate gives disproportionate power to this tiny clique:

> The political mandate has been likened to the power of attorney that is familiar in private law. But in private relationships, delegations of powers and capacities always presuppose that the principal has the broadest freedom in choosing his representative. Now in practice, in popular elections, that freedom of choice, though complete theoretically, necessarily becomes null, not to say ludicrous. If each voter gave his vote to the candidate of his heart, we may be sure that in almost all cases the only result would be a wide scattering of votes. When very many wills are involved, choice is determined by the most various criteria, almost all of them subjective, and if such wills were not co-ordinated and organized it would be virtually impossible for them to coincide in the spontaneous choice of one individual. If his vote is to have any efficacy at all, therefore, each voter is forced to limit his choice to a very narrow field, in other words to a choice among the two or three persons who have some chance of succeeding; and the only ones who have any chance of succeeding are those whose candidacies are championed by ... *organized minorities*. (*RC*: 154)

The reference to organized minori*ties* highlights an important point. Mosca acknowledges that the ruling class in a parliamentary system will normally be divided into two or more parties competing with one another for popular support at the polls. It follows (Friedrich please note) that what Meisel called 'the three C's' – cohesion, consciousness, conspiracy – cannot be attributed to the ruling class *as such*, but only to the various groupings that comprise it. (Meisel 1958: 16)

Neither does Mosca seek to deny that elections have an effect on the policy-making process:

> The great majority of voters are passive ... in the sense that they have not so much freedom to choose their representatives as a

limited right to exercise an option among a number of candidates. Nevertheless, limited as it may be, that capacity has the effect of obliging candidates to try to win a weight of votes that will serve to tip the scales in their direction, so that they make every effort to flatter, wheedle and obtain the good will of the voters. In this way certain sentiments and passions of the 'common herd' come to have their influence on the mental attitudes of the representatives themselves, and echoes of a widely disseminated opinion, or of any serious discontent, easily come to be heard in the highest spheres of government. (*RC*: 155)

He even maintains that, if the electorate could be limited to intelligent and educated people, then one of the chief assumptions of the liberal system – 'namely, that those who represent shall be responsible to the represented' – could be rendered 'not wholly illusory' (*RC*: 413). Even in its least prepossessing forms, the parliamentary process 'provides a way for many different social forces [interest groups] to participate in the political system' and influence public policy to some degree (*RC*: 258).

Still, Mosca never deviated from his view that the 'sovereign people' are a fiction, that we can never attain more than *apparent* democracy', and that a minority , however divided internally, will always retain 'actual and effective control of the state' (*RC*: 335, 331). But this control will be limited by the very nature of the representative system, which 'would function very badly if all free activity on the part of individuals were suppressed, and if individuals were not fairly well protected against arbitrary acts on the part of the executive and judiciary powers'. Overtly repressive measures, by curtailing public debate and therefore exposing the sham of democratic rule, would threaten political stability. Such measures, however, are unlikely to occur in a parliamentary regime. Because representatives, who alone make laws, are obliged to flatter and cajole the 'common herd', the system itself provides the 'maximum guarantee' of civil liberties (*RC*: 470).

Mosca's analysis of liberal representative government was neither 'tautological' (Friedrich) nor 'quasi-metaphysical' (Dahl) nor self-evidently wrong. Indeed, Mosca's arguments were implicitly accepted by later academic *defenders* of parliamentary democracy, some of whom admitted that democratic elections express what 'is largely not a genuine but a manufactured will', since 'the will of the people is the product and not the motive power of the political process' (Schumpeter 1942: 263; see also Sartori 1962: 77). Joseph Schumpeter declared that this manufacturing process 'is exactly analogous to the ways of commercial advertising'. He went on to elaborate: 'We find the same attempts to contact the subconscious. We find the same technique of creating favourable and unfavourable associations which are the more effective the less rational they are' (Schumpeter 1942: 263). Slogans, half-truths, marching tunes, razzmatazz, backroom deals, deliberate distortions, bribes, rigid party discipline – these are not avoidable deviations from democratic purity. On the contrary, they 'are the essence of politics' (1942: 283). While Schumpeter concedes that the competitive element in the parliamentary system does allow for some measure of responsible government and citizen choice – and is therefore 'democratic' – he also urges us to recognize that voters are inevitably manipulated and do not themselves decide policies or issues. Western democracy amounts not to popular rule but to a system of *limitation* and *control* of power.

Schumpeter, without mentioning Mosca, substantially endorses his assessment of what actually happens in parliamentary systems. But unlike his Italian predecessor, Schumpeter was willing to call this *real*, as distinct from *apparent*, democracy. Leaving aside their contention that popular sovereignty is, strictly speaking, impossible, I find it hard to resist the conclusion that Mosca and Schumpeter were right about the constricted nature of 'democracy' as presently practised. In our highly centralized Western societies, where popular participation is kept to a minimum, where rational debate is replaced by slick advertising techniques, and where remote bureaucracies and multi-national corporations make major decisions concerning the distribution of resources, no one can afford to be sanguine about the actual degree of popular control. The gap between liberal democratic rhetoric and empirical reality remains wide. And yet, as Mosca/Schumpeter realized, this rhetoric is not entirely without foundation. Those who wish to reform or discard the existing political order should not lose sight of its virtues. They must, moreover, find a way of refuting or at least circumventing Mosca's most powerful argument, later taken up by Schumpeter: that the mass of ordinary people are neither willing nor able to develop a serious interest in public affairs, and that their readiness to defer to manipulative politicians and bureaucrats becomes more pronounced as issues grow more complex. In the face of this apparent truth, comforting clichés – human nature is essentially social, participation is an educative process – seem less than adequate. Mosca has diagnosed the Achilles' heel of radical democratic theory; it is up to radical democrats to find a convincing remedy. As he reminds us, the fact that we can discover serious failings in what exists does not mean that a superior alternative is available.

We turn, finally, to Mosca's critique of Marxism, which – though anticipating arguments made years later by F.A. Hayek and others – has prompted remarkably little scholarly comment. The critique takes two forms. First, Mosca attacked Marxism as a defective method of analysis, a dictatorship of abstractions, where 'historical truth' must always triumph over refractory empirical reality. In particular, he opposed the Marxist attempt to reduce politics and religion to what Lenin referred to as 'concentrated economics'. Ever the empiricist, Mosca adduced several historical examples to show that important changes have occurred in human societies – changes that have radically altered political constitutions and 'formulas' – without any simultaneous or approximately simultaneous modifications in methods of economic production. There is no need to list all his examples here. Two from ancient Roman history should suffice to convey the flavour of his argument. The changeover from the republican to the imperial form of government took place, he notes, 'without the slightest change' in forces or relations of production. And what about the fall of the Western Empire, a major catastrophe in the history of civilization? To him, 'it is clear enough that the system of economic production remained identical before and after the barbarian invasions'. Central to his argument is his insistence that religious beliefs and political doctrines themselves contribute greatly toward determining historical events. How else, for instance, could one account for the 'age-long struggle between papacy and empire' during the Middle Ages, a struggle totally inexplicable on economic grounds? Mosca sums up with a passage that strikingly adumbrates the idea of 'structural causality' associated with Louis Althusser's brand of Marxism:

The error of historical materialism lies in holding that the economic factor is the *only* factor worthy of consideration as cause, and that all other factors have to be regarded as effects. Every great manifestation of human activity in the social field is at the same time both cause and effect of the changes that occur in manifestations of the same activity – cause, because every modification in it influences other manifestations, and effect, because it feels the influence of modifications in them. A rather crude comparison may serve to make the point clearer. No one would deny that, if the brain is diseased, the entire human organism ceases to be in its normal state. But the same thing might be said of the digestive system, of the respiratory system and of any essential organ in the body. It would therefore be a fallacy to conclude that *all* diseases were brain diseases, or diseases of any other particular organ. It is evident that the individual's health depends on the proper functioning of *all* his organs. (*RC*: 440–4)

We can safely assume that the epigones who solemnly praise Althusser for his theoretical 'discovery' have not read their Mosca.

Having affirmed the complex interaction of so many different factors in the historical process, he wastes little time in rejecting the Marxist claim to predict the future. In his opinion, of course, the role of 'chance' in human events cannot be calculated in advance, and therefore exact predictions are impossible. If, however, one accepted Marx's 'single-track doctrine' of economic determination, prophecy of a limited kind might be possible in principle, since economic variables are quantifiable. But once other causes are admitted into our analysis – especially intangible ones, like human ideas – we must conclude that the future is open-ended (*RC*: 446–7).

While one may cast doubt on Mosca's interpretation of historical evidence (see Meisel 1958: 312), nowadays even Marxists accept the essential falsity of economic determinism. And while Mosca's criticisms of historical materialism were not *substantially* different from those of his contemporaries, Bernstein and Croce, he nevertheless provided interesting variations on general themes. From the perspective of modern politics, however, Mosca's assault on Marxist utopianism and collectivism is of greater interest.

Writing some twenty years before the Russian Revolution, Mosca asks

> whether, with the realization of the communist (or of the collectivist) system, justice, truth, love and reciprocal toleration among men, will hold a larger place in the world than they now occupy; whether the strong, who will always be at the top, will be less overbearing; whether the weak, who will always be at the bottom, will be less overborne. That question we now answer decidedly with the word 'no'. (*RC*: 283)

This is indeed a crucial question, equally important to the Marxist and to the dispassionate seeker for truth. But, straightaway, Mosca could be accused of assuming precisely what needs to be proved: namely, that the strong will always be on top and the weak always at the bottom of a social pyramid. Our author's reply would be simple. The theory of the ruling elite is as applicable to a Marxist or socialist state as to any other type of rule, and therefore what is true of class societies will equally apply to the so-called classless society. It too would 'beyond any doubt be managed by officials'. For the sake of argument, Mosca assumes that these officials (or most of them) 'would be elected exclusively by universal suffrage'. Given that 'the selection of candidates is itself almost always the work of organized minorities', the outcome is unavoidable: a small oligarchy ruling in the name of the majority. To those who would object that this happens because of the present capitalistic organization of society, where owners of great fortunes have a thousand means, direct or indirect, for manipulating the votes of the poor and buying the obedience of politicians, Mosca retorts that even in a communist society 'there would still be those who would manage the public wealth and the great mass of those who are managed'; and the former 'would undoubtedly be far more powerful than the ministers and millionaires we know today'. Why? The abolition of private property and the advent of central economic planning would destroy the 'multiplicity of political forces ... all independence and all possibility of reciprocal balancing and control'. He thus offers what has since – with the wisdom of hindsight – become a classic argument against state socialism:

> As things are today, the office clerk can at least laugh at the millionaire. A good workman who can earn a decent living with his own hands has nothing to fear from the politician, the department secretary, the deputy or the minister. Anyone who has a respectable position as the owner of a piece of land, as a businessman, as a member of a profession, can hold his head high before all the powers of the state and all the great landlords and financial barons in the world. Under collectivism, everyone will have to Kowtow to the men in the government. They alone can dispense favour, bread, the joy or sorrow of life. One single crushing, all-embracing, all-engrossing tyranny will weigh upon all. (*RC*: 284–5)

According to Mosca, such disastrous prescriptions for the future are intimately linked to a faulty analysis of the present. Marxists, in their belief that private property is the root of all evil, betray their crude economic determinism, which prevents them from seeing that political power possesses its own internal dynamic and is in no sense reducible to unequal ownership of the means of production.

Though a fierce critic of socialism, Mosca makes no attempt to defend the moral virtues of capitalism. Quite the reverse. One does not, he points out, need the 'algebraic demonstrations of Marx' to prove what readily strikes the eye of the most casual observer, that 'enjoyment of the good things of life has not been proportioned even to the value, let alone to the difficulty, of the work that is done to produce them .... Between the service that an individual renders to society and the reward that he receives there is almost always a wide, and often a glaring, discrepancy'. The problem for socialists is not that their critique of capitalist society is wrong; it is that their alternative is utopian – and utopias, *whatever their content*, pose a threat to liberty:

> *No social organization can be based exclusively upon the sentiment of justice....* It is natural that things should be that way. In his private and public conduct no individual is ever guided exclusively by his sense of justice. He is guided by his passions and his needs.... Human sentiments being what they are, to set out to erect a type of political organization that will correspond in all respects to the ideal of justice, which a man can conceive but can never attain, is a utopia, and the utopia becomes frankly dangerous when it succeeds in bringing a large mass of intellectual and moral energies to bear upon the achievement of an end that will never be achieved.... Burke remarked more than a century ago that any political system that assumes the existence of superhuman or heroic virtues can result only in vice and corruption. (*RC*: 287–8)

Political doctrines which promise perfection and absolute justice are very likely to lead to much worse social effects than doctrines less entrancing in appearance. For utopias, by definition, 'take no account of the complicated and difficult structure of human nature, but try to adapt the organization of society to a single, one-sided, absolute concept and establish it upon a single exclusive principle'. Whether this principle be the 'will of God' or the 'will of the people' or the 'brotherhood of man' or whatever, its establishment will obliterate 'the multiplicity of political forces', the system of formal or informal checks and balances that alone prevent tyranny (*RC*: 292). Marxists should be forewarned that utopian dreamers tend to become armed prophets, intolerant of natural human diversity. 'So far in history', Mosca writes, 'freedom to think, to observe, to judge men and things serenely and dispassionately, has been possible ... only in those societies in which members of different religions and political currents have been struggling for dominance'. Intellectual and moral monopoly is infallibly associated with political monopoly. Where a single truth prevails, freedom dies. This, he tells us, is an empirical fact, which utopian collectivists can counter with nothing more than pious hopes (*RC*: 196). The Marxist plan to abolish private property – harmful in itself – is therefore symptomatic of a deeper disorder: the manic desire to build a realm of perfect harmony, free from the complications and confusion of life as we know it.

It is not easy to find fault with Mosca's arguments. Pluralism and collectivism are indeed strange bedfellows – and the problem of combining the two principles remains a tricky one for radical socialists, who have so far only managed to solve it rhetorically. Of course, a diehard Marxist of the old school might argue that 'a multiplicity of political forces' is valuable only if Mosca is right about what he describes as 'our imperfect human nature' (*RC*). Mosca's answer seems unanswerable. If human nature is inherently good, then who is responsible for the existing, corrupt society? The collectivist argument stands up only if we assume 'that society is not the result of the natural and spontaneous activity of human beings but was set up by some superhuman or extrahuman will, which amused itself by giving us laws, institutions and morals that have poisoned and upset the innate goodness, generosity and magnanimity of the seed of Adam' (*RC*: 289).

Notwithstanding his opposition to socialism, in all its varieties, Mosca was far from being opposed to change as such. No political scientist, in his view, could see it as anything but inevitable, even natural:

Complete immobility in a human society is an artificial thing, whereas continuous change in ideas, sentiments and customs, which cannot help having its repercussions upon political organization, is natural. To prevent change, it would be necessary to destroy all influences from the spirit of observation and inquiry, from the growth and spread of knowledge, from accumulating experience; for such influences make it inevitable that new manners of thinking should mature, and new manners of feeling, and these necessarily corrode faith in ancestral teachings and weaken the traditional concepts that form the foundations of the political structure of the forefathers.

The way to defeat socialism, therefore, is to channel the energies it has unleashed into a creative renewal of the status quo. Coming from a foe of universal suffrage, this call for adaptation may ring false to some ears. What does one make of a 'reactionary' who professes admiration for 'the spirit of observation and inquiry'? But Mosca, rather like Lampedusa's Sicilian Prince, understood that things must change in order that things can remain the same:

Things being as they are, there is only one way to avoid what is called the death of a state or a nation ... That way is to provide for a slow but continuous modification of ruling classes, for a slow but continuous assimilation by them of new elements of moral cohesion that will gradually supplant the old. In this case, probably, as in others, the best results in practice are obtained by a sound balance between two different and opposite natural tendencies, between the drift toward conservatism and the urge for innovation. In other words, a political organism, a nation, a civilization, can, literally speaking, be *immortal*, provided it learns how to *transform itself continually without falling apart*. (*RC*: 461–2)

One might add that Mosca himself maintained 'a sound balance between two different and opposite' tendencies within his own mind: the empirical bent he inherited from Machiavelli, and the regressive instincts he derived from his privileged Sicilian background.


CONCLUDING REMARKS

Norberto Bobbio has made a useful distinction between two types of political realism. One, resting upon the counterposition of 'real' and 'ideal', scorns utopian escapism, ridicules the search for final solutions; the other, based upon the counterposition of 'real' and 'apparent', unmasks the hidden aspects of power, de-mystifies the status quo (Bobbio 1977: 9–10). Mosca is a most unusual thinker in as much as he combines, in one devasting and innovative analysis, both types of realism. In a sense, then, he should be much more popular and revered than he actually is, for he offers something for everyone. The radical can find sustenance in his indictment of bourgeois hypocrisy and liberal democratic mythology; the conservative can take comfort from his relentless assault on socialist pretensions. In fact, however, Mosca has succeeded in alienating just about everybody. To defenders of the established order, he is a pseudo-scientific subversive, undermining the mysteries of existence in language reminiscent of a demented *philosophe*. To reformers and revolutionaries, he represents the flowering of everything they exist to oppose – cynicism, contempt for the masses, a pessimistic belief in the eternal antithesis between man and society.

From a scientific viewpoint, Mosca's work leaves much to be desired. Crucial questions remain unanswered. For example, what is the precise relationship between the political bosses and the traditional 'ruling classes' – the bankers, the merchants, the industrialists? How exactly do we draw the line between 'real' and 'apparent' democracy? And, more fundamentally, how can Mosca be so sure that human nature is forever immutable? But, without endorsing his arguments in every detail, I would contend that the events of this century have justified his scepticism: neither capitalism nor socialism nor democracy has fulfilled its promises, and the melancholy Sicilian can help us to understand why. What's more, he teaches us that it is possible – indeed desirable – to deflate the myths that sustain the status quo without succumbing to the temptations of imaginative fantasy. The social critic deals in awkward truths; he (or she) need not and should not emulate the quack doctor, who claims to have a universal and infallible remedy for all diseases.

## NOTES

1. But, *pace*, Dahl, students of the imagery and illusions that constitute our social bonds need not be reduced to metaphysical speculation. Though normally unsusceptible to direct observation and measurement, the effects of ideology are not beyond empirical analysis. With the aid of counterfactuals, for example, we may be able to demonstrate how a society's routine assumptions and procedures prevent certain important issues from ever reaching the public agenda. For an excellent empirical study of how ideology permeates established practices and limits the scope of decision-making, see Crenson (1971).

2. There is, however, some controversy surrounding Gramsci's complaint about Mosca's 'elastic and variable' terminology – a complaint echoed by later commentators such as Bobbio (1977: 202). While Mosca does appear to use the terms *classe politica* (political class) and *classe dirigente* (ruling class) interchangeably, without regard for their different connotations, Ettore Albertoni disputes this common critical observation, arguing that by *classe dirigente* Mosca meant *all* ruling minorities (political, economic, religious, intellectual, military, bureaucratic). The *classe politica* is therefore a sub-species of the ruling class (Albertoni 1987: 16–17). I remain unconvinced. True, the second volume of the *Elementi*, published in 1923, can plausibly be read in this way; but the first volume (from 1896) cannot. There Mosca, apparently recognizing no distinction between the two terms, refers in at least two places to 'classe dirigente o classe politica' (Mosca 1953, Vol. I: 79, 84). Indeed, in the English version of the *Elementi*, the two Italian terms are both translated as 'ruling class'. One might dismiss this as a translator's error, were it not for the fact that the English edition was read and approved by Mosca himself (Mosca 1939: xli of editor's introduction).

REFERENCES

Albertoni, E.A., *Mosca and the Theory of Elitism*, trans. by P. Goodrick (Oxford: Basil Blackwell, 1987).

Bobbio, N., *Saggi sulla scienza politica in Italia* (Bari: Laterza, 1977).

Bottomore, T., *Elites and Society*, (Harmondsworth: Penguin, 1966).

Crenson, M.A., *The Un-Politics of Air Pollution: A Study of Non-Decision-making in the Cities* (Baltimore: Johns Hopkins University Press, 1971).

Croce, B. (20 November 1923). *La Critica* XXI: 377.

Dahl, R., A Critique of the Ruling Elite Model, pp. 126–35, in A. Pizzorno (ed.), *Political Sociology* (Harmondsworth: Penguin, 1971). The article was originally published in *American Political Science Review* (1958) 52: 463–9.

Friedrich, C., *The New Image of the Common Man* (Boston: Beacon Press, 1950).

Gramsci, A., *Note sul Machiavelli*, Vol. 4 of *Quaderni del Carcere* (Turin: Einaudi, 1949).

Gramsci, A., *Selections from the Prison Notebooks*, ed. and trans. by Q. Hoare and G. Nowell Smith (London: Lawrence and Wishart, 1971).

Mannheim, K., *Ideology and Utopia* (London: Kegan Paul, 1936).

Meisel, J., *The Myth of the Ruling Class* (Ann Arbor: University of Michigan Press, 1958).

Mosca, G., *The Ruling Class*, trans. by H.D. Kahn (New York: McGraw Hill, 1939). This English translation combines the two volumes of Mosca's *Elementi di scienza politica* (Vol. I: 1896; Vol. II: 1923). Pages 329–494 of the English edition refer to Vol. II of the original edition.

Mosca, G., *Elementi di scienza politica* (two vols, 4th edn) (Bari: Laterza, 1953).

Parry, G., *Political Elites* (London: Allen and Unwin, 1969).

Sartori, G., *Democratic Theory* (Detroit: Wayne State University Press, 1962).

Schumpeter, J., *Capitalism, Socialism and Democracy* (New York: Harper and Row, 1942).

Vico, G., *The New Science*, trans. by T.G. Bergin and M.H. Fisch (Ithaca, NY: Cornell University Press, 1961).

# 5 Pareto's Concept of Demagogic Plutocracy

Despite his status as a founder of modern social science, Pareto receives little scholarly attention. In particular, his penetrating discussion of 'demagogic plutocracy' (his term for the liberal state) has been strangely ignored by analysts of Western, or 'bourgeois', democracy. While Marx's scattered and inconsistent remarks on 'the capitalist state' have spawned a vast literature, Pareto is lucky to be acknowledged in a footnote. Consider the exemplary case of David Held, a theorist of great repute, who managed to write a 321-page textbook called *Models of Democracy* without once mentioning Pareto's name.[1] Why has Pareto been 'put in quarantine'?[2] One reason is surely the irritating nature of his masterwork, *Treatise of General Sociology* (published in 1916).[3] Even his admirers describe this work as 'monstrous' – disorganized, unnecessarily long, full of pedantic distinctions, and continually interrupted by digressions, and by digressions within digressions.[4] He never missed an opportunity to break the thread of exposition in order to pursue some bright idea or display his arcane erudition. But a fuller explanation of Pareto's 'quarantine' requires us to look at the social psychology of intellectuals. Few writers managed to antagonize their potential public quite as much as he. Optimistic moralizing, of a kind favoured by progressive intellectuals, was his principal target; and he was relentless in exposing the double standards and faulty logic of its purveyors.[5] Yet, while he disdained moral preaching, he had the unpleasant scoffing habit of the moralist (in the classical sense of the term), who dispassionately lays bare human vices. When hearing politicians or activists pontificate about 'morality' or 'social justice', Pareto felt an irresistible urge to count the spoons. To 'worshippers of the Goddess Reason',[6] he was a slanderer of mankind, a master of despair.[7] Another reason for Pareto's unfashionableness is his disturbing association with fascism. It appears that he welcomed Mussolini's triumph, and some see fascism as the 'logical fulfilment' of his political philosophy. Pareto, they say, was the 'Karl Marx of Fascism' – a status which has earned him terrible maledictions.[8] Like the carrier of an infectious disease, he is studiously avoided by those who adhere to the interpretative principle of 'bad man, bad theory'. This principle is of course childish and logically nonsensical, since even bad people can produce good (or interesting) theories. Neither can it be a sufficient cause of Pareto's 'quarantine', given the exponential growth of the Nietzsche industry in recent years. But Nietzsche, though a proto-fascist, was precociously 'postmodern'. Pareto, with his scrupulous regard for logical and empirical methods, is considered 'old-hat' by the arbiters of academic fashion. In what follows, an attempt will be made to prove them wrong, at least with respect to the concept of demagogic plutocracy. First, however, I must set out the basic theories that underpin this concept, and also summarize Pareto's objections to Marxist analysis.

## NON-LOGICAL ACTIONS

What had impressed Pareto in observing the social behaviour of mankind was the prevalence of 'non-logical' actions over 'logical' ones. Briefly, acts are non-logical when the subject acts without explicit knowledge of the purpose of his action, or, having such knowledge, chooses means which, in the light of better information, are unlikely to achieve the purpose. By contrast, actions are logical when the consequences anticipated by the subject are identical with the consequences that might reasonably be anticipated by a disinterested observer of the act.[9] Non-logical actions are governed by sentiments, or 'residues', which 'correspond to' or 'manifest' human instincts, just as mercury in a thermometer manifests the presence of heat. Residues are not themselves psychological drives, but rather symbolic expressions of such drives. The desire for sex is an instinct; sexual puritanism is a residue – a basic and essentially invariable attitude or sentiment.[10] Pareto was struck by the way that sentiments, throughout history, had been hidden by pseudo-logical constructions. The main function of reason was not to dominate the passions or sentiments but to disguise them. Men and women, having a hunger for logic, will usually try to give a reasoned explanation or justification of acts they do from obscure or unconscious motives.[11] Rationalistic reformers assume that we first think, first formulate ideas and theories, and then act accordingly. For Pareto, behaviour follows the reverse process: commission precedes rationalization. The theories or rationalizations that give a logical veneer to our activities Pareto terms 'derivations'. In a manner reminiscent of Marx, he sought to discover, beneath the superstructure of professed values, the underlying structural reality – the real purposes and motives of human actions. Where he differed from Marx was in the explanatory primacy he assigned to human psychology: both conduct and belief stemmed from the same residual root. Whether we choose to be communists or nationalists, liberals or fascists, depends primarily on sentiment, though we often pretend otherwise. Reason, as embodied in the scientific method (or the 'logico-experimental' method, in Pareto's idiom), can help us to get from A to B, but it cannot determine whether B is a desirable destination. The conflict between competing ethical systems is incapable of rational resolution. Committed as he was to the scientific method, Pareto refused to offer therapeutic theories. Rather, he saw himself as an heir of Machiavelli, separating morality from political analysis.[12]

It is sometimes assumed that Pareto, by describing human activities as 'non-logical', was somehow trying to denigrate them, and to elevate the 'logico-experimental' method as the be-all and end-all. To Bellamy, for example, he was guilty of 'crude utilitarian rationalism'.[13] It is true that the Paretian category, 'non-logical', included behaviour and reasoning that were downright *illogical* and contrary to experience. But it also included ideas and actions – such as those connected with religion – that could be neither verified nor refuted, and were in this sense beyond criticism.[14] Whatever form it took, the non-logical realm was, for Pareto, an essential component of existence. We need ideals or myths for consolation, to give meaning to life, to explain the unexpected or the unusual. He was adamant that we should distinguish between the logico-experimental truth of certain theories and their social utility, since the two things often stand in flat contradiction.[15] So far from being a crude utilitarian rationalist, he attacked the utilitarian rationalists for their crudeness. In his estimation, the concepts which different individuals have about their own good and the good of others are essentially heterogeneous and incommensurable, and there is no way of reducing them to a rational unity. Judgements about social utility will always be vague and contestable, for they will depend upon the value-coefficients that are used in rendering diverse utilities homogeneous. The admirer of the 'superman' and the lover of equality will obviously arrive at very different conclusions concerning the utility of a particular distribution of income or power – and there is 'no criterion save sentiment for choosing between one and the other'. Another complicating factor is the internal complexity of the concept of utility itself. We can, for example, aim to maximize the 'utility *of* a community' or the 'utility *for* a community'. The former arises when the community is considered, 'if not as a person, at least as a unit'. The latter refers to community viewed as a collection of individuals. Take the matter of population increase. This will undoubtedly be a good thing if we think of the utility *of* the community as regards prestige or military power. But if we desire the maximum of utility *for* the community, we will consider the living conditions of individual citizens, which might be diminished by overcrowding or rising unemployment.[16]

A further criticism of Pareto is that he ignored the findings of 'holistic' sociology: social determinism, the power of collective beliefs and social practices. Pareto, it is argued, reduced the mechanics of the social and political process to a number of archetypical psychological responses, and thus assumed that 'everything is the same everywhere'.[17] It must be conceded that Pareto's discussion of residues and derivations stresses similarities, not differences. He believed, for instance, that differing religious rituals revealed the existence of certain universal residues: the baptism of Christians, the sacrifices of the pagans, the ablutions of the Muslims all express the same underlying sentiments and needs. His was a protest against historicism and its belief in the uniqueness and individuality of each society or epoch. However, to say that Pareto ignored the impact of social norms on human conduct is wide of the mark. It is simply misleading to describe him as a psychological reductionist. While he saw human psychology as the *principal* factor in social life, it was only *primus inter pares*. Nor could it be divorced from the social context. Sentiments, he believed, were *both* innate *and* socially acquired. In various passages, he made it clear that social practices themselves encourage the diffusion of sentiments appropriate to their continued functioning.[18] Borrowing from general systems theory, Pareto saw society as a system of mutually interdependent phenomena, moving from one state of equilibrium to another. According to this mechanical model, the 'form of society is determined by all the elements acting upon it and it, in turn, reacts upon them. We may therefore say that a reciprocal determination arises'.[19] These movements and counter-movements adjust themselves to one another to produce a state of equilibrium – but a *dynamic* equilibrium, since the system 'is constantly changing in form'.[20]

## PARETO AND MARXISM

Pareto's insistence on replacing the concept of one-sided causality with that of mutual interaction or functional correlation underlies his critique of Marxism. Legend has it that Pareto caused Lenin graver worry than any other anti-Marxist writer.[21] Still, Pareto's critique is tempered by a certain affinity. Of the 'founding fathers' of sociology, Marx was the only one he esteemed. The English edition of the *Treatise* is over 2,000 pages in length, yet the names Weber and Durkheim do not appear it all! Comte and Spencer, though given due consideration, are contemptuously dismissed as mere metaphysicians.[22] Marx was placed in a different category. As we have seen, Pareto borrowed some of his themes: the priority of practice over theory, the need to unearth the hidden reasons behind actions or verbal statements. But the German, he thought, had gone astray in substituting relationships of cause and effect for relationships of interdependence. Marx's error was not his stress on material interests – this, on the contrary, 'was a notable forward step for social science', bringing out as it did the contingent character of morals and religion.[23] Marx, however, claimed too much for his insight. Turning a blind eye to experience, he failed to see how material motivations are themselves modified by other factors, such as residues or ideologies. Marx compounded his error by coupling his economic determinism with a simplistic theory of 'class struggle'. The classes, into the bargain, 'were reduced by a dichotomy somewhat cavalier to two' – 'capitalists' and 'proletarians'.[24] 'Class', Pareto maintains, is an aggregative concept, incorporating a diversity of groupings under one heading. For example, the label 'capitalist' applies to both *entrepreneurs* and owners of savings. Yet, on some matters (e.g. interest rates), the needs of the two groups are 'diametrically opposed'.[25] How can the liberal state be an 'instrument' of a 'class' that is divided in its interests and perceptions? Nevertheless, Pareto acknowledges that the theory of class struggle contains a grain of truth; for in all societies at all times, there exists a minority of persons who seize the goods of others, sometimes by legal and sometimes by illegal means.[26] This, in brief, is his doctrine of 'spoliation'. The 'class struggle', then, is a 'real factor'. But it is not confined to only two classes; it occurs between an 'infinite number of groups' with different interests – and these groups need not be economically defined. Spoliation may also be based on nationality, race, language, religion and sex.[27]

Notwithstanding its scientific discoveries, Marxism, as an integrated system of analysis, is demonstrably false; its logical sophistries, Pareto insists, can 'deceive no one who is not already disposed to be deceived'.[28] Why, though, were so many people willing to be 'deceived'? He agreed with his friend Sorel that Marxism was best interpreted not as a science but as a form of 'social poetry', providing the proletariat with one of those great social myths which have incited men to action through the ages. The beatific vision of communism was 'akin to the golden age of the millenarians ... lost in the mists of the future'.[29] Indeed, Pareto saw Marxism as a kind of lay religion, spread by tireless apostles, exhibiting a faith in the principles of Marx equal to that of the early Christians in the gospel. Marxism, like any other religion, expresses the persistent human need for abstractions, or ideal images. As a Machiavellian realist, Pareto could hardly accept Marx's prophecy that class struggle would eventually be resolved in a peaceful and harmonious future where spoliation gives way to cooperation. For Pareto, it matters little what the economic system or the official principles of government might be – the effect will always be the same: the exploitation of one segment of the community by another. And the despoiling elite will, in the normal course of events, capture the machinery of state – the better to achieve its nefarious purposes.[30] All revolutions simply replace one oligarchy with another, and a communist revolution would be no exception. While newly ascendant elites often proclaim their submission to the 'popular will', the 'small and humble' soon discover that they have merely exchanged yokes: 'whether universal suffrage prevails or not, it is always an oligarchy that governs'.[31]

POLITICAL ELITES

The governing elite keeps itself in power by resorting to two methods, force and guile. The distinction between the two methods of government corresponds to Machiavelli's famous antithesis between the lion and the fox. Political elites divide naturally into two families, one of which deserves to be called the family of the lions and the other the family of the foxes. In Pareto's scheme, the various political elites, the lions and the foxes, are characterized primarily by the types of residues they embody. Lions are rich in sentiments that reflect instincts of 'aggregate-persistence'. Such persons are idealistic, but unimaginative and intolerant. Enamoured of expressive 'wholeness', and fearful of dissident voices or behaviour, they are inclined to use force and even violence to attain their objectives. Foxes, on the other hand, are abundantly endowed with residues that manifest the 'instinct for combinations' – the propensity to take disparate elements out of their familiar contexts and unite them together in novel combinations. Possessed of considerable imagination, foxes strive to maintain political power through bargaining and manipulation. A political system ruled by foxes is likely to be participative, liberal, urban, and technologically advanced. Such a system would conventionally be called a democracy; Pareto prefers the term 'demagogic plutocracy'. Although he never deviates from his belief that 'popular representation' is a 'fiction'[32] in our so-called democracies, he admits that it is a necessary fiction, since the masses tend to be idealistic and literal-minded (i.e. lion-like). They are effectively guided, affirmed Pareto, not by naked interest but by 'living faiths'. While democracies do not officially align themselves with this or that religious faith, the 'sovereignty of the people' functions as an *ersatz* deity. 'King Demos, good soul, thinks he is following his own devices,' but from the days of Aristotle down to our own, he is more or less 'bamboozled'.[33] Though the people may reign, they never govern.

If a governing elite could apply force and persuasion in the appropriate proportions, it could, in principle, maintain itself forever. No elite, however, has ever succeeded in doing so. 'History is the graveyard of aristocracies.'[34] Pareto thus offers a dual hypothesis, which he feels is confirmed by historical evidence. To wit, an elite of lions will be deficient in the spirit of innovation and compromise, and this shortcoming will eventually undermine its ability to keep the masses quiet; conversely, an elite of foxes will lack the will-power to use force, and this can, in the fullness of time, erode its authority to the point of social anarchy. In his analysis of demagogic plutocracy, Pareto wants to demonstrate that the vulpine arts of the governing class are proving disastrous, that we are approaching the end of an historical cycle, which may see a successful uprising by a new leonine (communist or fascist) elite.

Before reaching middle age, Pareto was an intransigent democrat *à la* Mazzini. While he enthusiastically supported free markets he also defended universal suffrage, as well as the rights of workers to combine and strike to improve their conditions. By the turn of the century, however, extension of the franchise and the rise of organized labour had caused his opinions to change. The cynicism he had once directed against the reactionary bourgeoisie was now turned against the workers and their phoney champions, who were – to his mind – substituting one form of spoliation for another. His views on these 'democratic' developments are nowhere collected into one comprehensive statement. They must be gathered, mainly, from the last two (very long) chapters of the *Treatise*, and from various post-treatise writings.

For Pareto, the essence of modern democracies is the patron-client relationship, a relationship based for the most part on material interests. His paradigm was the Italian *'consorteria'* of parties that ruled in his day, but he thought that this analysis applied to most, perhaps all, parliamentary systems. What he had in mind was a network of 'patrons', each of which has clienteles consisting of sub-patrons, and so on. the system is pluralistic, comprising a vast number of mutually dependent hubs of influence and patronage. These power-centres are forever quarrelling and competing with one another but nevertheless display sufficient cohesion to warrant calling them a class. Such cohesion, however, is not to be confused with conspiratorial or tight organization. The idea that the ruling class is a 'concrete unity' or a metaphorical person is, in Pareto's view, a Marxist fairy-story.[35] For one thing, this class embraces the leaders of all the constitutional parties – those of the Left and those of the Right. Nor does it rule by deliberate and concerted stratagem. The road it follows is, instead, 'the resultant of an infinitude of minor acts', each occasioned by particular circumstances, leading collectively to consequences that no one foresees. Society is a reality *sui generis*. The chief determinant of what happens is 'the order, or system, not the conscious will of individuals, who indeed may in certain cases be carried by the system to points where they would never have gone of deliberate choice'.[36] Here, as elsewhere, Pareto insists on the great complexity of social action, and on the need for replacing the notion of linear causality by that of reciprocal determination: the multiple and unpredictable combinations of actions and reactions are bound to produce unintended effects. Such cohesion as exists within the ruling elite is a systemic requirement. Since all its members are actuated by economic self-interest and a desire to retain influence, they naturally tend to act in a common direction without any preconceived design.

Though the governing class does not have a single will, it does contain 'a smaller, choicer class', which 'practically exercises control'. In parliamentary regimes, this inner governing body will consist of the political 'bosses' of the main parties, whose task is to aggregate the demands of the various clienteles.[37] In pursuit of electoral success, leaders of the different parliamentary parties will compete with one another in this aggregative endeavour. Promises can be made, in the knowledge that government provides a vast panoply of means to fulfil them: tariffs, public works, tax policy, devaluation of the currency, government contracts and subsidies, social welfare benefits, minimum wage guarantees, closed-shop rules, legal immunities for trade unions – all help to keep the various clienteles happy. Corruption – either by 'honours' or illicit payments – usually plays a lesser role than these 'legitimate' forms of bribery, though it attracts disproportionate opprobrium.[38]

## 'SPECULATORS' AND 'RENTIERS'

Who exactly composes the governing class? In a dazzling leap of imagination, Pareto sees it as an unholy, though tacit, alliance of bourgeoisie and organized working people against the fixed income groups of the community. Although businessmen and labourers do not always share common interests,[39] these apparently antagonistic 'classes' actually live in symbiosis, agreeing inflationary wage settlements and jointly demanding subsidies and tariffs, which must be paid for by the rest of the population through higher taxes and prices. Plutocrats may rule, but only through demagogic appeals to the interests and sentiments of ordinary folk. Pareto expands on this point by drawing a distinction between two 'classes' – 'speculators' and 'rentiers'. The former are chiefly *entrepreneurs* or financial traders – adventurous risk-takers, rich in combination instincts. They are adept at winning concessions from fox-like politicians, who see them as soul-mates. Confusingly, Pareto includes in this 'S' category not only the risk takers themselves but all persons depending upon them – lawyers, engineers, workers, politicians – and deriving advantage from their operations. In other words, he lumps together all individuals whose incomes are essentially variable and dependent upon ingenuity and political connections.[40] Ill-chosen though it may be, the word 'speculators' describes Pareto's governing class.

Arrayed against the 'speculators' are the 'rentiers', another promiscuously inclusive term, comprising all those who live on fixed or near-fixed incomes:

> In this category, roughly, will be found persons who have savings and have deposited them in savings-banks or invested them in life-annuities; then people living on income from government bonds ... or other securities with fixed interest rates; then owners of real estate and land where there is no speculation; then farmers, working people, clerks depending upon such persons and in no way depending upon speculators.[41]

A poor old-age pensioner, for example, will have an economic interest resembling that of members of the 'capitalist' class who live on fixed incomes in the shape of returns on debentures and rents. The same pensioner will find, on the other hand, that his or her interests conflict with those of unionized workers in a protected industry. This group of workers can secure high wage increases from their employers because these are in a position to pass on such wage increases to the consumer (e.g. the pensioner) in the form of higher prices. Indeed, inflation may even be to the advantage of the tariff-protected businessman, as it depresses real interest rates and – certainly in the short term – raises profits.[42] For the pensioner, however, the effect is similar to being set upon by armed bandits.

Without the 'downtrodden' rentiers, the economy would grind to a halt. It is they who supply the savings and the tax revenues to support the money-making schemes of the speculators. And yet, as dull, unimaginative types, replete with instincts of aggregate-persistence, rentiers lack the manipulative and rhetorical skills to win concessions from the political elite. The 'pork barrel' remains more or less closed to them, as the trade unions and employer organizations jointly manipulate the state to exact tribute from everyone else. While Pareto, unlike the Marxists of his day, did not underestimate the power of politicians, he believed that the public authorities were increasingly acting as mere ratifying bodies for the exploitative policies of the 'producer' groups. He also remarked upon the frequent willingness of the victims to cooperate in their own spoliation. Short of vulpine shrewdness, they allowed their vision to be 'clouded by sentiments' favourable to the speculating class.[43]

Psychological explanations for the passivity of the rentiers did not, it seems, fully satisfy Pareto. He thus offered what might appear to be a contradictory argument, one that foreshadowed the 'rational choice' explanations of modern political scientists.[44] The intensity of human activity, he reminded us, is not proportional in the same degree to losses as to gains: 'if, in a nation of thirty million, it is proposed to levy one franc per annum on each citizen and to distribute the total to thirty individuals, these latter will work night and day for the success of this proposal, while it will be difficult to get the others to bestir themselves sufficiently to oppose the proposal, because, after all, it is only one franc!'

Furthermore, the 30 individuals who benefit from this largesse will do so because they form an identifiable group. And for a group to form, let alone exert effective pressure, it 'must not be too widely dispersed' and 'must have an easily recognizable common characteristic, such as the same race, the same religion, the same occupation, and so forth'. This is why consumers, for example, 'can scarcely ever organize themselves successfully to resist the producer combines'.[45] To organize scattered and diverse individuals with low-intensity preferences is virtually impossible. But in a demagogic plutocracy, those who have no organizational power have no bargaining power. By virtue of their social and geographic dispersal, they neither occupy a strategic position within the system nor possess the potential to cause serious conflict or disruption. They can be, and are, effectively ignored by the powers-that-be. Policy emerges out of a complex network of visible and invisible exchanges between the various bargaining agents who represent vested interests in the particular policy area. This segmented decisional process has dire consequences. Not only does it alienate 'the silent majority', it also produces short-sighted and incoherent policy. The repeated surrender to vested interests leads to a paralysing disproportion between current expenditure and long-term investment.

On Pareto's reading of history, spoliation rarely meets with truly effective resistance from the despoiled. What brings an end to a particular form of exploitation is the destruction of wealth consequent upon it. 'History shows us', he writes, 'that more than once spoliation has finished by killing the goose that lays the golden eggs'.[46] Demagogic plutocracy administers daily doses of poison to the capitalist goose. Too much attention is paid to allocating wealth rather than creating it. Instead of concentrating all their efforts on improving efficiency, capitalists devote precious energy and resources to lobbying for protective duties and other gifts from the public. The competition which favours initiative and economic expansion gives way to bureaucratic dependency.[47] Unions, for their part, use legal immunities to preserve outmoded jobs or to prevent non-union workers from working at non-inflationary wage levels.[48] Other citizens are bought off with public employment, communal facilities, and income maintenance programmes.[49] In general, political needs take priority over economic needs. The cumulative effect of controlled markets and uncontrolled public expenditure is macro-economic distortion. Massive public debts accumulate and these are inevitably accompanied by higher prices and interest rates. Worse, rising taxes exhaust the incomes of ordinary, non-speculating investors.[50] Creative accounting, along with the printing of new money, can disguise the appalling state of public finances for a while, but eventually the consequences of profligacy must be faced. The funds available for investment begin to dry up.[51]

In Paretian analysis, hyperactive, interventionist government also has a corrosive effect on public morale. When so much of the population depends on state handouts, an ethic of greedy discontent inexorably takes root, since most people can always point to someone or some group who enjoys more influence or more patronage or simply bigger handouts than they. The idea that one should *earn* one's benefits or privileges is gradually consigned to the dustbin. Moreover, the constant bestowal of government favours, by undermining the work ethic, stimulates a debilitating and hedonistic egoism. People increasingly indulge their tastes for immediate gratification: they squander savings and incur debts. Eventually, they will be forced to use their earnings to retire debt, and consumption will decline. This will exacerbate the problems caused by the shortage of funds for investment.[52]

Pareto takes perverse pleasure in demystifying the 'non-logical' derivations that serve to justify the redistribution of income by a meddlesome state. For him, as we have seen, concepts like 'justice' and 'morality' lack any logico-experimental basis; they 'have no precise objective reality, being only the product of our mind'.[53] Their meanings are therefore inherently 'indeterminate and transitory'. Such concepts are normally defined in accord with 'the sentiments of some collectivity at a given point in time'. When times, and sentiments, change, so do the definitions.[54] Pareto is especially amused by the transformation in the meaning of 'liberty'. Once it stood for the reduction of state restrictions which deprived the individual of the power to dispose of his person and property as he wished. Now, Pareto claims, it signifies precisely the opposite. Coercion for purposes of 'efficiency' or 'social justice' is christened with the name of 'liberty'.[55]

Pareto's analysis of demagogic plutocracy is not entirely negative. A nation without speculators would, after all, be a poor nation. They alone have the initiative and energy to carve out economic opportunities. And at certain stages in economic development, government subventions and protective tariffs are positively conducive to industrial growth, since they afford time to effect the necessary accumulation of capital in order to enable national industry to compete in world markets. In addition, fox-led governments, for all their chicanery, might reasonably be given credit for maximizing the utilities of individual citizens – at least in the short run. Net beneficiaries of state indulgence are many, and their benefits are often great. Here we can make use of Pareto's intriguing antithesis between utility *of*, and utility *for*, a community. Maximum utility *for* a collectivity – that is, the greatest satisfaction for the greatest number of individuals – is a matter of giving everyone what he desires as far as possible. Egoistic or material interests and the interests of the present will prevail. But the maximum utility *of* a collectivity will depend on the health or well-being of that collectivity understood as an organic whole. This might require individuals to sacrifice their private interests (e.g. protective tariffs or inflationary wage increases) to communal needs. Pareto had little time for those followers of Bentham and Rousseau who, while arguing from opposite perspectives, nevertheless agree that there is no *real* contradiction between the collective good and the individual good.[56] The capitalist class, too, often conflates these different types of utility when it wants the labouring class to make sacrifices for the (alleged) public good. Such losses, it is said, become gains when one takes into account the *indirect* utility that accrues to individuals living in a prosperous/strong/orderly society. But, argues Pareto, it is not always the case that indirect advantages outweigh direct sacrifices. From the viewpoint of the organized worker, for example, the indirect harm he suffers because of his inflationary wage settlements may be quantitatively smaller than the direct benefit he derives from his 'selfish' (to Pareto) actions.[57] If we pursue this line of reasoning, we can grasp how demagogic plutocracy may maximise utility *for* the community even when destroying the utility *of* the community.

Both types of utility, however, will diminish when the economy falls into depression or deep recession. At this point, the counter-productive nature of the demagogic strategy will become obvious. It is all very well to 'conquer by gold, not by steel', but what happens when the gold runs out? Previously contented clients become disenchanted, as their expectations are dashed. The authority of the state, based as it is on bribery, begins to evaporate. By squalidly buying off potential adversaries, the top politicians sacrifice the mysterious aura, the 'dignity and respect' that evoke the sentiment of deference in the masses.[58] This emergent 'legitimation crisis' poses a knotty problem for the ruling elite, because foxes are unwilling or unable to use force in the required measure. Such pacifism, Pareto believes, is misguided. All laws and institutions must be sustained by a judicious blend of force and consent; where one or the other is forgone, the result will be either incipient anarchy or naked despotism. Pareto saw the former as a real danger in modern society: 'The bourgeois state is tottering, and the power of central authority is being eroded.'[59] Centrifugal forces are beginning to prevail.

He illustrated this point by reference to trade unions, for which he developed an obsessive hatred. They were, in his view, a law unto themselves. Dissatisfied with their *official* legal immunities, the unions proceed to demand (and receive) *unofficial* ones. In Italy, trade union members destroy the property of their employers and beat up black-legs under the benevolent paternal gaze of the public authorities, who do nothing to stop such out outrages. Pareto compares the situation to the rise of feudalism: the *de facto* authority of kings disappeared, to be replaced by an elaborate system of immunities. The trade union bosses are the new barons, paying ritual obeisance to the *ideal* central authority, while ignoring it in practice. In the face of union power, the upper strata of the ruling elite have shown themselves to be 'cow-ardly', according to Pareto.[60] Their plight filled him with a mixture of pity and contempt. He was fond of quoting an old Italian saying: 'Play the sheep and you will meet the butcher.' The butcher, in this case, might be the 'silent majority'. Weak demagogic governments parcel out operating autonomy to power blocs, special interests and (suppos-edly) subordinate organizational units. Once central authority disinte-grates in this way, the silent majority find that they are no longer protected by the 'sovereign' power. Increasingly, they fear less for their pocket-books than for their safety and peace, as crime and trade union 'justice' become harder to avoid. The system moves into dise-quilibrium – one would therefore expect centrifugal forces to be coun-tered by a swing back to centripetalism.[61] Writing in 1920, Pareto alerted his readers to the authoritarian movements (Bolshevik and nationalist) waiting in the wings. The rentiers, the non-union workers – all those who have had to pay the price for the pluto-democratic system 'will eventually rebel'.[62] Ever the sceptic, he was reluctant to predict the timing or the exact magnitude or even the effectiveness of this rebellion. After the March on Rome, however, he saw Mussolini's rise to power as striking confirmation of his theory.

CRITICAL REFLECTIONS

However, uncongenial this theory of the liberal state may be, it would be difficult to deny its perspicacity. Pareto pioneered propositions and ideas which have since become widely influential or commonly accepted. One can mention his pluralistic model of the policy process, his masterly analysis of why 'diffused interests' are ignored, his emphasis on vertical as well as horizontal divisions in society, his abandonment of the notion of simple cause-effect in favour of variables standing towards one another in varying states of mutual dependence. He offers an original combination of insights from

Marxist and anti-Marxist sources. On the one hand, he accepts that power in modern society is dispersed; on the other, he recognizes the systematic disadvantages inflicted on those outside the unofficial constellation of power, which bypasses the formal circuits of representation. Moreover, as Finer pointed out, his concept of a 'patron–client' regime can be a useful tool of comparative analysis, helping to isolate 'unsuspected affinities between apparently diverse regimes'.[63] The patron–client relationship is meant to be a defining feature of Mediterranean political anthropology, but Pareto demonstrates its relevance to 'Protestant' democracies as well. Last but not least, his rigorous dissection of the concept of utility, though mysteriously ignored by political theorists, could dissipate the persistent fog surrounding such catch-phrases as 'national interest' and 'public good'.

Yet, anyone attempting to encourage closer study of Pareto's ideas comes up against a formidable barrier: his reputation as an advocate or, at least, a 'precursor' of fascism.[64] Do we really want to be instructed on the nature of the liberal state by a man whose theory could have been formulated by Il Duce himself? By way of reply, it might be asked why we should judge the value of a theory by facile consideration of the personal merits of its author. But the issue is more complex, for the interpretation of Pareto as a proto-fascist depends upon a *defective understanding* of his theory. *Prima facie*, he would seem to have a case to answer. Mussolini did hail Pareto as his inspirer and teacher, and insisted on making him (against his wishes) a senator for life. There is no doubt that his contempt for the moralistic approach to politics, along with his *exposé* of democratic ideals like 'justice' and 'liberty', meshed with Mussolini's world-view. Pareto and the fascists had enemies in common – speculators, Marxists, trade unionists, progressive politicians – and used almost identical language in championing the interests of 'savers', those sturdy pillars of social order. But these overlapping likes and dislikes should not be allowed to conceal a profound divergence in underlying philosophy. Fascism's attack on demagogic plutocracy was fuelled by a totalitarian hatred of individualism, as that concept was conceived by classical liberals. Rampant egoism, Mussolini declaimed, was destroying the organic solidarity of the nation. By contrast, Pareto's contempt for demagogic plutocracy stemmed from a desire to safeguard liberal individualism against the encroachments of the leviathan state. His primary interest was to strip all governments, whatever their complexion, of as many powers as possible.[65] To uncritical lovers of democracy, he pointed out, as did Tocqueville before him, that the threat to freedom came from the *extent*, not the *source* of state power. Collectivism was his principal dread, and – let us be clear – he denounced *all* forms of collectivism by name. Though socialism was his main target, he also inveighed against nationalism, racism, and anti-semitism. These were 'blind revulsions with no more reason in them than in the action of a child belabouring the inanimate object it has stumbled against'.[66] Considering such evidence, Sidney Hook, himself a leading anti-fascist, dismissed all talk about Pareto being the prophetic defender of fascism as 'sheer poppycock'.[67]

But if Pareto was such a good liberal, why do commentators denounce his 'glorification of force'[68] and his 'apology for the will to power'?[69] Here we encounter a straightforward, if widespread, misreading of those passages in the *Treatise* where he pronounces on the necessity of using public power to preserve liberty and constitutional procedures. In fact, he makes it clear (to any careful reader) that force should be used sparingly – and only against *illegal* opposition, not legal dissent.[70] To be sure, Pareto was a consistent and outspoken supporter of freedom of expression, a value he pointedly defended in a number of articles written *after* Mussolini's ascent to power.[71]

Perhaps, though, there is an implicit connection between fascism and the often *virulent tone* of Pareto's critique of demagogic plutocracy. Borkenau expresses a typical standpoint when he describes this critique as 'a violent manifesto against democracy'.[72] If democracy is a sham, a disguised form of despotism and exploitaton, then why bother to defend it against the fascist assault? According to Luigi Montini, Pareto thought that the 'majoritarian fetish' was destroying bourgeois freedoms and standards. Small wonder, then, that he welcomed fascism as the only possible saviour of values he held dear – sound money, public probity, market discipline, personal responsibility. Pareto thus became a fascist by default.[73] This argument is not easily dismissed. In the early months of fascism, he was definitely more inclined towards adherence than towards aversion – though the same can be said for other liberals, including Croce, who were later to become stern opponents of Mussolini's regime.[74] The totalitarian nature of fascism was not self-evident in those embryonic stages. And one can assume that, had he lived beyond 1923, Pareto too would have become a vociferous critic of the regime. For, contrary to received opinion, he did not believe that fascism was the only acceptable alternative to communism or demagogic plutocracy. The *Treatise* contains a little-noticed footnote where he actually set forth his personal preference concerning political systems:

The best government now in existence, and also better than count-
less others that have so far been observable in history, is the government of Switzerland, especially in the forms it takes on in the small
cantons – forms of direct democracy. It is a democratic government,
but it has nothing but the name in common with the governments,
also called democratic, of other countries such as France or the
United States.[75]

From this passage we may infer that Pareto favoured devolved and
minimal government, where the 'fiction' of representation is replaced
as much as possible by direct consultation with the people. Whether
the Swiss model could have been transplanted into large countries like
Italy is debatable; and how he managed to reconcile his praise for this
model with his customary cynicism about popular rule remains less
than clear. But it is unfair to say that he presented 'a violent manifesto
against democracy' *as such*.

For Richard Bellamy, however, Pareto is not so easily exonerated.
While acknowledging that he never explicitly forsook the 'liberal
belief in the rights of the individual against all forms of authority',
Bellamy focuses on the dangers implicit in Pareto's relativistic
approach to political values. Since no political goal could be regarded
as more rational than any other, 'social utility was the only standard by
which [Pareto] could judge a particular regime'. He consequently
deprived himself of any objective grounds for isolating what was or
was not an abuse of power. In other words, his liberalism rested on
insubstantial metaphysical foundations.[76]

This is a subtle but inconclusive argument. The question whether
moral relativism favours despotism or tolerance is difficult to
resolve.[77] But, on the face of it, the view of values as subjective preferences would seem to be more naturally linked with individual autonomy than with the imposition of collective purposes. Certainly,
Pareto thought so. In an article published just before his death, he
cautioned the fascists as follows: 'Not persecuting any religion, not
wanting to impose any, seems the best and wisest procedure for governments'.[78] (Pareto was, as usual, using 'religion' in the broad sense,
to include ideologies.) A relativistic despotism is hard to imagine in
modern circumstances. All recent dictatorships have tried to mobilize
the masses by appealing to some moral absolute; in the case of
fascism, it was the priority of the nation or race. At any rate, Pareto
may simply be right when he claims that concepts like 'justice' or
'liberty' are essentially contestable. There is not now, nor is there ever

likely to be, an intersubjective consensus on what these concepts mean in practical terms. But this is hardly an argument for nihilistic indifference to abuses of power. Those who doubt the ontological existence of a natural moral order, discoverable through reason, are not thereby precluded from expressing moral preferences or from supporting these preferences with logical and empirical analysis. In my opinion, Pareto's evident satisfaction following the victory of fascism was inspired by intellectual vanity rather than theoretical affinity. He delighted in telling friends that Mussolini's triumph validated the forecasts of his theory.[79] And this theory, as an explanation (not justification) of fascism's popular appeal, surely deserves more attention than it has hitherto enjoyed.

The appropriate criticism to level at Pareto, I think, is not that he was a mindless relativist but that he was inconsistent in his relativism. It is a common observation that the anti-metaphysical doctrines of 'scientific' thinkers like Comte and Marx usually contain unconscious metaphysical elements. Pareto was no exception. As a Machiavellian pragmatist, he always declared his firm opposition to 'essentialism'.[80] Why should any one conception of the 'human essence' be superior to any other? Why, in particular, should socialists proclaim that the human need for association is 'essential', while the pursuit of self-interest is 'unnatural'? A good question – but by reversing the terms, we could direct it at Pareto himself. For his theory of spoliation *assumes* that state intervention, in order to tame or 'rationalize' market forces, destroys some natural order of things based on free and voluntary transactions. The free market itself, however, necessarily depends upon state action to protect the 'haves' from the 'have-nots'. Pareto should have reflected more deeply on the words of his mentor, Adam Smith: 'The affluence of the rich excites the indignation of the poor, who are often both driven by want and prompted by envy to invade their possessions. It is only under the shelter of the civil magistrate that the owner of that valuable property ... can sleep a single night in security.'[81]

To want to exclude government from participating in the distribution of wealth, when the present distribution exists precisely because of it, seems a desire of staggering incoherence. What is more, the operation of the market presupposes an historically defined ethical context, regulating economic interchange and attaching varying degrees of value to different types of activity. State protection of property could only be effective within the framework of such a consensus, since – as Pareto himself informs us – force by itself is inadequate as a method of social control. *Pace* Pareto, the free market is not the automatic and spontaneous expression of human cooperation; it is an elaborate artefact, and therefore cannot provide an absolute standard by which to judge liberal democratic regimes.

Pareto's metaphysical commitment to *laissez-faire* capitalism explains the apparent irrationality of his invective against trade unions. For example, he was outraged when workers reacted to industrial disputes by withdrawing their labour power; yet he was equally outraged by legal restrictions on the exportation of capital. It was unacceptable for workers to deprive the national economy of *their* 'property' (i.e. labour), but perfectly acceptable for capitalists to do likewise with *their* property (i.e. capital).[82] For this reason, it is impossible to agree with Carlo Mongardini when he describes Pareto's writings as an extended 'critique of power'.[83] Pareto had a blind spot: he could not see that huge concentrations of property were every bit as oppressive as huge concentrations of state power. Anyone who wishes to cast aspersions on his scientific credentials can find plenty of ammunition. On balance, though, we can concur with H. Stuart Hughes's description of Pareto as a 'belated French *philosophe*', a sceptical man of reason battling against obscurantism.[84] His aim was to demystify inflated rhetoric and dangerous illusions. That he could not entirely free himself from his own myths does not substantially detract from his incisive, though insufficiently explored, contribution to liberal political thought.

## NOTES

1. Cambridge: Polity Press, 1987. In addition, see Andrew Vincent's highly regarded *Theories of the State* (Oxford: Blackwell, 1987), which mentions Pareto once in passing.
2. J. Freund, *Pareto: la teoria dell' equilibrio* (Bari: Laterza, 1976), p. 1.
3. English translation by A. Bongiorno and A. Livingston under the title, *The Mind and Society* (London: Jonathan Cape, 1935). The Italian title was *Trattato* (Treatise) *di sociologia generale*.
4. G.H. Bousquet, *Pareto: Le savant et l'homme* (Lausanne: Payot, 1960), p. 149.
5. V. Pareto, *Mind and Society* (henceforth *MS*), para. 933.
6. Ibid., para. 2206.
7. 'Everywhere and everlastingly human beings brutally ill-treat, slaughter and destroy their kind.' *Fatti e Teorie* (1920), in V. Pareto, *Sociological Writings*, trans. D. Mirfin and ed. S.E. Finer (Oxford: Basil Blackwell, 1966), p. 294.

164     *The Machiavellian Legacy*

8. J.W. Vander Zanden, 'Pareto and Fascism Reconsidered', *American Journal of Economics and Sociology*, 19 July 1960, p. 408; R.V. Worthington, 'Pareto: the Karl Marx of Fascism', *Economic Forum* (Summer and Fall 1933).
9. *MS*, para. 150.
10. Ibid., paras 870, 875.
11. Ibid., para. 154
12. Ibid., paras 2239, 2394; and V. Pareto, *The Transformation of Democracy*, trans. R. Girola and ed. C.H. Powers (London: Transaction Books, 1984), p. 28. Originally published in 1921 under the title, *Trasformazione della democrazia*.
13. R. Bellamy, *Modern Italian Social Theory* (Oxford: Blackwell, 1987), p. 26.
14. *MS*, para. 70.
15. Ibid., paras 72, 843.
16. Ibid., paras 2133–5, 2143.
17. W. Stark, 'In Search of the True Pareto', *British Journal of Sociology*, XIV (June 1963), pp. 111–12; M. Ginsberg, 'The Sociology of Pareto', in *Pareto and Mosca*, ed. J.H. Meisel (Englewood Cliffs, NJ: Prentice-Hall, 1965), p. 96; F. Borkenau, *Pareto* (London: Chapman & Hall, 1936), ch. 3; and N.S. Timasheff, *Sociological Theory* (New York: Random House, 1957), pp. 159–66.
18. *Les Systèmes Socialistes* (1902), in Pareto, *Sociological Writings*, p. 124; *Manuel d'Economie Politique* (1909), in Pareto, *Sociological Writings*, pp. 148–9; and *MS*, paras 1091 and 1690.
19. *MS*, para. 2060.
20. Ibid., para. 2067.
21. H. Stuart Hughes, *Consciousness and Society* (St Albans: Paladin, 1974), p. 78.
22. *MS*, paras 6, 1537.
23. Ibid., paras 829, 1884.
24. Ibid., para. 830.
25. Ibid., para. 2231.
26. *Cours d'Economie Politique* (1896), in Pareto, *Sociological Writings*, p. 117.
27. *Les Systèmes Socialistes* (1902), in Pareto, *Sociological Writings*, p. 140.
28. *MS*, para. 1543.
29. *Les Systèmes Socialistes* (1902), in Pareto, *Sociological Writings*, p. 138.
30. Ibid., p. 139.
31. *MS*, para. 2183
32. Ibid., para. 2244.
33. Ibid., paras 2253, 2183–4.
34. Ibid., para. 2053.
35. But it's a fairy-story whose authorship is often attributed to Pareto! Tom Bottomore, for example, in his influential *Elites and Society* (Harmondsworth: Pelican, 1966), complains that Pareto (unlike Mosca) was blind to the 'heterogeneity' of the elite (p. 12). For some people, a ruling elite is *by definition* conspiratorial and self-conscious. (See R. Dahl, 'A Critique of the Ruling Elite Model', *American Political*

*Science Review*, LII, 1958, pp. 463–9.) Maybe they read Pareto with this preconception in mind.

36. *MS*, para. 2254.
37. Ibid.
38. Ibid., paras 2265, 2257.
39. Ibid., para. 2231.
40. Ibid., para. 2233.
41. Ibid., para. 2234. Borkenau finds it odd that Pareto, having accused Marx of simplifying a complex reality by dividing society into 'capitalists' and 'proletariat', should commit precisely the same error with his division between 'speculators' and 'rentiers' (*Pareto*, p. 141). The criticism is a fair one, though Pareto does acknowledge that the dividing line between the two 'classes' is blurred. (*MS*, para. 2235).
42. *MS*, para. 2231.
43. Ibid., para. 2250.
44. See, in particular, M. Olson, *The Logic of Collective Action* (Cambridge, Mass.: Harvard University Press, 1965).
45. *Les Systèmes Socialistes* (1902), in Pareto, *Sociological Writings*, pp. 141–2.
46. Ibid., p. 142.
47. *Cours d'Economie Politique* (1896), in Pareto, *Sociological Writings*, p. 119.
48. Pareto, *The Transformation of Democracy*, pp. 43–6, 66.
49. *MS*, paras 2228, 2255, 2309.
50. Pareto, *The Transformation of Democracy*, p. 60.
51. *MS*, paras 2306–7.
52. Pareto, *The Transformation of Democracy*, pp. 65–7.
53. *Manuel d'Economie Politique* (1909), in Pareto, *Sociological Writings*, pp. 148–9.
54. Pareto, *The Transformation of Democracy*, pp. 25, 31; *MS*, para. 401.
55. *MS*, para. 1554.
56. Ibid., paras 1486–92, 1608–9.
57. Ibid., para. 2134.
58. Ibid., paras 2228, 2307, 2309, 2059.
59. Pareto, *The Transformation of Democracy*, p. 71.
60. Ibid., pp. 43–6, 66.
61. *MS*, para. 1210.
62. Pareto, *The Transformation of Democracy*, p. 47.
63. Finer, 'Introduction' to Pareto, *Sociological Writings*, p. 80.
64. Borkenau, *Pareto*, p. 174.
65. *MS*, para. 2267.
66. *Cours d'Economie Politique* (1896), in Pareto, *Sociological Writings*, p. 121. See also *MS*, paras 1050, 2390.
67. 'Pareto's Sociological System', *The Nation*, CXL, 26 June 1935, p. 747.
68. Vander Zanden, 'Pareto and Fascism Reconsidered', p. 408.
69. R. Aron, *Le Machiavelisme, doctrine des tyrannies modernes*, cited in G. Busino, *Gli studi su Vilfredo Pareto oggi* (Rome: Bulzoni, 1974), p. 77.
70. *MS*, paras 1050, 2175, 2246.

71.  For references, see J. Lopreato and R.C. Ness, 'Vilfredo Pareto: Sociologist or Ideologist?', *Sociological Quarterly* (Winter 1966), p. 36.
72.  *Pareto*, p. 136.
73.  *Vilfredo Pareto e il fascismo* (Rome: Volpe, 1974), pp. 15, 216 in particular.
74.  Fascisms's temporary hold on the liberal imagination extended beyond Italy. Many American liberals also welcomed the fascist takeover. Unlike Pareto, however, they tended to be 'new liberals', disillusioned with the atomistic, contractual approach of the Lockean tradition. See J.P. Diggins, *Mussolini and Fascism: the View from America* (Princeton: Princeton University Press, 1972), pp. 220–39.
75.  *MS*, para. 2240.
76.  *Modern Italian Social Theory*, pp. 22, 33.
77.  For an excellent analysis of the philosophical issues, see M. Ginsberg, *On the Diversity of Morals* (London: Heinemann, 1962), ch. 3.
78.  *Il Secolo*, 17 May 1923; quoted in D. Fiorot, *Politica e scienza in Vilfredo Pareto* (Milan: Edizioni di Comunità, 1975), p. 214.
79.  Fiorot, *Politica e scienza in Vilfredo Pareto*, p. 212.
80.  See, e.g., *MS*, para. 69.
81.  *The Wealth of Nations: Representative Selections*, ed. B. Mazlish (Indianapolis: Bobbs-Merrill, 1961), p. 252.
82.  Pareto, *The Transformation of Democracy*, pp. 45–8.
83.  *La sociologia di Vilfredo Pareto fra otto e novecento* (Genoa: ECIG, 1984), p. 60.
84.  *Consciousness and Society*, p. 266.

# Index

and Pareto, 148–50
McLellan, David, 64
Medici, Lorenzo de' (the
Magnificent), 7
Meisel, James H., 126, 127, 134
Michels, Robert, 132
Mill, John Stuart, 74
Mongardini, Carlo, 163
Montini, Luigi, 160
Mosca, Gaetano, **126–44**
his elitism, 133–7
and Gramsci, 55, 63n, 94, 127, 143n
and Machiavelli, 2–3, 25–6, 32,
35–6, 51–2, 55, 132, 142
on Marxism, 137–41
his methodology, 128–33
and Pareto, 2, 25, 35–6, 38–9,
51–2, 55, 164n
on 'political formula', 131–2
his positivism, 35–6, 127
on science, 35–9
Mussolini, Benito, 126, 145, 158, 159,
162

Newton, Sir Isaac, 31, 34
Nietzsche, Friedrich, 21, 146
Numa, 20

Olschki, Leonardo, 27–8

Parel, A.J., 29–31, 61n
Pareto, Vilfredo, **145–66**
elites, theory of, 150–5
and fascism, 145, 159–62
and Machiavelli, 2–3, 25–6, 32,
35–6, 51–2, 55, 147, 150
and Marxism, 148–50
and Mosca, 2, 25, 35–6, 38–9,
51–2, 55, 164n
on residues and derivations,
146–8, 150
on science, 35–9
and utilitarianism, 147–8
Parry, Geraint, 127, 129
Patrizi, Francesco, 15
PCI *(Partito Comunista Italiano)*,
106, 107, 108, 109

Péguy, Charles, 83–4
Pellicani, Luciano, 125n
Piccone, Paul, 76
Plato, 47
Plekhanov, Georgi, 17, 69, 74, 75–6,
101
Pole, Cardinal Reginald, 5
Pontano, Giovanni, 15
Popper, Karl, 132
positivism, 35–9, 82–3, 86–7, 127
Poulantzas, Nicos, 114
PSI *(Partito Socialista Italiano)*, 108,
109

Renaissance, 5, 7–16, 29–30
Ricardo, David, 95
*Risorgimento*, 6, 83
Robespierre, Maximilien, 96
Rolland, Romain, 83–4
Rome and the Romans, 7, 20, 22, 29,
31, 32, 41–2, 43, 44
Rucellai, Cosimo, 57n

Salutati, Coluccio, 12
Salvadori, Massimo, 107
Schumpeter, Joseph, 135–6
Scipio, 33
Second International, 75
Smith, Adam, 162
Soderini, Piero, 33
Sorel, Georges, 66, 83–4, 149–50
Spencer, Herbert, 25, 149
Spinoza, Baruch, 65–6
Stalin, Joseph, 112, 113
state, theories of, 1
Strauss, Leo, 56

Therborn, Goran, 114
Togliatti, Palmiro, 106
Tolstoy, Leo, 96
Tronti, Mario, 65
Turati, Filippo, 76

Valla, Lorenzo, 48
Vico, Giambattista, 100, 129
Vincent, Andrew, 163n
Virgil, 41